The
INTERPRETATION
of
SCRIPTURE

BY

James D. Smart

THE WESTMINSTER PRESS

PHILADELPHIA

PRINTED IN THE UNITED STATES OF AMERICA

CONTENTS

ABBREVIATIONS

PREFACE

The title of this book is perhaps too comprehensive. It might lead *It does indeed!* some readers to expect an orderly explication of rules for the interpretation of Scripture, in short, a hermeneutic, with full discussion of philological, literary, historical, and theological problems. Attention, however, is focused on a narrower area, the specific theological and historical problems that seem to require consideration and clarification most urgently today. A more accurate title might have been " Prolegomena to Biblical Theology," since the primary concern is to bring into the open certain questions that are preliminary to the development of a Biblical theology and to theological exposition but that seem to be passed over too lightly or even ignored at times in the literature of Old and New Testament theology.

The consideration given to the views of Rudolf Bultmann and Karl Barth may seem out of proportion, but the disproportion is the consequence of the author's conviction that most of the issues that confront us today in Biblical scholarship come to their sharpest expression in the work of these two men. By the thoroughness with which they follow out the implications of their thought they help us to see our own problems in a clearer light. Also it has been inevitable that many books that bear upon the subject have received either too slight notice or none whatever. The scope of the subject, extending over both Testaments, is so vast that one would require much more time than has been available to master all the literature. The criticisms of the views of some scholars may be in a measure unjust because of a failure to take into account all that they have said in all their writings.

No apology is made, however, for the emphasis upon the sharp

9

antithesis between various approaches to the interpretation of Scripture. There is a politeness in the world of scholarship, particularly in our English-speaking world, that conceals or de-emphasizes the differences in viewpoint, or even proceeds upon the assumption that it is possible to synthesize the best elements from the work of all competent scholars. This can lead to serious confusion. The issues that confront us today in Biblical scholarship have to be seen with clarity and thought through with decisiveness. They are not to be lightly reconciled by even the most synthesis-prone mind.

Chapter IV, though it concerns itself with typology, allegory, and analogy, is actually a continuation of the discussion of the unity of Scripture. Chapter V, on the image of God, may seem at first sight to be an alien intrusion, interrupting the orderly discussion of the problems outlined in Chapter I, but it is introduced at this point to give concreteness to the problems that have been discussed. It is only in the process of actually interpreting Scripture that the significance of the problems and the implications of the principles can be rightly seen. An abstract discussion of them seems to hang in the air. It might be more in place after Chapter III, but in that position it would have broken the discussion of unity.

The historical chapters, VIII and IX, would be unnecessary if there existed in English any adequate history of the last two hundred years of Biblical interpretation. The existing histories which in brief compass deal with twenty centuries of interpretation can give the modern period little more than a passing glance. I am well aware that my sketch can make no claim to comprehensiveness. My only hope is that it is sufficient to provide a background for the discussion of our present urgent problems so that we may see them not superficially but in the perspective of two centuries of debate. I have found nowhere in English or German a history that combined into one story the developments of scholarship in both Testaments, yet it is only reasonable that they should be closely related and should throw light on each other. Also there is need to set the history of interpretation more deeply in the context of the history of theology as a whole, much more deeply than I have been able to do. In these chapters I have made considerable use of material that appeared in my two essays on "The Death and Rebirth of Old Testament Theology" in the *Journal of Religion,* January and April, 1943.

I would express my thanks to Prof. Louis Martin, of the faculty of Union Theological Seminary, and to Dr. Paul Meacham, the editor of The Westminster Press, for criticism and suggestions that were of value in the revision of the manuscript.

JAMES D. SMART

Union Theological Seminary
New York City

— translations of
   (1) Kraus'-
   (2) Kümmel (p. 241

⌈ I ⌉

THE MYSTERY OF THE SCRIPTURES

THE PECULIAR and unique character of the Scriptures is nowhere so apparent as in their ability to hide their meaning, sometimes for long periods, from even the most intelligent and earnest of men, and then suddenly to disclose their meaning with revolutionary consequences in human life. This is experienced both in the history of the church and in the history of individuals.

The history of Biblical interpretation is the story of how the church has over and over again had to rediscover the Scriptures. While retaining possession of the Book, and even while it makes frequent use of the words of the Book, the church may for a time cease to understand what the words mean, so that they are as though written in a foreign language of which the key has been lost. Then one day *the Key* the key is found again; the words are translated afresh, and the Bible speaks with its own life-transforming power into the valley of dry bones that church and world for want of God's word have become.

Rabbinic Judaism cannot be accused of neglecting the Scriptures, and yet the testimony of Paul, once a rabbi himself, is that the rabbis, with all their diligent searching of the Scriptures, were not able to see what was there for them. A veil was over their eyes (II Cor. 3:14). They discerned a law of God that they were obliged to observe and a form of religious worship that to them was the only true worship, but God himself in the fullness of his mercy and grace and the awfulness of his judgment was hidden from them. They were able to build for themselves a reasonably noble and secure structure of religion and ethics out of the teachings of Scripture and to draw from the same source a reasonably comforting assurance concerning their relation with God. But there had ceased to be for them, through the medium of Scripture, that radical confrontation with God in which dimensions and possibilities of life are disclosed that shatter all existing structures and open up a totally un-dreamed-of future. The prophetic vision of God, which always led to exceedingly disturbing visions concerning man, had been lost. But with John the Baptist in part, and with Jesus in utter decisiveness, the prophetic vision, and more than the prophetic vision, was found again, so that the Old Testament Scriptures were read with new eyes and their message was heard as a word that had power to create a new life for man.

It will perhaps reinforce this illustration of how the meaning of Scripture can be hidden if we consider how little influence Second Isaiah, the greatest prophet of Israel, had upon the shaping of the religion of his people in the five centuries between his time and that of Jesus. His ministry and message in the dark years of the sixth century B.C. were like a lightning flash of revelation lighting up the whole purpose of God for Israel and for mankind. He had disciples and through them his mission would have some immediate impact upon the life of Israel. But in the general character of Judaism as it had taken shape by the second century B.C. there was little sign of his influence. His consciousness of Israel's destiny as the servant of God through whom God's saving purpose must be brought to its triumph among the nations was not communicated to his country-men. In the intensity of his hope in God and in his recognition that no response to God is worth anything unless it makes a man do something about God's poor, he seems fairly knocking on the door of the Christian gospel, and yet it was five hundred years and more before he was heard in such a way that the content of his words shaped the life of a people. His writings were carefully preserved and undoubtedly were read, but not until his words and insights were taken up into the message and mission of Jesus did they have their appropriate power. He had to wait centuries to be understood.

It would be grossly unfair, however, to leave the impression that only in Judaism has there been blindness such as this. It has happened over and over in the history of the church. In the Middle Ages the Scriptures were held in high honor. They were studied with great care. Belief in their infallible truth was a fundamental article of faith which a man would not deny if he hoped for eternal salvation. But the context in which they were read and studied was such that they had little freedom to say anything that would seriously set in question the established order of religion and morals. They were subjected to the religious institution, with its code of doctrines and practices. Allegorical interpretation, hallowed by centuries of use, proved a serviceable instrument with which to find in Scripture the meaning that would be most in harmony with the mind of the church. Thus, again, the radical word of Scripture, in which all human institutions both religious and secular are brought under the judgment of God and so have their deepest dilemmas and sicknesses laid open to the mercy of God, ceased to be heard. The Bible had to be rediscovered, and at the heart of the Reformation of the sixteenth century, which shattered the whole existing religious and social order of Europe, lay the reopening of the Bible.

Again, what has been the driving force in the historical and critical research of the last two centuries except the consciousness of unearthing behind the ancient records of Scripture a story that had never rightly been heard before? It had been buried, and most completely buried when the church in its zeal to exalt the Scriptures so emphasized their divinity as to deny the actuality of the human element in them. In asserting their character as the word of God, it had refused to let the human beings, to whom and through whom the revelation came, be really human. The great and abiding achievement of historical scholarship has been to discover and establish the human character of the Scriptures.

So obsessed, however, did scholars become with the importance of this discovery that in a very large degree they lost sight of the divine character of Scripture. It became for them the human story of man's religious and ethical achievements. Revelation became merely a synonym for religion. The Bible, critically evaluated, became an important source and support for the intelligent modern man's structure of religion and ethics. But it ceased to be a point at which he expected in any real sense to be confronted with the revelation of God as prophets and apostles were confronted with it. The Bible was assimilated into the religious and ethical order of modern cultural Protestantism so completely that it became unthinkable that the Bible should ever again in Protestantism be the source of an explosive judgment and creative promise such as was experienced in the sixteenth century. (This is discussed more fully in Chapter IX.) It followed inevitably that the Bible was forced into the background in Christian preaching and in the lives of Christian people, even though physically it remained and remains very much in the foreground. It can be said of Biblical scholarship in the early years of the twentieth century that very largely the Bible as a revelation of God in any radical sense had been lost from sight in spite of the intelligence and devotion that was being expended in the investigation of every part of it. Something more was needed than philological, historical, and literary expertness combined with religious and ethical earnestness. A key to its meaning was missing. But since the twenties of the present century there has been a revolution among Biblical scholars. Many now see that, whatever else the Biblical records may be, their own primary claim must be taken with complete seriousness: that they embody a witness to a decisive and unique self-revelation of God to man. So it is that in recent years a considerable number of books about the Bible have been published with the words "rediscovery" and "recovery" in their titles, and Biblical studies in general in theological seminaries are experiencing a renaissance of interest. We seem to be in the midst of a period in which the Bible is disclosing its meaning afresh, though the developments thus far in the American church and in our American theology would incline us to restraint in claiming that the Bible as a radical and life-shaking revelation of God has as yet begun really to be heard.

This experience of the church through the centuries can be paralleled in the experience of individual Christians and particularly in the experience of those who spend their lives in the study of Scripture. Years of sustained research in the language, literature, and history of the Bible may bring a sense of mastery over the materials, but let this man who thinks himself a master in Scripture be confronted by the simplest and most well-intentioned congregation of human beings who expect him to tell them what God has to say to them now through these Scriptures, and all his sense of mastery vanishes in a moment. He has to wait before the text of Scripture like a child who knows nothing of himself and has to be taught his A B C's in this new language of revelation. Perhaps after a time he begins to pride himself upon the fact that he has learned and even in some measure mastered this language of revelation. The Bible has become an open book to him in a totally new way. He can discourse freely concerning its theological significance and its relevance for life. All its parts fit neatly into an ordered theological system. The new meaning of Scripture has been discovered and absorbed into an improved religious and ethical viewpoint. The mystery is revealed and there is no longer any mystery to make one apprehensive. He can proceed with confidence in the interpretation of Scripture and feel a reasonable security in his theological discernment — until one day again the familiar texts open themselves to him in such a way that it is as though he had never really seen what they meant before, and he has to start all over again to spell out the meaning of all the texts. What kind of book is this that the scholar, even after forty years of intensive study, should feel that he has constantly to be making a fresh start in his entire investigation? — or that the church after nearly two thousand years should have to reread it as though it had never seen it before!

This strange and mysterious quality in Scripture is a sign pointing to its hidden center. It seems to be religious literature similar to the religious literature of peoples other than the Hebrews; it seems to consist of historical records, sagas, legends, gospels, letters, which one should be able to understand in the light of their origin; but, in the midst of all else that the Scriptures are, they are the embodiment of a revelation of God to man, in which God, when he truly reveals himself, actually comes to man as the living God that he is,[1] actually claims his right to sovereignty over all things in human life, and actually discloses himself in love to those who receive him as their God. Truly to know the Scriptures is therefore to know God in the most intimate, personal, and unconditional way. That is why the meaning of Scripture has constantly to be rediscovered by the church and by individuals. To master the meaning of Scripture would be to master the meaning and the reality of God! But in our knowledge of God and in all other knowledge that is dependent upon our knowledge of God (such as our knowledge of ourselves and of our

---

[1] Sigmund Mowinckel, *The Old Testament as Word of God,* pp. 41, 43, emphasizes the character of revelation in the Old Testament as well as in the New Testament as divine self-giving.

fellow men), we have to confess with Paul that at present we see as in a glass darkly. Only in the consummation of the Last Day have we the promise that we shall see face to face and know as we are known. All our knowledge of God is broken and incomplete. To our dying day we have to be children with God, willing to be led step by step into new understanding and new relationships. Therefore, it is only to be expected that in our dealings with Scripture we should be conscious not just once but repeatedly of having our blindness taken away and of being given new eyes with which to behold all things. At the center of Scripture is the unfathomable mystery of the grace, the mercy, the truth, and the judgment of God, which lays a restraint upon us and cautions us to a humility in all our interpretations and yet at the same time draws us on with the promise that even the slightest penetration of the mystery has far-reaching consequences for the whole of life.

The Recognition of the Mystery in Biblical Scholarship

Historical-critical scholarship in its concentration upon the human story in the Scriptures succeeded in a large measure in dissolving the mystery. The material embodied in the documents might be said to have been brought under control. Their religious content was available to the scholar, and his task was to describe it with scientific accuracy. That in the midst of his task he should become aware of an actual confrontation with God which would break through all his categories of religious explanation and force him to rethink his entire religious viewpoint was not anticipated, and no place was provided for it in the conception either of Scripture or of Biblical scholarship. The final goal of the Old Testament scholar was to write a history of Israelite and Jewish religion. In New Testament research the supreme achievement was to describe the variety of religious phenomena in the primitive church within the context of the religious beliefs and practices of the surrounding world. The Biblical scholar counted himself a historian of religion and not a theologian. It was his responsibility, upon the basis of what he found in the texts, to describe as accurately as possible the religious life reflected in the Bible in all its manifold variety. The theological question of the validity of particular beliefs and practices was not his responsibility but belonged rather to the systematic theologian, although he might in the manner of his descriptions and in the placing of his emphasis indicate his own preferences.

For various reasons (which will be considered more fully in a later chapter) there began in the twenties and thirties of this century a revolt against this approach to Scripture. Its earliest and most vigorous expression was in Karl Barth's commentary on Romans in 1919 in which a Swiss village pastor dared to deal with Scripture not just as the record of ancient religious phenomena from which certain values might be extracted for a modern day but as witness to a revelation of God which is as strange and new and revolutionary in the twentieth century as it was in the first. His interest was not in describing the religion and religious ideas of Paul but in translating Paul's words into twentieth-century words through which Paul might really say in our time what he was saying in his own time. The startling novelty of Barth's procedure to theologians and churchmen was an indication of how completely they had ceased to expect from Scripture anything more than light on the various aspects of the problems of religion, including the problem of belief in God. The revelation of a God whom man did not already know in the higher expressions of religion and ethics was unthinkable. Yet here the claim was made that the intention of Scripture was just such a revelation, one that both in Biblical times and in our time would cut diametrically across the established patterns of religion and life.[2] Therefore, a science that would deal adequately with the content of Scripture had to be one that was no longer embarrassed by the factor of revelation but was equipped to take account of it in all its varied manifestations.

The basic question raised by Barth is whether the records of Scripture are merely records of Israelite, Jewish, and Christian religions enabling us to reconstruct the religious life of these people during certain decisive periods in their history, or whether the claim they make for themselves is valid: that in them is the deposit of a unique and final revelation of God through which alone God can be rightly

[2] Millar Burrows, *An Outline of Biblical Theology,* p. 4: " Biblical theology is not to be identified with the history of religion in the Bible. History asks what the religion of the ancient Hebrews and early Christians was; Biblical theology asks what was God's judgment on that religion, and what significance it has for us. The Bible contains not only a historical record but also an interpretation and critique of the history from the point of view of the divine will."

known and served today. If the latter is true, then the Biblical scholar, unless he is to regard his investigations as merely preliminary and peripheral contributions to Biblical understanding, can no longer limit himself to historical description but has also to do the work of a theologian, interpreting the theological content of the documents that he investigates.

Since 1919 there has been widespread recognition and acceptance by scholars of the necessity that they should be theologians as well as historians, and the discipline of Biblical theology has gradually established itself, though not without opposition. Representatives of a purely historical approach who have no sympathy with the theological interest have sometimes spoken of " the Biblical theologians " as though these were always to be found in some one theological position, most likely in the neighborhood of Karl Barth. Actually, scholars of widely diverse origins — Lutheran, Reformed, Anglo-Catholic, Roman Catholic, Jewish — have recognized the need to go beyond the historical to the theological in the investigation of Scripture. Far from there being any monotonous sameness in their productions, the problem at present is the extreme diversity of their approaches and their conclusions. If anyone expects the Biblical theologians suddenly to produce an authoritative Biblical theology, validated by its demonstrable Biblical origin and thereby making unnecessary any further discussion of our theological problems, let him read the New Testament theologies of Bultmann, Stauffer, Cullmann, and Richardson in quick succession and he will be freed from his illusion. Also, in Old Testament theology where so many volumes have appeared recently, there is a lack of clarity about what is being attempted.

Theological interest throughout the church and revived concern about the message of the Bible created a demand for theological summaries of the Old and New Testaments before sufficient work had been done in the area of theological exegesis on which all such summaries must be built. Ludwig Köhler, in the preface of his *Old Testament Theology,* tells how he was forced to write it by the demands of his students to have the contents of the Old Testament presented to them in a form that would make it relevant to contemporary theological discussions. In this haste to reap the harvest quickly, some earlier stages of cultivation have been neglected. A number of

His problem is unanswered question about Biblical Theology—

basic questions have been left unconsidered or have been skimmed over in a superficial manner, questions to which some decisive answer must be given before Biblical theology can find its right context and character. In fact, its character will be in a large measure determined by the answers it gives to these questions. Moreover, each new volume on Old or New Testament theology assumes some answer to each of these questions but without any clear or adequate discussion of what is involved either in the question or in the answers. T. C. Vriezen, in an introductory section of his *An Outline of Old Testament Theology,* has at least recognized the importance of the questions and given them some consideration but too briefly to do justice to the importance of the issues. We turn, therefore, in this and following chapters to extensive considerations of the unanswered questions about Biblical theology.

The first such question, which has far-reaching implications, has to do with the relation between the two Testaments. That they stand together in one Bible is not an accident, the consequence merely of the events narrated having all taken place within a single nation; rather, it is a sign of a deep organic unity between the two. But what is the nature of this unity? Is it merely a unity of language and thought-forms within which quite different theologies come to expression? Or is it a unity of content in which all the parts are in their own way essential and bear witness to a single revelation of God? The answer to these questions is decisive for the form of Biblical theology. If the Bible is a unity in the latter sense, then what is called for is a theology of the Bible rather than a theology of each of the Testaments. A theology of the Old Testament would by its very nature be deficient, since it would leave out of consideration the most important and decisive events in the story of Israel in which the whole story comes to its climax, the advent of Jesus and the birth of the new Israel. No scholar would dream of writing a theology of the Old Testament without giving serious consideration to Second Isaiah. Is it not an even greater and more disastrous error to leave out of consideration the One who claimed to be bringing the whole history of Israel to its fulfillment? Likewise, a theology of the New Testament, based only on the documents of the New Testament, would condemn itself to being only a fragment of the whole if the revelation of God in Jesus Christ is not the whole revelation but only the final stage and climactic fulfillment of a work of God that compassed the whole historic life of Israel. The very fact that a scholar undertakes only an Old *or* a New Testament theology, while in part it may be due to the limitations of specialized scholarship, may also contain within it an assumption concerning the relation of the Testaments to each other.

A second question which needs clarification is the relation of historical to theological understanding. Some historical scholars seem to think that, while historical understanding is a serious scientific attempt to determine what the words of a text were intended to mean by the person who wrote them, theological understanding ceases to take the text with the same seriousness, does not let itself be bound by philological and historical considerations, and proceeds to find in the text all manner of edifying truth that the original writer never dreamed of. Let it be said emphatically that eisegesis is bad interpretation both in the theologian and in the historian. But the historian is naïve in thinking himself less subject to the possibility of eisegesis than the theologian. No one is able to read any text except as the person that he is and his perception of its meaning is influenced by his personal point of view, his convictions on the subject with which the text deals, and the total philosophy and theology which forms the context of all his ventures in understanding. *Both* historical and theological interpretation have therefore a subjective element in them that is inescapable and can be minimized only when first it has been recognized. Since theological interpretation presses more deeply into the subject of which the text speaks while historical interpretation tends to focus more upon the illumination of the text by outward events and environment, the former is perhaps somewhat more in danger of eisegesis. Both, however, are equally concerned with determining what the text really says, and the line between them may at some points grow very vague and hard to discern.

A third question, which has received more consideration recently than the others and is of more urgent importance in the church — and in theology — than appears on the surface, is that of the authority of the Bible, from which the question of the canon of Scripture is inseparable. Perhaps the Biblical theologian, when he omits the subject from his volume, considers it a question reserved for the systematic theologian in his treatment of the church's doctrine of Scripture. But surely what is primary here is to discover what authority Scripture claims for itself, or, to be more accurate, for the God to whom it witnesses. Its authority is not to be conceived as one that is wholly fixed upon it and defined by action of the church; rather, the action of the church is the recognition of an authoritative voice that it has heard in Scripture. The question of the authority of Scripture is the question of the nature of the revelation and the nature of the God who is revealed and the relation of that revelation and that God to the life of the church and to the life of the world. Therefore, we have a right to expect the Biblical theologian to tell us something of what the Bible has to say concerning its own authority.

A fourth question, concerning which there is widespread confusion in the mind of the church and in which a Biblical theology should bring clarification, is closely related to the foregoing and has to do with the inspiration of Scripture. In what way is it inspired more than any other noble human literature? Are its authors inspired but not the text, or are both authors and text inspired? Does inspiration of the text make it infallible and impeccable so that everything narrated in it must have happened exactly as it is described? Is the assertion of the divine inspiration of the text inconsistent with the free investigation of the text by historical-critical scholarship? Does the prophet or apostle who claims direct divine inspiration for his word have the same conception of inspiration as the interpreter who regards every word and even the punctuation of Scripture as directly inspired by God? No one can be unaware of the deep schisms in the life of the church, schisms across which some members of the church family can hardly speak to each other, caused by the failure of the church to reach any thoroughgoing agreement concerning the nature of the inspiration of Scripture. Could such schisms have continued so long if Biblical interpretation had been able to make plain what the Scriptures themselves really claim to be their inspiration? And do the recent Old and New Testament theologies enable Scripture to speak for itself on this subject, or do they leave us still in our paralyzing dividedness?

Yet another point at which clarification is needed is the relation between Biblical theology and systematic theology. The impression is created at times that if and when Biblical theology has provided an adequate account of what the Bible teaches concerning God, man, the relation of man to man, the nature of Jesus Christ and his saving work, the church and all such essential themes, this will be, for those who desire it, a satisfactory substitute for systematic theology. In short, the expansion of the task of the Biblical scholar into the theological realm seems to encroach upon the area traditionally assigned to the systematic theologian. The student of theology is only too often inclined to think that, since his Biblical instructors have initiated him into a theology that has the prestige and authority of being directly Biblical, it is superfluous to explore the intricate paths of systematic theology. All he needs in order to be a " minister of the Word " to his congregation is his Biblical theology.

Such thinking is possible only when it is forgotten that the hearing of God's word in the Scriptures and the proclamation of that word in the contemporary situation are not two tasks that can lightly be merged into one but constitute two major and complex problems of the church's ministry. The words and thoughts of Jeremiah or of Paul cannot be transferred directly into the modern situation. When we speak today we speak as men of the mid-twentieth century with nineteen centuries of human history and development between us and Paul and nearly twenty-six centuries between us and Jeremiah. All that has happened during those centuries cannot be brushed away with a wave of the hand. All that we say is conditioned by the history that lies behind us, and all that men hear from us is conditioned by the history that they and their ancestors have undergone. Jeremiah spoke not a timeless message but a word of God for Judeans in the years of the breakup of their kingdom. And Paul spoke into the problems of the Jewish and the Gentile churches of the first century. *We* must speak, however, a word from God into the specific situations of *our* era. We are not likely to do it unless we take with full earnestness the contemporary problems of theological existence, recognizing how deeply webbed into the theological dilemmas of our time are both our own and our people's life. The revelation that comes to expression in the writings of Jeremiah and of Paul has actually to be heard afresh in the totally new situation of the modern world and has to find embodiment in preaching that is *our* preaching, in actions that are *our* actions, and in a theology that is *our* theology. In short, the Bible does not present us with a ready-made theology which relieves us of the necessity of intensive theological thinking in terms of our own situation.

Biblical theology has its focus upon the text of Scripture, not contenting itself with merely explicating the ideas that are found there but taking us through the text into a participation in the life of God with his people and thereby giving the words their true depth of meaning. Systematic theology has its focus upon what we say and do and are as the people of God today in continuity with Israel and the New Testament church, bringing all our words and actions and our very existence to the test of whether or not they are valid witness to the same God to whom the Scriptures bear witness. The two cannot live in separation from each other because each is essential to the other. Through systematic theology the Biblical scholar becomes aware of the sharpness and importance of theological distinctions and is made conscious of his own theological presuppositions. Through Biblical theology the systematic theologian hears more distinctly the Biblical witness in which is disclosed the criterion of what constitutes a true gospel and a true church. Both are concerned with the translation of the gospel out of an ancient into a modern situation. At some points the borderline between the two is hard to see, but both have an indispensable function to fulfill and neither dare displace the other. The delusion that by means of a Biblical theology one can bypass the whole complex task of systematic theology can lead only to a naïve type of Biblical preaching that congratulates itself that it is proclaiming genuine Biblical words and ideas, in fact, a genuine Biblical theology, when actually to the hearers it is as though their minister were speaking in a foreign language or an unknown tongue.

THE SUBJECTIVE FACTOR IN BIBLICAL THEOLOGY

Mention has already been made in passing of the inescapability of the subjective factor in both historical and theological interpretation of Scripture. This needs much more careful consideration particularly in America, where the idea still persists very widely among Biblical scholars that complete objectivity must be their ideal,[3] that

---

[3] M. Burrows, *op. cit.*, and Otto Baab, *The Theology of the Old Testament*, anticipate no serious difficulty for scholars in attaining objectivity in their evaluation of the content of Scripture.

in so far as they fail to attain it their investigations are unsuccessful, and that only a scholarship that has given up all hope of getting at the truth can take any other attitude. W. A. Irwin, in his presidential address to the Society of Biblical Literature and Exegesis, in December, 1958,[4] received considerable applause when he charged Biblical theologians in general with abandoning the only truly scientific basis for Biblical exegesis. " We are not theologians . . . ; primarily we are historians. . . . Our function, for which we have been trained, on which our entire activity converges, is to tell as accurately and fully as possible just what happened and what was understood about that happening and its meaning for man's life, in those centuries of the ancient world which were so determinative for the course of the human career." The historian is to tell us what happened " but even more what was said and thought and — here is the important matter — felt; in other words, the total of the faith and practice of Israel and of the early church." Dr. Irwin is quite willing to recognize that the objectivity of the historian is never perfect. " All history writing is filtered through the prejudices and purposes of the historian." " Every scholar has presuppositions, or a bias." But these presuppositions he interprets as the enemy of true scholarship, which must be overcome. " Our prejudices are a dead weight of our past against which every honest scholar must struggle with might and main while he tries desperately to see truth as it is." The one hope we have is that in the community of scholars the varying biases will cancel each other out. Religious convictions are included by him in the category of prejudices and biases that obstruct objective and scientific scholarship. Thus the Christian scholar must put aside his Christian convictions in reading the Old Testament, and the Jewish scholar his Jewish convictions, so that they both may read it without presuppositions, and, seeing only what is really there, arrive at identical conclusions!

But who is this scholar without presuppositions? He is essentially an abstraction who never has existed in the past, does not exist in the present, and, from all that we know of human beings, will not exist in the future. Certainly Dr. Irwin himself has not attained this objectivity. He has provided us with an excellent example of the dilemma of the scholar who claims to have attained this scientific

---

[4] Published in JBL (March, 1959).

ideal in an essay which he contributed to the volume *The Study of the Bible Today and Tomorrow* (1947) edited by H. R. Willoughby. The essay is entitled "Revelation in the Old Testament."

Dr. Irwin's basic assumption, which appears constantly in the essay, is that "divine revelation" is merely a religious or Biblical name for rational conclusions concerning the phenomena of life reached by empirical processes. He nowhere admits the modernity of this equation but presents it as self-evident from Scripture itself. It is surely not unfair to suggest that prophets and apostles alike would be at least mildly surprised to be told that what they took to be a direct revelation of a transcendent God was merely the voice of their own empirical reason. The idea that Isaiah, in his call-experience narrated in Isa., ch. 6, "actually did come in contact with unseen reality," that is, with a supernatural God, is termed "this facile interpretation." Such visions as that of Isaiah's are said to belong in the same class with the trances of primitive shamans and "for religious knowledge they are of dubious worth." "The test of their religious validity lies in their conformity with the highest standards and ideals that we know." *Our* standards and ideals provide the absolute criterion of what is or is not valuable or valid in the Biblical phenomena! "Isaiah's great vision, then, was not a source of religious knowledge. Briefly, the vision constituted the prophet's inspiration. But his revelation had its source elsewhere. . . . The content of the unusual phenomena in the ecstatic ' vision ' and the common teaching of the prophet day by day thus alike derive from mental and spiritual activity such as are characteristic of normal human thinking. . . . The source and origin of the prophets' knowledge of God lay in their own human endowment of thought and feeling. . . . . They pondered deeply, devoutly, and long on the issues of their days, and they were profoundly concerned about them; out of such activity there came to them the convictions which they have set down for us as revelations of the will of God." Isaiah's experience "was a part of the quest, pursued by thoughtful men in all ages for a reality deeper than the transient things of the common days." One may wish to ask why the pondering of Isaiah and Amos and Jesus and Paul should have had such notable consequences in comparison with the thoughtful and earnest pondering of millions of other men in all ages. That mysterious fact remains undiscussed.

Behind this conception of revelation as taking place in "normal intellectual processes" lies an identification of the spirit or reason of man with the divine. "The mystery of man's being is that he is shot through with that reality which we call the divine." Paul is represented as saying on Mars' Hill that "God is in man by nature." This divine element in man has made him struggle upward from the primitive clod and has generated in Israel "an uneasy aspiration which led it ever upward to nobler concepts of God and man." But one may legitimately question whether there is any historical evidence that Israel ever arrived at the concepts of God and man and revelation that Dr. Irwin attributes to it. The transcendence of God is intrinsic to the Old and New Testaments alike. God is God and man is man, always in relation with each other but never with any confusing of one with the other. The idea of a man whose reason is divine is historically located in Greece and not in Israel, and when it invades Israel, as it eventually does, it comes as an alien force.

Having identified revelation with reason, Dr. Irwin can recognize no limits to revelation, since reason is universal in man. An authoritative Biblical revelation is impossible. The canon of Scripture is an absurdity. "Divine revelation is a process as wide as the race and as long as time. . . . The voice that spoke through prophet and sage in ancient Israel has been heard by men everywhere since first the race emerged from its brute ancestry." Thus, other religious books than the Bible must be for us "valid revelations of God." In fact, since revelation and reason are one, all products of human reason since the beginning of time must surely be accounted valid revelations, and it is not clear by what criterion Dr. Irwin is able to assert, as he does, a definite superiority of the Bible among all other phenomena.

One may legitimately question whether he found his understanding of revelation empirically in the Bible. That the theological ideas implicit in his viewpoint are those which were dominant in a rationalistic and naturalistic theology that was widely current in America in the earlier decades of this century is not accidental. Had he frankly acknowledged to himself these assumptions that conditioned his approach, it would have been more possible for him to recognize and describe in the Biblical authors a concept of revelation that differed radically from his own. As it is, he has dismissed the really distinctive features of their conception as peripheral in order to find in them what is for him the only valid revelation of God. It would seem that the claim of absolute scientific objectivity in interpreting Scripture involves the interpreter in an illusion about himself that inhibits objectivity and makes eisegesis inevitable.

The question must now be asked whether Jewish or Christian scholars are capable of putting aside their Jewish or Christian convictions and presuppositions without thereby ceasing to be Jews and Christians and becoming some other kind of human being with some other kind of convictions and presuppositions — most likely rationalists of some sort. Surely it is fair also to ask whether our ablest Jewish and Christian scholars have actually come to common conclusions in their exegesis of the Old Testament. It is not difficult to be objective about the events of David's reign or the analysis of the documents of the Pentateuch, but would Jewish and Christian scholars be satisfied with each other's most honest exegesis of Gen., ch. 12, or Isa., ch. 53? *Does* the Old Testament mean the same thing to the Jew as it does to the Christian? *Can* it mean the same thing to a rationalist agnostic who chooses to specialize in ancient Hebrew literature and history as it does to the Jew or Christian for whom the Old Testament is in some way a revelation of God?

The assumption must also be challenged that religious convictions are an obstruction to the scientific investigation of Scripture, so that it is scientific only in so far as the convictions are put aside. The natural scientist is not made less scientific by the fact that in the progress of his investigation of some aspect of nature and from all that he has learned of the world and life he begins to have a coherent philosophy within which he interprets the phenomena of nature. Nor does the secular historian become a less competent historian when he recognizes frankly that he has certain convictions concerning the meaning of the human story and that his whole approach to the phenomena of history — the selection of the period about which to write, the selection of events to be considered within the period and his way of seeing those events — is influenced at every point by his convictions. The historian without any particular convictions (if he can be conceived at all) would be a historian without any eyes with which to see and a human being without any interest in himself or his fellow men to motivate his research. Convictions are the product of interest and concern and are therefore an important part of the equipment of the scholar.[5] This is true in every realm. Which is likely to come closer to understanding Shakespeare, the scholar who attempts to divest himself of all his own prepossessions so that Shakespeare's play may make an impression upon him as upon a *tabula rasa,* or the scholar who, in full possession of all that he himself knows and believes, enters into dialogue with Shakespeare, not just hearing but hearing and answering?

From within the Bible itself we meet more than once with the assertion that faith is essential to understanding. According to the prophets, Israel's repudiation of its covenant with God brought upon the nation a blindness that made the people unable either to understand God's dealings with them in the past or to interpret rightly what was happening to them in the present. According to Paul, it was not until a man's eyes had been opened by faith in Jesus Christ and his mind enlightened by the Spirit that was the Spirit of Christ that he could rightly discern the meaning of the Old Testament. This opens to us a subject that needs more detailed consideration: to make clear how the presuppositions of faith, far from destroying the scholar's ability to be faithful to his object, actually make possible a greater objectivity than can be achieved in any other way.

An even more important question is whether the historian is capable of performing the task a purely historical Biblical science assigns to him. He is to tell us what happened, what was said, what was thought, what was felt. He is to set before us the reality of faith and practice both in Israel and in the early church. And he is to do this without becoming a theologian or using theological categories of thought! Let us put this to the test by applying it to the events that from the beginning were central to the very existence of the Christian church — the death and resurrection of Jesus. Their centrality is evident in all the early Christian literature, and the space assigned to them in the Gospels indicates their prominence in Christian worship and thought. But what can the historian

---

[5] Rudolf Bultmann asserts this with great force and clarity in his essay on "The Problem of Hermeneutics," in *Essays Philosophical and Theological* (1955), and in an essay on "The Problem of a Theological Exegesis of the New Testament," in *Zwischen den Zeiten* (1925), p. 334.

who refuses to be a theologian tell us about the death and resurrection of Jesus? What can he, as a completely objective historian, and strictly not as a Christian believer or theologian, see in those events? Must it not be a totally impenetrable mystery for him how a Jewish itinerant preacher, dying the death of a criminal after a brief and inconclusive mission that was confined to Palestine, could so quickly become the focal point of a movement that set out to conquer the world? As a historian, he has to suspend judgment concerning the resurrection stories by which the church explained the miracle of its origin. This dilemma of the historian is particularly evident in Goguel's *Birth of Christianity,* where, on the basis of the evidence, he has to conclude that the birth of Christianity is inexplicable apart from the belief of the early Christians that their master Jesus was risen from the dead and was alive, and yet as a critical historian he feels compelled to discount the reality of the resurrection as an event in history. This is the embarrassment that the Bible throughout its whole length and breadth furnishes for the historian. All its most important happenings are of a kind that, because they have to do not just with the actions of men but also with the actions of God, result in a peculiar kind of record. How are events to be narrated in which not just men but also, and above all, God is active? Does God's participation in the event make it something other, something perhaps less, than a historical event? Must the historian in loyalty to his science refuse to recognize the possibility of events in history in which God acts? And does he therefore disqualify himself from ever being able to understand the kind of history of which the Bible is full? These are important questions which cannot be lightly dismissed. It is sufficient at this point merely to say that the historian who claims to be an interpreter of the Scriptures, a Biblical scientist, must be a sufficiently open-minded scientist to let his subject matter determine the character of his approach. If the Scriptures confront him with theological realities, i.e., mysteries — and it is not unreasonable surely to suggest that they do — then he will need theological as well as historical and literary equipment in order to deal scientifically with their full content.

THE INTERDEPENDENCE OF HISTORICAL AND
THEOLOGICAL INTERPRETATION

The assertion that a purely historical approach is unable to comprehend the full reality of content with which Scripture confronts us because it is able to take account only of human actions, human thoughts, human words, and human feelings and is embarrassed by references to divine actions, thoughts, words, and feelings, may lead to an unwarranted depreciation of historical research in the understanding of Scripture. The theological approach by its nature gives the primary place to what the Scriptures reveal of God, as he is in himself, in his relation with man and in his relation to the whole of human history. It may thus seem to provide a means of laying hold directly upon what is most significant in Scripture for the life of man and of the church, without the painful necessity of working through all the literary and historical problems that have occupied the attention of scholars for the last two centuries. The student who has struggled through the intricate maze of problems that is provided by the text of Genesis and has come away with the impression that this is nothing more than the folklore of an ancient Semitic people, impressive in some of its literary excellences but wholly antiquated in its ideas of God and man, and who then has a theologian lay open to him the rich significance of those very chapters for the Christian's understanding of himself and his world in relation to God, may become impatient with the earlier process. Why bother with all the literary and historical questions when the text itself can speak so directly and plainly to our modern need? But when interpreters, even though they be highly intelligent theologians, begin to divorce the theological from the historical as though the theological were of itself a new and superior route to the meaning of Scripture, the way is opened for all manner of uncontrolled perversions and we are on the road back to the situation of the Middle Ages when by means of allegory each theologian could make Scripture say whatever he wanted it to say. Historical and theological interpretation must be inseparable, each dependent upon the other.

The dependence of the theological upon the historical is easiest to recognize. All interpretation must have as its first step the hearing of the text with exactly the shade of meaning that it had when it was first spoken or written. First the words must be allowed to have the distinctive meaning that their author placed upon them, being read within the context of his other words. Then each word has to be studied in the context of the time in order to determine not only what meaning it had for the author but also what meaning it would have for those to whom it was addressed, the two not always being identical and both playing a part in the origin of the text. The religious, cultural, and social background is of the greatest importance in penetrating through the words to the mind of the author, but it must not be assumed that he used words always with the same significance as his contemporaries.[6] The omission of any of these disciplines is a sign of lack of respect not only for the text and its author but also for the subject matter with which it deals. One of the great achievements of historical scholarship of this painstaking kind is that it lets Paul be Paul, and Isaiah Isaiah, and Amos Amos. Let it be neglected and quickly all the Biblical witnesses become mingled together in a theological mishmash. It guards rightly against a theology being foisted upon Isaiah of which there is no evidence in his words. A theological interpretation that does violence to the intention of the original writer is not to be tolerated.

The other side of this interdependence is not likely to be recognized so readily — the dependence of the historical upon the theological. The discernment of the theological significance of a text may throw important new light upon the historical and literary problem. An illustration of this may be found in the exegesis of Isa., chs. 40 to 66. Until recently Old Testament scholars had little or no appreciation of the intense eschatological expectation of Second Isaiah, an expectation of a day of vindication when God would gloriously reveal his sovereignty in the affairs of men. It corresponds closely to the eschatological hope in the midst of which the early Christians lived. When the prophet in glowing language heralded

---

[6] E. F. Scott, *The Fourth Gospel*, assumes much too readily that the author of John's Gospel adopted Philo's concept of the Logos, thereby confusing his own message. He might first have inquired whether the author of the Gospel had his own distinctive use of Logos, which embodied a critique of all contemporary usages.

the coming of God to his people, a new exodus, the creation of a
new heaven and earth, this was formerly dismissed as merely a
poetic way of announcing the return of a number of Jewish exiles
from Babylon to Jerusalem. But now we see how eagerly he
awaited God's coming, how he lived and taught others to live in
hope, and by the confidence of his eschatological expectation was
kept steadfast in his prophetic witness. The words come alive in a
new way when this is understood. Theological penetration results
thus in a truer estimate of the historical significance. Perhaps the
most familiar example, however, would be the new appreciation of
the meaning of Gen., ch. 3, in recent more theologically perceptive
commentaries. An earlier historical approach understood the mythological features that appear in Gen., chs. 2 and 3, as indications of
the religious naïvete of the Yahwist. He was represented as thinking
that in the earliest days on earth knowledge of good and evil was
gained by eating the fruit of a tree, temptation was embodied in a
serpent who walked upright and talked, and God himself went
walking about his garden on earth in human form. One would not
expect the modern church to receive much in the way of religious
guidance from such a barbarously primitive thinker. But more historical and literary justice is done to the Yahwist by scholars who
evaluate him as a theologian with profound insight into the relations between God and man, for whom the mythological elements
are of a much more sophisticated character, being intended to represent enduring realities rather than curious ancient happenings.
If Second Isaiah with his transcendent conception of the creator
God could portray him as sitting on the circle of the firmament
above the earth, stretching out the heavens as a tent for himself, and
beholding men as grasshoppers on the earth below, surely the Yahwist in his picturing of the intimate relations between God and man
could let God go walking in the garden where man was hiding
from him without being accused of being crudely primitive. The
aim of both historical and theological interpretation is to let the text
speak in its own way, and in this each is constantly in need of the
other.

The question may yet be raised: May there not be a meaning in
the words of Scripture that was not fully known or understood by

the person who spoke or wrote them? Since a prophet received his message from God, could it not be true that even the prophet himself did not grasp the full significance of what he was saying? The historical scholar is likely to deny any such possibility, since its admission would seem to open the door to eisegesis of the rankest kind, the interpreter being able on this basis to allege that *his* interpretation was in the mind of God when he spoke to the prophet even though it was not consciously in the mind of the prophet. Exegesis that has to justify itself in this way must always be looked upon with something more than suspicion. And yet it must be recognized that the Biblical records, because they have to do with God and with the purposes of God for humanity through all the ages, constantly point to realities that are far beyond the conscious grasp of any human being. The writers themselves are conscious of the mysterious depths of the word that comes to them out of the unseen and that they speak as best they can to the people of their time. That word contains within it for Second Isaiah the purpose of God for Israel that binds together past, present, and future into a unity. The future has not yet come, and he does not know its exact shape, yet it is already present and ready to come and known to him in its essential character in this word of God. God will one day redeem the world from its darkness and evil and bring joy in place of sorrow; but for the fulfillment of his purpose he has to have a servant-people who will be willing to pay any price, in life and in death, in faithfulness to God and his purpose. Here Second Isaiah was peering deeply into the central truth of all existence that was not to have its triumph until Jesus Christ died upon his cross. It would be false in the exegesis of Isa., ch. 53, to say that the prophet was writing with his eye upon the cross of Jesus Christ. And yet it has to be said that, writing in his own time concerning what he knew of how God brings his purpose to its victory in the midst of humanity, he said actually much more than he was conscious of saying, and we do no violence to his words when we see in them an intimate relation to an event that was not to take place until more than five hundred years later. Perhaps the safeguard at this point is that we should never mingle together and so confuse what can be said to have been in the mind of the author with the deeper implications of his utterances that have emerged at a later time. To deny the possibility of these deeper implications of the text would be to deny that the word of the prophet is really the word of a God whose purpose comprehends the whole of human history; in short, it would be to deny the mystery of Scripture and to reduce all its words to no more than human words.

⌐ II ⌐

THE PROBLEM OF INTERPRETATION

I T BELONGS to the essential nature of *historical* interpretation that it widens the distance between the Bible and the modern world. The more thoroughly it accomplishes its task the more completely it removes the Biblical documents into worlds of human existence that very emphatically are not *our* world. We unconsciously modernize the patriarchs, the prophets, Jesus and Paul, in our reading of Scripture, letting the elements fall away that are peculiar to their age and strange to ours, and focusing our attention upon those more universally human features which seem to convey readily the meaning of the ancient story. The perils of this seemingly common-sense procedure are nowhere more evident than in biographies of Jesus in which the author proceeds with confidence to extract from the Gospels a life portrait of Jesus that will make him a vivid, admirable, and meaningful human figure to the modern age.[1] But in the process he ceases to be a Jew living in the milieu of the Judaism of the first century A.D. and becomes a high-minded citizen of some modern culture. For Renan he was one who would have been quite at home among the intellectuals of France in the mid-nineteenth century; for Bruce Barton he was a robust type of American idealist. The perversion of meaning in these instances is easy to recognize and has often been pointed out, but what is rarely recognized is that the same modernizing and distorting process goes on constantly and unconsciously in the use that is made of all Scripture by Christians. Therefore, it is important in the preservation of the integrity of the Scriptures that scrupulous care should be exercised to determine as far as possible the meaning of the text in its original

[1] H. J. Cadbury, *The Peril of Modernizing Jesus.*

situation. No matter how strange it may make the figures of Jesus or Paul or Jeremiah or Abraham we must let them be distinctly themselves in all the particularities of their historical existence if their words, or words about them, are to have their proper shades of meaning.

This has inevitably certain distressing consequences. To take just one instance, Jesus becomes plainly a person who *believed* in the existence of demons which took possession of people and made them both mentally and physically sick. His entire work of exorcism rests upon that belief which he shared with the people of his time. We do not share that belief, at least not in its ancient form, and were he to appear among men today believing with the same intensity in demons and offering to expel them, most of the churches that bear his name would be highly embarrassed. Yet that does not mean that his exorcism of demons was a superstitious practice, that in his dealing with demons he was not dealing with realities, or that that aspect of his ministry has no significance for the modern church. But just quietly to forget that Jesus had anything to do with demons makes him something less than the Jesus to whom the New Testament bears witness.

However, when the historian has done his work conscientiously and the gap between the world of the Bible and the world of our day has become a gaping chasm, the church with full right demands that scholarship go a stage farther, bridge this chasm, and show how the word of the Bible in spite of its time-bound quality is still a word of God to man in the present day. Far too often in the past the Biblical scholar has taken the attitude that the problem of the contemporary meaning of the Biblical text lies outside the purview of his responsibility, that his task is solely the historical one of determining "*wie es eigentlich gewesen*," the character of the events and words in their original occurrence. The determination of what the text means for man *now* has been regarded as merely the task of applying in present-day life the truths and principles that have been laid bare by the historical investigation, a task that can safely be left in the hands of preachers and professors of homiletics. The assumption that still continues to be made in many quarters is that exegesis is a historical, perhaps also a theological, task, requiring a full equipment of specialized Biblical and theological scholarship, but that exposition, being largely the application of the results of scholarship, can dispense with such equipment, calling rather for knowledge of the world of our day, resources of literary illustration, and other homiletical gifts.

W. A. Irwin, in the address cited earlier, shows some confusion concerning this problem. In one place he says that it is not the function of the Biblical scholar "to deal with the ultimate truth entailed," since he is purely a historian but, on the same page, that the Biblical historian and Biblical theologian alike "can do no more than present the realities of the ancient revelation," and, in his conclusion, "that to us as Biblical scholars have been committed the oracles of God." The scholar speaks, and "from there onward it is all a question of what happens in the individual consciousness." Clearly he sees no need of any discipline that will address itself specifically to the problem of interpretation in the contemporary world. He assumes that not only the modern preacher but modern man in general can bridge the gap between the two worlds. A closer examination of the misunderstanding and misinterpretation of Scripture in the contemporary church and world might make him, and others, less optimistic. They need to ask themselves why so many ministers, who have been trained to read the Bible historically and critically during their years in college and seminary, find themselves at a loss to know how to make its contents meaningful to the people to whom they minister. Preachers and teachers become lost in the chasm that scholarship has left gaping open between the original and the contemporary situation.

Fortunately during the century since historical-critical scholarship first began to make its way in the English-speaking world, many Old and New Testament scholars, however capable they might be as historians, and however they defined their task, remained deeply conscious of their responsibility to the church and were concerned in their historical interpretation to show also the relevance of the text for contemporary religious discussions. Robertson Smith, in his earliest writings, showed a remarkable combination of critical scholarship with evangelical doctrine. The tradition continued in such men as A. B. Davidson, George Adam Smith, James Denney, A. C. Welch, and others in Scotland and in a succession of men in the wake of Westcott, Hort, and Lightfoot in England. This succession of scholars forms a chapter in the history of interpretation that deserves more attention than it has received. It must be recognized, however, that this evangelical tradition in Biblical scholarship in England and Scotland kept the historical problem from appearing in its full sharpness, and because it never came through to an adequate understanding of the relation of the historical to the theological, it tended to confuse the two and so failed to do full justice to either. German scholarship, with its more logically consistent and thoroughgoing character, by 1870 was demanding the exclusion of theological considerations from Biblical research in order to make it possible to arrive at more scientifically objective results. In 1882 Wellhausen transferred from the theological to the philosophical faculty in Greifswald because of his desire to prosecute his investigations without any consciousness of theological responsibility. This conception of an untheological Biblical scholarship came to dominate the scene in the first quarter of the present century not only on the Continent but also very widely in Britain and America, and, if unchecked, would eventually have relegated the Biblical documents to the limbo of ancient religious literature, chiefly of interest to academic specialists, and no longer to be taken seriously by the church as an authoritative revelation of God to modern man. This may seem an extreme statement, but a more careful documentation of it will be attempted in a later chapter (Chapter IX).

Exegesis and Exposition

T. C. Vriezen, in his *Outline of Old Testament Theology,* has a brief section on the relation between exegesis and exposition which he entitles " the homiletic use of the Old Testament," an indication that he assigns the problem to the preacher and does not grasp the necessity for it to be faced first of all by the exegete. " The preacher's attitude," he says, " is (formally, at any rate) fundamentally different from the standpoint of the exegete. As he is the witness, the preacher stands in an immediate personal relation to what is proclaimed in the Bible and speaks about it from this close relation in spiritual unity with it." He is "completely dependent on the Biblical message; but this obedience to the subject matter in some respects frees him from the letter, from the form in which the message comes to him." " By understanding the matter (*die Sache*) one may rise above the Word as a historical datum; and exactly in that way one may fulfill the Word." By "rise above" he means that the church must draw out implications that go far beyond anything stated in Scripture (he gives as examples the rightness of the abolition of slavery and the social equality of man and woman). The preacher is preserved from erratic interpretations as he "goes beyond" Scripture by maintaining "a scrupulous theological and exegetical conscience" and by devotion to grammatical, historical, and critical exegesis. He needs also to be "critical of a great deal of modern eisegesis of the Bible, coming from various sides, the results of which often contain all kinds of dogmatic presuppositions which the preacher must be able to discern." [2]

Vriezen is here pointing directly at the problem that is of such deep concern for the church. The preacher and teacher cannot merely take over the words of Scripture or the ideas of Scripture *simpliciter* as their word from God for the modern situation. Upon the basis of Scripture they have again and again to say something that cannot be found in Scripture. Biblical preaching and teaching is not just a repetition of Biblical words but is a ministry in which a modern man attempts to speak in a modern situation in modern language and thought-forms the same essential word from God that was spoken in an ancient time and in ancient languages and thought-forms by prophets and apostles. This is exposition in distinction from exegesis. But Vriezen assumes that the two can operate largely in separation from each other. The scholar is the exegete and the preacher the expositor. The preacher takes over from the scholar the results of his exegesis as he faces the task of going prophetically beyond Scripture. It is taken for granted that historical scholarship, without ever giving its mind to the problem of the present meaning of the text, will have made quite clear for the preacher what the meaning of the text was. This provokes two questions: first, whether the Biblical scholar can or does content himself with historical exegesis, that is, with defining what the words meant at their point of origin; and secondly, whether he is able to say what the message and meaning of a text *was*, unless, like the preacher, he "stands in an immediate personal relation to what is proclaimed in the Bible" and wrestles with the problem of translating not just the words but also the reality of

---

[2] T. C. Vriezen, *An Outline of Old Testament Theology*, pp. 111–115.

thought and life behind and in the words into terms that are relevant to the existing theological (i.e., life) situation.

The separation of exegesis from exposition that Vriezen assumes, only the preacher combining the two, reflects the existing practice. *The Interpreter's Bible,* confronted with the problem of providing a commentary that would deal not only with the original meaning of Scripture but also with its present meaning, followed the practice of assigning exegesis to Biblical scholars and exposition mainly to preachers who might or might not have special training to equip them for independent work in exegesis as well as in exposition. Again the premise seems to be that exegesis establishes the meaning of the text while exposition applies this established meaning to the contemporary situation. Fortunately, often in the commentary the lines are crossed, the exegete doing valuable exposition and the expositor showing himself an able exegete.

There is unlikely to be any argument about the dependence of exposition upon sound exegesis. Exposition that has no careful rootage in the original significance of the words of the text is erratic and dangerous. Exposition is inseparable from exegesis. But when one reverses this sentence and states that exegesis is inseparable from exposition there is likely to be strong protest. Yet the question must be faced: Has the exegete any access to the original meaning of the text except *by way of the present meaning of the text for him?* It is an illusion to think that there is any scientific device by means of which the historical scholar can bypass all present meanings of a text, and, leaping over the centuries between, can penetrate the mind of the ancient author and state decisively what significance he placed on each of his words. He would not interest himself in the text at all if it did not have some present meaning for him. This is a hermeneutical problem that exists more widely than merely in regard to texts of Scripture. R. G. Collingwood, in his *Autobiography* (1937) and his *The Idea of History* (1946), takes issue with the positivist school of historians, who never get past the " outside " of history, and explores the question of how one is to reach the " inside " where history is fashioned. His conclusion is that the historian has access to the past only by way of its present existence in himself and his contemporaries. He can discover the inner meaning of past events only because the past is *his* past, and as he reads texts that come from it

Collingwood

cf. criticism of Collingwood on p. 302; improper use of...

they have meaning for him. All history is the history of thought, and there must be a re-enactment in the historian's mind of the thought whose history he is studying. Past and present cannot be cut apart without the past becoming a corpse and the exegete's task merely one of historical dissection. Only the exegete who takes seriously the question, What does this text mean *for me now?* has any hope of getting inside the mind of the original author in order to understand what the words meant *for him then.*

Exegesis and exposition are inseparable and yet they remain two tasks and not one. When they are no longer distinguished, we are in danger of identifying what we say on the basis of the Biblical text directly with what the Biblical author said. There must ever remain a distance between the two in spite of the fact that the identity of their essential content alone gives the exposition validity and authority. Barth, in his *Romans* of 1919, attempted to show that the only way in which to get at the original meaning of the text was by an exposition that dared to say in the language and thought-forms of the twentieth-century world what Paul said in his own way in the first century. Exegesis and exposition were blended into one, which laid Barth open to the charge that he was attributing to Paul thoughts that never entered into the mind of man before the nineteenth or twentieth century. Barth's protest was against an exegesis that thought it could perform its task adequately without ever looking closely at the really dangerous question of the present meaning of the text. It seemed to him that an exegesis of that kind always stopped short of dealing with the actual content of the text, which is a word from God to man in which man is judged and redeemed. He established his point that exegesis in separation from exposition is futile, and yet the character of his achievement gave warning that exegesis and exposition must remain in tension as well as in union with each other. In short, there must be an ever-renewed dialogue between the interpreter and the text in which the interpreter gives the text freedom to speak with its own unique accents out of its ancient situation. At the same time he must claim for himself the freedom to bear his witness in the modern scene in oneness with the Biblical witnesses because of the entire dependence of his faith upon them, and yet speaking with his own unique accents as a modern man to modern men. Biblicism asserts the authority of Scripture in such a way that the interpreter is robbed of the freedom that must belong to him if he is to have fellowship with prophets and apostles as servant together with them of the Word and the Spirit of God; is allowed only to parrot the words of Scripture and is not encouraged to dare in his own day the venture of speaking God's own word after him. The opposite error into which men frequently fall by reaction is the assertion of a freedom to know and declare the truth in independence of the witness of Scripture.

Two examples may illuminate this strange freedom of the interpreter which he possesses in spite of remaining a servant under the authority of a sacred tradition. Paul shocked his fellow Christians in Jerusalem by the freedom with which he reinterpreted the gospel for the Gentile world. He did not let himself be hindered by words of Jesus such as " Go not into the way of the Gentiles " or attitudes of Jesus such as his conformity at many points to Jewish customs. He made no attempt merely to repeat the preaching and teaching of Jesus. So radically do his thought-forms differ from those of Jesus that he has often been accused of being the great misinterpreter of Jesus. And yet there is a unity between Paul and Jesus that vindicates his assertion: " I live; yet not I, but Christ liveth in me." As an interpreter he was bound and yet free. He could be faithful to the gospel only by saying all things differently. John Calvin's doctrine of preaching illustrates the same principle. He recognized three forms of the same revelation, the original revelation of God to the first witnesses, the record of those witnesses in the text of Scripture, and the preaching of the church in which the revelation became actual in the contemporary world. The third was not for him merely an application of the second, but was the finding of words that in dependence upon the revelation of the Scriptures and by the inspiration of the Holy Spirit would let God speak into the ever-new situations of human life the same judging, redeeming Word by which he first established his Kingdom among men and called his church into being.

THE PROBLEM OF SUBJECTIVITY IN INTERPRETATION

We have already introduced the problem of subjectivity and suggested both its inescapableness and the tendency of American scholars to minimize its importance. The element of subjectivity is present in all perception. What we perceive is always a fusion of the object with elements that are already present in the mind. We interpret our impressions by means of knowledge that we already possess. But sometimes, particularly with people, we receive false impressions because the picture of them that we have in our minds is so strong that it resists any new discovery concerning them. Thus what we have in our minds is at one and the same time the possibility of understanding and the source of misunderstanding. Men who are experienced in preaching should be acutely aware of this problem because they have frequent illustrations of the fact that what their people hear is not directly what the preacher says but what he says filtered through and colored by the religious mind which they bring to the hearing. Sometimes they are unable to understand a preacher at all because the meaning he places upon the words he uses is so different from the meanings to which they are accustomed. The problem arises also in the reading of Scripture. The passage read is Matt., ch. 5, and the people hear the words, " Blessed are the meek: for they shall inherit the earth." But for them the word " meek " means "soft," " weak," " pliable," a Caspar Milquetoast who lets himself be a doormat for everyone. Therefore, what they hear is, " Blessed are the doormats: for they shall inherit the earth," something quite different from what Jesus intended and an utter perversion of the gospel. All Scripture is open to this kind of misunderstanding.

Subjectivity is inescapable. But how, then, are we to arrive at objective knowledge? What is to prevent all our interpretations of Scripture from being reduced to purely subjective impressions? The two scholars in whose writings this problem has been most provocatively discussed are Rudolf Bultmann and Karl Barth, but others have made significant contributions. When Barth's *Romans* appeared, Bultmann astonished his New Testament colleagues by welcoming it as a revolt against the sterility of an exegesis that labored under the illusion that it could by historical means define the content of a text with scientific exactitude. He and Barth were agreed that it is impossible for any interpreter of Scripture to be uninfluenced by his theological and philosophical convictions and that scholars who claim to achieve this are guilty of an unconscious dishonesty. The interpreter must be a " whole " man, not an abstraction of a man who tries to approach his subject matter as though he had no strong convictions or attitudes in regard to it.

The danger inherent in this development was that theological interpretations would be regarded as purely, or largely, subjective. The meaning of Scripture would be its meaning for this or that theologian. Thus, theological exposition, instead of penetrating to the one word of God in Scripture that brings all Christians into fellowship with one another, would give each segment of the Christian community the license to read its own theological convictions out of the text of Scripture. An essay by Otto Eissfeldt in 1926 pointed definitely in this direction. He recognized the necessity that there should be an Old Testament theology that would concern itself with making clear the significance of the Old Testament for the Christian church of our day, but he saw no hope that theological judgments concerning present meanings would ever attain any measure of objectivity such as seemed to him possible in purely historical judgments.[3] He called, therefore, for two disciplines which should be maintained in separation one from the other. In determining what the documents signified in the situation of their origin the scholar should operate as a historian with a scientific methodology that would reduce the subjective factor to a minimum. But in determining what the documents have to say with divine authority to our own day, and particularly in the life of the church, the scholar must unashamedly read them as a theologian of the church, and necessarily the outcome of his reading will be influenced in a high degree by the theological tradition to which he belongs. Old Testament theologies must be expected to display a subjectivity that would be shameful and unscholarly if it appeared in a history of Old Testament religion. The best that could be hoped for, then, would be a series of Old Testament theologies, each showing what some one church hears today in the Old Testament. The only control on this subjectivity would be that exercised by the purely objective and scientific study of the religious phenomena of Old Testament times. Eissfeldt assumed that the scholar as a historian possesses an objectivity that he loses at once when he becomes a theologian. Neither in sacred nor in secular spheres, however, do the facts support that assumption. The theologian need not be the creature of subjective influences any more than the historian. For both of them the recognition of their subjective in-

[3] O. Eissfeldt, " A. T. Religiongeschichte und A. T. Theologie," ZAW (1926).

volvement may mean not capitulation to uncritical subjective judgments but rather a greater degree of control over them and liberation from what might be their distorting effect.

Bultmann, in an essay on " The Problem of a Theological Exegesis of the New Testament" (*Zwischen den Zeiten,* 1925), asserts that the interpreter has no possibility of hearing anything new from the text, anything that he does not already know, until he surrenders his neutrality and acknowledges that the exposition of the text must go hand in hand with the self-exposition of the exegete. Exegesis that merely interprets the text in its original historical situation cannot get beyond words to meaning, and therefore ignores the ultimate content. Psychological penetration is not adequate to reach this final distance, for it takes us only into the experience of the author and not into the reality of the object with which the author is concerned. Psychological studies have only preparatory value. The surrender of neutrality comes with the conscious acknowledgment of our standpoint in which we become ready to hear from the text a word that has as yet no place within our understanding and that will demand of us a decision that will involve our whole being. " The only guarantee of the objectivity of the exegesis, that is, that in it the reality of the history comes to expression, is just this, that the text impinges as reality upon the exegete himself."

The relation of the interpreter to the text Bultmann likens to the relation between two human beings. Theological exegesis is not a new methodology by means of which the text may be compelled to disclose its meaning. Nor is there ever the possibility of exhausting the text. Rather, as in human relations, one is confronted with a reality that constantly discloses new possibilities. The dilemma of the exegete is that, man's relation with God being the substance of the text of Scripture, there can be no ultimate disclosure of meaning except to faith, and yet faith is an impossibility until Scripture has spoken. The dilemma is overcome by the fact that the exegete stands within the tradition of a church that has already heard God's Word and so brings to his task a faith and obedience that are God's gift to him through the church.

A later essay on " The Problem of Hermeneutics," written in 1950,[4] shows a significant difference in its explanation of the inter-

[4] R. Bultmann, *Essays Philosophical and Theological.*

preter's subjectivity. As before, Bultmann demonstrates masterfully the impossibility of historical understanding unless the interpreter brings to the text not a mind that is a *tabula rasa,* but rather a passionate interest in the subject because of its significance for his own existence, together with questions that have arisen from his personal involvement. But now what the interpreter brings to the text is called "a preliminary understanding," and since this preliminary understanding determines in a large degree what he finds in the text, it is of the utmost importance that it should be shaped with care. Here Bultmann calls to his aid what seems to him to be the most helpful philosophy of our day, the existential philosophy of Heidegger, to assist in the task of clarifying the self-understanding of the exegete which contains within it his understanding not only of himself but also of his world, his fellow man and God. Where, in 1925, the exegete received his preliminary understanding from his involvement in the church's faith, which was in its origin a response to the word of Scripture, in 1950 he was told to look to existentialist philosophy for it. Then, in confrontation with the text, let him become aware of the points at which the text itself sets his self-understanding in question, and in dialogue with the text let him expect the disclosure of the truth.

Fuchs

Emil Fuchs, a disciple of Bultmann, has developed existential interpretation into a special theory of hermeneutics. (*Hermeneutik* [1954]; *Zum hermeneutischen Problem in der Theologie* [J. C. B. Mohr, 1959].) The description of his method is made doubly difficult to understand by its own complexity being expressed in terminology drawn from the philosophy of Martin Heidegger. The focus of his concern is with what we have called theological exposition. It must not be any mere edifying practical application of the text but rather a scholarly translation of the truth embodied in the New Testament statements into the very words that this truth compels us to speak to our fellow men in the present day. The words of the Biblical text cannot be our words because they belong in a world different not just in thought but also in self-understanding from ours. Fuchs is also concerned that we let the text retain the full character that it had in its own world, not revising it or eliminating elements from it in order to make it more congenial to our modern world. He values Bultmann's project of demythologizing because it makes us conscious of the strangeness of the mythical forms of expression and thought that belong to the Biblical world. At the same time he takes with complete seriousness the task of speaking in words that have integrity in our world the same truth with which the Biblical authors were concerned. The crucial point for Fuchs seems to be that to speak the same truth today that was spoken in New Testament times sets one in the same dangerous exposed situation in which the original spokesman for God stood. The existence of the Biblical text does not make our task easy or safe or less costly. We are bound to the Biblical text in our exposition and yet we must depend not on it but wholly upon the God with whom we are confronted in our situation today. It must be *our own* word from God to our fellow man that we speak, helped to it by the Biblical text. Thus far we follow. But this is only the first step.

Existential interpretation according to Fuchs is a hermeneutical method to effect the translation of the truth embodied in the Biblical text into living and relevant truth for man today. To translate mere conceptions and ideas is too superficial, since the reality that is expressed in the words compasses the whole of man's existence. The mythological statements that mean nothing to us were for the New Testament man essential expressions of reality. But if we are to translate this reality into terms meaningful for us, we must establish some basis for comparison. Fuchs finds this in the self-understanding of the New Testament man which can then be readily compared with the self-understanding of man today. But this end is not easily achieved. The first requires the translation of the mythical expressions in the New Testament into terms of man's self-understanding; the second requires an existential analysis of the modern man that he may become conscious of his own self-understanding and so may be open toward the text of the New Testament and ready to hear from it a word that will transform his existence. Both processes, however, as they are developed, attain the complexity of higher mathematics, so that the conclusions when they emerge seem to come forth from an impenetrable cloud of obscure sequences. Fuchs lays open problems that theological exegesis cannot ignore but the road to their solution that he proposes seems to make the mastery and acceptance of existential philosophy a prerequisite for engaging in the task of exegesis and exposition.

Barth

Karl Barth [5] would agree with Bultmann and Fuchs in recognizing that no interpreter sees the Bible except through the screen of his own theological, philosophical, psychological, sociological, economic, and political presuppositions. He has to see it and hear it as the man that he is, a man whose life is embedded in the total religious and cultural life of his time. There is no spectator position beyond all such human involvements that can be adopted by even the most disciplined scholar. The claim of complete or nearly complete objectivity is to Barth a laughable delusion. The fear of being an eisegete rather than an exegete merely paralyzes the interpreter, so that he fails to hear and to respond to Scripture with his whole being. He can know what the Biblical witness meant to say originally only when he has really heard and responded to what it is saying now. But Barth disagrees with Bultmann when the latter asserts the positive and preparatory significance of the interpreter's theological and philosophical perspective for the understanding of Scripture. According to Barth, God reveals himself to us in his Word not because of any readiness or peculiar receptiveness to be found in us but always in spite of the resistance in which our whole being stands to God. Because we are sinners and unbelievers, even though we may be highly accomplished theologians and philosophers, God's coming to us in revelation and redemption is always an act of sheer unmerited grace. Nothing we can do or think, no standpoint we can take, can prepare us to respond to God or to understand his truth. God may speak his word through Scripture more plainly to the hostile agnostic than to the devout believer. It is true that what each man hears will be profoundly affected by whatever may be the character of his existence and by where he happens to be in his understanding of the world and himself. But his ability to understand Scripture will increase not through any conscious attempt on his part to secure in himself a standpoint in harmony with Scripture but through the reshaping of his mind and spirit and his total understanding of life by what he hears in Scripture itself. It is God himself who, through his Word and Spirit, creates in man the necessary presuppositions and the perspective for the understanding of Scripture.

This difference between Bultmann and Barth has far-reaching effects upon their interpretations of Scripture. Though Bultmann, like

[5] K. Barth, *Dogmatik* I, 2, pp. 513 ff.

Barth, insists that the perspective of the interpreter must be corrected constantly by what is heard in Scripture, just as any scientist must be prepared to correct his methodology and adapt it to the nature of the object of investigation, it is really only what he defines as the kerygma in the New Testament, the word of redemption that has its locus somehow in the cross, that is authoritative for Bultmann. It is, therefore, possible for him to interpret almost any element in the Biblical content as mythological and unacceptable until demythologized, so that he is left free in some measure to draw his basic theological conceptions from other quarters. For Barth there is no such freedom. The whole of the Scriptures, Old and New Testaments, have to be heard if we are rightly to receive the revelation of God. In them we meet with an understanding of God, of ourselves, of our relation with our fellow men, and of the nature of our world and of all life that is unique and can be known from no other source. It is because of its absolute uniqueness that the revelation of Scripture must communicate not only itself but also the possibility of receiving and comprehending it, so that to take any other knowledge gained from other sources as a basis for understanding the message of Scripture can issue only in the misunderstanding of it.

For Barth the possibility of understanding Scripture lies before all else in the fact that the Biblical authors bear witness to a reality (*Sache*), which is, through them, accessible also to modern man. What they write about primarily is not something that had its existence only in the ancient world. God, the response of man to God in faith, and the confrontation of man with his fellow man, are not time-bound realities but remain constant in all ages. The interpreter is not limited, therefore, merely to describing how Paul thought and felt about God, as though he had no knowledge of Paul's God except through the mind of Paul. Rightly hearing the witness of Paul, he himself comes into a direct relation with the God whom Paul worshiped, and the life of faith and hope and love of which Paul speaks becomes his own life, so that, knowing with this immediacy and directness the realities with which Paul was concerned, he is able to understand what Paul was talking about. The route to understanding is thus not by a psychological penetration into the inner life of the man Paul, in which the scholar remains essentially a spectator of Paul, but rather by letting the words of Paul point us to the object of Paul's concern, so that they convey a knowledge of this object (which, being God, is more active subject than object) which in turn will illuminate the words. In short, the route to understanding Paul is by way of God, the living God of both Paul and the interpreter. But also the route to understanding God is by way of Paul. Paul bears his witness to what God has done and is able to do through Jesus Christ and the power of the Spirit. But only as we receive that witness in faith and have our own lives laid open to the redemptive action of God's Spirit in and through Jesus Christ have we the necessary basis from which to interpret the words of Paul. Paul spoke as he did because through Jesus Christ he had received the Spirit of God to indwell his whole being and to illuminate his understanding of all things. Without the same Spirit possessing us, we cannot read his words with his meaning in them.

For Barth, as for Bultmann, exegesis is a dialogue between the text and the interpreter, a dialogue that must be taken up ever anew by a humanity that knows its own sin and blindness. The content of the text for Barth is not a human self-understanding that mediates an understanding of God, but God's self-revelation in which alone man has a true understanding of himself, so that genuine confrontation with the text is the confrontation of blind and sinful man with the sovereign and gracious God. To this meeting man can bring only his own emptiness, hunger, and thirst. No matter how far he has gone in the Christian life, he remains always a beggar at God's table. No philosophical clarification of perspective can equip him for the task of interpretation. Perhaps Barth does not give sufficient scope to philosophy as the means whereby a man becomes conscious of his presuppositions. But this is because he knows how easy it is to pass from a philosophical preparation for the revelation to a philosophy that becomes a criterion of truth standing above the revelation. How easily this can happen is evident on the last page of Bultmann's 1950 essay, where he insists that we are forbidden to consider anything true " which contradicts the truths actually presupposed in the understanding I have of the world — the understanding which is the guide for all my activity." Here the human self-understanding has become the final authority. Also, for Barth the consciousness of one's presuppositions is Christian self-knowledge that is the concomitant of knowledge of God rather than a philosophical self-knowledge that comes from intellectual self-examination. It might be said, then, that in the dialogue with the text of Scripture, Barth depends upon God speaking in and through the text to overcome the subjectivity of man and to bring him into a relation with God in which he will know the truth, while for Bultmann it is man rather than God who must take the initiative, since only when man has distilled the truth from all its time-bound expressions does a genuine confrontation with it become possible. Hence the urgency with which he launches his program of demythologization. The pearl of kerygmatic truth must be separated from the shell of Scripture that in decisive confrontation with it men may claim for themselves their true life in God.

An Ever-unfinished Task

An exegesis and exposition of Scripture, for which the content of Scripture is a revelation of God in which the true life of man is disclosed, is a task that must constantly be undertaken afresh. Only when the dimension of revelation is dismissed, or when God ceases to be a living God who speaks and acts and is reduced to the stature of a shifting idea in the minds of a succession of men, is it possible to think that a reasonably complete description of what Scripture contains can be set down in print. No man can ever know what will need to be spoken to the man who will come after him. That man will live in a new situation and will be a different man who will have to hear for himself. The word of God is not a set of truths and principles and rules, which, when once known, can be transmitted from man to man from that time on. Men have tried it again and again, and each time the words in which an age of great and vital faith expressed its truths and principles have become chains around the bodies and souls of the men of a succeeding age, robbing them of their freedom to hear for themselves and to find their way as men of a different age. The interpreter of Scripture, however he may profit by the labors of the past, must know himself to be ever standing on the threshold of new disclosures and new insights into the text of Scripture.

It is significant, therefore, of the character of Biblical scholarship in the first quarter of this century that it was able to have such confidence in the solutions it had already found for its problems. The great discoveries had been made by the giant pioneering scholars of the nineteenth century. The really exciting revolutionary developments lay in the past. The twentieth-century scholar had only the humbler task of gleaning the corners of the field. Ernst Käsemann, in an essay on "New Testament Questions of Today," [6] recently drew attention to the fact that in Germany in 1914 so many New Testament problems were regarded as settled and the ones that remained were so difficult that a scholar choosing a thesis for his academic promotion was usually advised to select one from the church fathers, while today all questions are wide open to research and no one cares to speak of "assured results."

The earlier point of view is reflected in H. P. Smith's *Essays in Interpretation* (1928) and the more recent one in Robert M. Grant's *The Bible in the Church* (1948), both of which sketch in outline the history of interpretation. The standpoint of Smith throughout is that for centuries the church floundered in its attempts to understand Scripture, occasionally catching a glimpse of a right approach, as in the school of Antioch and in some features of Reformation exegesis, but that with the advent of historical, critical scholarship the problem was solved in principle. There might have to be revisions and extensions of the method at some points in order to make it more comprehensively scientific, and different scholars might continue to arrive at slightly different results in matters of detail, but on the whole the problem of interpretation had been so completely resolved that it could no longer be regarded as a problem. The continued application of the method would gradually establish once and for all the meaning of Scripture. Grant's book reflects a quite different outlook. All confidence in the finality of results in Biblical scholarship is gone, and the adequacy of the methods of the past are set in question. He shows how scholars are being forced beyond a purely historical approach and are having to forge a new methodology in order to deal more adequately with the content of Scripture as a revelation of God. This consciousness results in a different attitude in two directions. The recognition that our best modern interpretations are only relatively adequate and are likely to be superseded by others produces a more sympathetic attitude toward earlier interpreters whose methods were imperfect, such as Origen and the Reformers. In spite of the in-

---

[6] E. Käsemann, "Neutestamentliche Fragen von Heute," ZTK (1959), p. 1.

adequacy of their methodology it is possible that they penetrated to meanings in Scripture that are hidden from us, so that we can profit from the careful study of their commentaries. On the other hand, the prospect is laid open of future developments as important as any that have taken place in the past. In the last chapter of Grant's book a picture is drawn of divergent developments, each of which is exploring some new avenue of interpretation.

The objection is likely to be made that interpretation is here being reduced to a subjective process in which we have no hope of ever knowing what Scripture itself says, since we can never get beyond what it has meant to each of a series of interpreters. Certainly it is true that we dismiss the possibility of any scholar's ever being able to speak the last word concerning the meaning of any part of Scripture. We envision a future in which the church in dialogue with Scripture will find meanings in it that are hidden from us today. We have to be prepared for today's most confident judgments to be set in question tomorrow. But when we say this of Biblical interpretation we are merely recognizing that it belongs not among the natural sciences but among the disciplines of theology. We are asserting no greater degree of relativity in Biblical interpretation than exists in theology as a whole. The truth in theologies of the past is not reduced to the subjective opinions of a series of individuals when we recognize that each of them was deeply involved in the life and culture of its own era and gave not final answers for all time but honest answers for its own time. The theologians had to speak as the men they were, each in an era that posed the issues of life and of theology in a way peculiar to itself, each confronted with perversions of the Christian faith different from those of other eras, each a human being involved in some measure in the sins and blindnesses of his own time. For the theologian to try to escape from his involvement, intellectually, religiously, socially, in the life of his time would be to make all his words empty abstractions that would have no meaning for any man in any age.

The theologian, then, speaks primarily for his own age, wrestling with the problem of truth and falsehood in relation to the issues with which his age is confronted. Thus, all his statements, no matter how great the truth that resides in them, have a time-bound quality. We do not expect any theologian of past or present to have delivered a statement of Christian truth that will be completely valid for all time; nor do we disparage his witness to the truth because it is something less than final. Finality we assert only of God's finished work of redemption and revelation in Jesus Christ, not of any of the interpretations of that redemption and revelation which have been formulated in the church. Why, then, should there be anything startling or disconcerting in asserting the relative and time-bound nature of all interpretations of Scripture? It is only because we have become accustomed to the claim that good scholarship is quite capable of telling us the meaning of Scripture with objective certainty, and we have taken for granted that it is scientific in a way that theology is not. Once we recognize that all interpretations of Scripture are shot through with theological assumptions and theological affirmations, even when they pretend to be most completely nontheological, and once we restore Biblical interpretation to its proper place as one of the theological disciplines, we shall lose all inclination to attribute to it, or to expect from it, a finality that is alien to the nature of theology. This means only that Biblical interpretation, like all theology, has its life not in a vacuum but in a specific historical situation in which human beings are confronted with the dilemmas of their existence and ask what the Christian faith has to say to them in the clarification, understanding, and solution of those dilemmas. Much as we may wish for a final certainty, and much as some Christians may try to persuade themselves that it is already available in some one historic theological statement, there is no answer that can be given to our question that will remain completely valid for all time. No matter how well the work of theology is done today, it has all to be done over again tomorrow in terms of the situation of tomorrow. For this reason, it is by no means a compliment to a theologian to demonstrate that he has not changed in any way during forty years; nor is it a compliment to a Biblical interpreter that what he said in the 1920's requires no revision in the 1960's.

There is always a certain danger that the recognition of this time-bound character of all theology will lessen the urgency with which men face the question of truth or falsehood in their own time. Since all theologies are only relatively true and will eventually be proved by later ages to have been in some measure false, should we take too seriously the differences between divergent theologies of our own time? Does not this make the passion with which men espouse some one theological position and reject all others slightly ridiculous? It should most certainly engender a humility that leaves the theologian open to be convinced concerning the inadequacies of his own position. But it does not lessen in any way his responsibility to follow the razoredge line between truth and error, affirming the truth at each step and rejecting the error. Irresponsibility in the slightest degree at this point destroys his very existence as a Christian theologian.

THE CHURCH AS THE INTERPRETER OF SCRIPTURE

The recognition that the meaning a scholar finds in Scripture is influenced inevitably by the presuppositions with which he approaches it makes the question *who* interprets Scripture of great importance. There is no better illustration of this than to consider what honest, thoughtful scholars make of the story of creation in Gen., ch. 1. There are some who approach it with the assumption that the terms " creator " and " creation " belong to an outdated Hebrew mythology and can no longer be used except poetically by any intelligent and well-informed modern man. Science has established the self-contained nature of the universe in all its movements, and any power exerted upon it by God must be exerted from within the life of man. From this viewpoint the chapter in Genesis becomes inevitably no more than a curious specimen of ancient cosmology, interesting as an expression of the Hebrew mind at a certain stage, but with no contributions to make to our understanding of our world or of ourselves. Since the author had a primitive conception of God, he must also have had a primitive and naïve conception of man; thus the making of man in the image of God is interpreted as signifying no more than that the god of Israel was thought to look like man. But let the interpreter be one for whom " Creator of heaven and earth " is an essential element of his faith in God, expressing not so much what happened at the beginning of time but the relation of God to the world through all time, and he approaches the chapter with a very different respect, recognizing behind the primitive and childlike features of the story a confession of faith in God as creator and a vision of man's destiny in relation to God and to the world that still has much to say to a modern Christian. There is no reason to assume that the first of these two interpreters is more objective than the second. Both are influenced in their estimate of the original author by their own present-day response to what he says.

If there were a methodology capable of eliciting the meaning of Scripture no matter who applied it, then it would make no difference whether Biblical scholars were believers in God or atheists, Christians, Jews, or Mohammedans, Roman Catholics or Protestants, immanentalists or transcendentalists. But because the ultimate content of Scripture is not merely religious phenomena or historical events or religious and ethical ideas and practices but witness to the reality of a God who can be known only where there is a response of faith and obedience, the character of the interpreter cannot be a matter of indifference. To the atheist, all the prophetic and apostolic visions of God are empty dreams, because to him the Unseen, which is the primary reality for every Biblical witness, is nonexistent. To the Jew, for whom the Messiah has not yet come, the central claim of the New Testament, that in Jesus' life, death, and resurrection, the long-awaited Messianic age broke in upon the world and created a totally new future for humanity, cannot be taken seriously, and the Old Testament cannot be interpreted as though in any way its promises had been fulfilled in Jesus Christ and the church. The Jewish scholar, or any scholar regardless of his religious viewpoint, may contribute much to the understanding of events, practices, and ideas in Biblical literature, but he could not be expected by the church to tell it what these Scriptures mean as revelation.

The Roman Church has consistently answered this question concerning the character of the interpreter of Scripture by insisting that only the church possesses the necessary understanding and faith to read the Scriptures aright and to draw from them their true meaning. What Scripture says cannot be left to the judgment of individual scholars, even though these scholars are thoroughly competent and loyal to the church's faith. The Holy See, which was instituted to guard the sacred deposit of Christian doctrine and therefore alone possesses the full depth of understanding of divine truth, alone is able finally to distinguish between a true and a false interpretation of Scripture. Our Protestant inclination is to repudiate violently this claim that the Scriptures must have an authoritative interpreter. We justify this reaction by pointing to instances in the past when within Roman Catholicism Biblical scholars have suffered severely for coming to conclusions that proved unpalatable to the Roman censor. Was not Luther himself forbidden by the church to find in his Bible the doctrines that he was preaching, and was not the Reformation fundamentally a liberation of the Bible from ecclesiastical domination and perversion that through it God might be free to speak his own word untrammeled in the church? Also, do we not find quite sufficient instances in our own Protestant past when the church has dealt severely with Biblical interpreters whose conclusions have not been acceptable to the existing mind of the church?

But must we, in order to escape such evils, go to the opposite extreme of complete individualism, allowing the church no place whatever in the process of interpretation? The Reformation principle of "the Bible its own interpreter," which was asserted in antithesis to the traditional subordination of the Bible to the church, has frequently in modern times been taken to mean "every man his own interpreter of the Bible," a sentiment that would not have been acceptable either to Luther or to Calvin. They had no intention of encouraging an indiscriminate individualism and were very well aware from the events of their own time that it could lead to a splintering of the church into sectarian fragments. They did not think, as many Protestants of our day seem to think, that the Bible could be left to interpret itself, all that was necessary being that a copy of it should be placed in the hands of every man. They knew the problems that "every man" was likely to meet in his attempt to understand Scripture, and they set great emphasis upon expository preaching and teaching as the church's guidance to "every man" in his understanding of Scripture. For the Reformers the church was still the authoritative interpreter of Scripture, but the relation between Scripture and church had been reversed so far as authority was concerned, the primary authority residing in the revelation of God in Scripture and the church's interpretation having always no more than a derived authority.

The problem, then, is to define the church's place in interpretation in such a way that it guards on the one hand against any interference with the freedom of critical scholarship to investigate the Scriptures and on the other hand against the intrusion into the church of alien doctrines under the guise of "the assured results of scientific Biblical scholarship." There must be no coercion of the scholar by the church, but neither should there be a more subtle coercion of the church by the scholar. Only a few years ago it took considerable courage for anyone, at least in wide sections of the church, to use the word " revelation " in anything except the most general fashion when " religion " was the word that alone had the approval of most scholars.

It may be helpful at this point to consider the relation in the Bible itself between the revelation of God and the " people of God " who in New Testament times were to be known as the church. Never in the Bible is there a disembodied revelation. Where God reveals himself in a word that manifests his purpose in the events of history, there has always to be a man who hears that word, remembers it, and communicates it to others. The revelation thus creates both a tradition and a people who are essential to the keeping alive of the knowledge that resides in the tradition. From the very beginning it was not sufficient that the tradition should be set down in writing, but rather it was essential that it should be remembered by a people. This we observe in both the Old Testament and the New. Moses received a revelation of the mind and will of God. It could have been set down in writing and distributed across the world. But at the heart of the revelation was the call of God for a people who would enter into a covenant or personal relation with him and in that relation be witnesses to the truth of the revelation. If all that was revealed to Moses was a code of religious and ethical principles, there was no need for the election of Israel. It was because it was the revelation of the *living* God and of the life that is possible in covenant or fellowship with the living God that there had to be not just sacred writings but also a people in whose very existence the meaning of the revelation would be manifest. The truth revealed to Moses could not be transmitted to later generations in any external or mechanical fashion; it had to be embodied in the life of Israel. And, as we well know, it was as Israel wrestled with the meaning of this revelation of God, which had been driven like an arrow into its heart, and constantly reinterpreted it to new generations that the record of the Scriptures came into being.

What happened in the New Testament is remarkably parallel. Had the gospel been a body of truths and principles concerning all things human and divine and nothing more, then Jesus would have been better advised to spend his time setting them down in writing instead of spending himself so recklessly upon those who gathered about him as he traveled through Palestine. That he wrote nothing on paper but committed his gospel entirely to the minds and hearts of his disciples was no accident but rather was what he had to do because of the nature of the revelation with which he was concerned. It could not be understood when merely stated in words but had to be embodied in a human life to be seen in its full reality. The heart of the revelation was a new relationship between God and man that opened a new kind of life to man. The relationship and the life were embodied in Jesus himself; they were concrete historical reality in him, but if they were to be communicated to mankind, they had to be embodied in a people, a community of human beings, and the witness of this community in its very existence would be essential to the understanding of the teaching. Thus, again, as in the Old Testament, the revelation was planted in the midst of a people; and as that people faced the situations and the decisions with which the revelation confronted them, it set down what it knew in Scriptures. In both instances the people of the revelation recognized the authority of the definitive record of the revelation that they possessed in Scripture, and had no inclination, because they had written these documents, to claim for themselves as an elect people an authority superior to Scripture. The word of Scripture was the criterion, or canon, of their life as a people of God. But at the same time, they were conscious of their high calling as witnesses in life to the truth proclaimed in Scripture. The truth of Scripture by its very nature could never be rightly understood in the world unless alongside the Scriptures there was a people in whose existence its meaning was being spelled out word by word.

What are the implications, then, of this intimate relation between Scripture and the church?

First, it reminds the scholar that the final and necessary translation of Scripture has to be spelled out in human flesh in the midst of a world that misunderstands it, questions it, denies it, and even hates it. There has to be a witness to God, to God's truth, to God's justice, to God's love, to man's hope in God, and to the futility of all life apart from God, a witness in the modern world that will so correspond to the prophetic and apostolic witness that it will be its legitimate continuation. And sometimes it is a witness that exacts the same cost of which there is abundant warning in Scripture. Always it is a witness that endangers life's commonest securities. But without it the Scriptures can never really be understood, and all our words of interpretation come to nothing. This is the goal of interpretation, and the scholar must know and be content that all his labors should in some way help the church to reach this goal.

Secondly, it suggests that the life of the church through the centuries provides a commentary upon the meaning of Scripture that dare not be disregarded without serious loss. The history of the church is in a very real sense the history of its understanding and misunderstanding of Scripture,[7] and in the midst of all misunderstanding there has always remained an understanding or the church would not have survived. It can be expected, therefore, of the Biblical scholar that he should have a respect and openness toward earlier interpreters, even though their method of approach may seem to him quite inadequate, not uncritical of them, lest he follow them in their misunderstandings, and yet not willing that any portion of the church's treasure of a true understanding should be lost.[8] The interpreter must therefore stand, not aside from the church, but in the full stream of the church's life. The tension that existed for a time between many Protestant churches and critical scholarship tended to make the scholar set a distance between himself and the church in order to protect the freedom of his scholarship, and this hiatus has often tended to harden into a tradition. The consequence can be that the scholar begins to draw his presuppositions and form his perspective from some other religious or cultural source than the historic life of the church. If, as has sometimes happened, he finds his spiritual home in the Hellenic tradition of humanism and his whole outlook becomes interfused with Greek conceptions of God and man, it is likely to have a profound effect upon his evaluation of many elements in Scripture.

[7] G. Ebeling, *Kirchengeschichte als Geschichte der Auslegung der Heiligen Schrift*, 1947.

[8] The revival of interest in the commentaries of Luther and Calvin is a sign of scholarly humility toward the past and can provide a significant enrichment of interpretation in the present. Both are careful scholars, within the limitations of their age, but both in their commentaries are also preachers and pastors of the church as well as scholars. The tendency in some quarters, however, to use Luther's or Calvin's exegesis in an uncritical fashion leads to unfortunate consequences.

This raises the problem of how the church is to deal with interpretations and interpreters that seem to endanger the very foundations of the Christian faith. It is strange and rather embarrassing that the church in the past has been most disturbed and has felt itself most endangered when some Biblical scholar has suggested that Moses could not have written the Pentateuch, or John the Gospel that bears his name, or that there are two Isaiahs, judgments that make no difference whatever to the spiritual condition of any human being and merely improve the intelligibility of the documents; yet so often the church has had no eyes at all to see the radical perversions of its doctrine and life that were obstructing its witness to the contemporary world. The impeachment of professors for no heresy in doctrine but only for being diligent historical and literary scholars is one of the most shameful episodes in the history of the church. But the doctrinal problem remains. What means has the church to guard against the introduction of false doctrines in the guise of " the findings of Biblical scholarship "?

The answer must be that theology itself, and in particular systematic theology, is the church's provision against false doctrine. The theologian is the watchman over the city of faith whose duty it is to see the enemy while he is yet afar off. It is his function to probe the presuppositions of the Biblical scholar (and of all others who speak and act on behalf of the church) and to test them by the criteria of truth that he possesses from within the Christian faith itself, not as a hostile critic but as a fellow worker in Christ, whose service to his fellow is the laying bare of assumptions that may until then have been unrecognized. All that he does is to ask, Is this what you consciously assume and is this the direction in which a really Christian faith compels you to go? Biblical scholarship in the nineteenth century was sorely in need of a critical service of this kind, and the same is true today. Nothing is so difficult as to be conscious of one's assumptions and one's theological direction, particularly if one stands in a tradition that has tended to neglect theological considerations. It is possible for a highly intelligent scholar to be very blind theologically. Perhaps there has been too sharp a division between the various theological disciplines, Old Testament scholars talking to Old Testament scholars, New Testament scholars talking to New Testament scholars, and systematic theologians to systematic theologians. The

apostles and from which the Christian church cannot separate itself without changing not just the character of its Scriptures but also the character of its own existence. Between these two are many different positions, some of which leave the relation very vague. In fact, the commonest position is that of deprecating all definite answers as " extreme " and leaving the question in complete vagueness. The uncertainty that prevails widely in the church concerning the relation of the Testaments to each other is a direct reflection of the vagueness of much of our Biblical and theological literature on the subject.

It should perhaps be emphasized that this is not a problem that concerns only Biblical scholars and systematic theologians but that it confronts us with great urgency in the practical life of the church. As long as ministers are content with a moralistic type of preaching and devotional meditations that require of the Scriptures little more than a convenient peg on which to hang the topic, the problem is not likely to arise. But when they begin to take in earnest not only their commission to preach the gospel but also the fact that the gospel is so bound up with the text of Scripture that they cannot preach it with confidence without becoming expositors of Scripture, they find themselves standing in frustration before the question, How are we to preach the Christian gospel upon the basis of an Old Testament text? Both in theology and in the practice of the church we have been proceeding for years as though we could continue to use both Testaments without saying anything definite about their relation to each other. The way in which until recently Old and New Testament studies were carried on in almost total independence of each other, as though each were a world complete in itself, helped to conceal the question. But now we have come to a point in scholarship and in the life of the church where the question can be neither concealed nor evaded.

If we recognize that doctrinal affirmations are made not only by duly constituted church courts but also by the visible order of things in the church, then we have to say that the church affirms the unity of the Testaments in the simple act of binding them between the covers of a single book, just as it affirms a sharply exclusive doctrine of the canon of Scripture as long as it continues to set the Bible alone on the reading desk in the sanctuary and to read only from it in Christian worship. In honesty, however, we have to acknowledge that these formal affirmations in the external order of the church stand often in contradiction to the conscious convictions of the Christian congregation. On both these points, the unity of the Bible and the absolute uniqueness of the Biblical revelation, there is great uncertainty in the mind of the church. In wide sections of Protestantism the Old Testament is quietly, perhaps unconsciously, dismissed as something less than Christian Scripture. An example of this occurs in the proceedings of one of the large American denominations. An important resolution of its national assembly reads: " Be it resolved: That we affirm our faith in the New Testament as a divinely inspired record and therefore a trustworthy, authoritative and all-sufficient rule of our faith and practice. We rededicate ourselves to Jesus Christ and call our entire denomination to the common task of sharing the whole gospel with the whole world." The Old Testament is not mentioned. To all intents and purposes much of the Old Testament has in our churches already been pushed into the background by both minister and congregation, only a few select passages appearing with any frequency. In services of worship where a lectionary is not used and there is only one Scripture lesson, invariably it is from the New Testament, and even where there are two lessons it is not uncommon to hear both read from the New Testament. It is the duty of the theologian, therefore, to ask which of these elements in the external order of the church corresponds to its actual faith, for a contradiction of this kind creates confusion in the church's life within itself and a loss of integrity in its witness to the world. It is intolerable for the church to seem to affirm in the formal order of its public worship something that in actuality it does not believe.

This problem of the unity of the Bible was thrust upon the European church with unusual force by political events in Germany in the 1930's. Both theology and church in Germany as in other lands had left this question in suspense for generations as though a decisive answer to it were not really necessary. But suddenly it became no longer a theoretical and academic consideration but an issue demanding decision in the concrete life of the church. The proposal was made to remove the Old Testament from the Christian Scriptures. Christians in general and theologians in particular had to ask themselves what the consequences would be for the life of the church if the Old Testament were removed from any place of authority or influence within it. And in that situation, where the Old Testament was under open attack, there took place a rediscovery of its significance for Christians. The attack itself served to reveal that the enemies of Christianity for some reason were more troubled by the Old Testament than by the New. And Christians under attack began to read the Old Testament as the early Christians read it, as the story of their own life, as the book out of which they were able to understand the tragic situations in which they were involved, but more than that, as the book through which God sustained them as a people in covenant with him in spite of every temptation and every disaster. They did not wait for permission from the theologians to read the Old Testament as Christian Scripture. It spoke to their need, and the voice they heard in it they recognized as the voice of their Lord. And it is a consequence of that experience of the church that German theologians today are wrestling with such seriousness with the relation of the two Testaments to each other.

The seriousness of the problem for the church in America, however, arises not from any external attack upon the Old Testament but from the church's inner uncertainty and embarrassment about what to do with the Old Testament. The historical investigation of the Bible has exposed to view a wide diversity of religious doctrines and practices from beginning to end of the Bible, so that to many scholars it has seemed impossible to find unity in either the Old Testament or the New Testament by themselves, much less in the Bible as a whole. Where is the unity between a worker of magic such as Elisha and a theologian-evangelist such as Second Isaiah, or between the approach to life of Ecclesiastes and that of the writer of Psalm 103, or between the priestly formulas of Leviticus and the preaching of an Amos who declares all ritual invalid if there is no obedience to God in the common affairs of life? Similarly in the New Testament, although the diversities are not so extreme, they are nevertheless present. The Letter of James cannot lightly be harmonized with Paul's letter to the Romans, nor the order of events in Paul's life as reported in The Acts with his own account in Galatians, nor the Gospel of John with the Synoptics. The unity of the New Testament documents in their focus upon Jesus Christ conceals from us sometimes the high measure of diversity that exists among them.

It is also a consequence of our historical approach that the Old and

New Testaments have been divorced from each other. The fact has seemed so obvious that it could brook no contradition that in the Old Testament we have the records of Israelite and Jewish religion while in the New Testament we have the records of the origin and early development of the Christian religion. These have been assumed to be separate religions, with Judaism bridging the gap between the others and in itself constituting a religion different from both. We have thus really three Biblical religions with genetic relations between them, but each distinctly different from the others. As a consequence, it has been standard practice very widely in Old Testament studies to deal with Old Testament books only as the records of Israelite religion and to regard it as an illegitimate intrusion of alien interests even to ask the question whether they are also Christian Scripture. Also in New Testament studies, since New Testament documents alone have to do with the rise of the Christian religion, it has often seemed unnecessary to pay much attention to the records of ancient Israelite religion. I. G. Matthews, in his *Religious Pilgrimage of Israel* (1947), represents the Old Testament as coming to its logical fulfillment in Judaism rather than in the New Testament and thus creates a deep and almost bottomless gulf between the two Testaments.

THE DEMAND FOR A DIVORCE

The discovery of the diversity of religious phenomena within the Bible has tended, then, to dissolve the marriage between the Testaments, but it has been in general a gentle drifting apart of the two and not a violent or abrupt rupture of relations. It comes, therefore, with something of a shock when we hear a number of distinguished scholars of our day demanding that the Old Testament be no longer regarded as Christian Scripture. But they are merely saying openly and in a provocative negative form what has been assumed in much of the Biblical scholarship of the past century and a half.

The most eminent spokesman for this viewpoint is Rudolf Bultmann. The peculiarity of his position is that, even though he denies that the Old Testament can be regarded by the Christian as an integral part of God's revelation to him, he insists that everyone who has even the slightest understanding of our historical involvement must know that we cannot retain Christianity and reject the Old Testament. " It is an Either-Or, both of them or neither of them." [1] Approaching the Old Testament from an existentialist standpoint and asking not what it means as an isolated phenomenon but what it means for him as a twentieth-century Christian, he comes to the conclusion that it has validity as an expression of the law of God under which a man must know he stands before he can rightly hear the gospel. But the Old Testament is not the only expression of the law of God. Paul recognized a law written in the non-Israelite conscience, and so we too must recognize all human declarations of what God requires of man as preparation for the hearing of the gospel. The Old Testament is not absolutely essential for this purpose, and its use in the church is justified only on pedagogical grounds. But this does not say quite enough. The Old Testament has become part of our existence as it has come to us from the past mingled together with the heritage of antiquity, so that it is one of the factors that we have to reckon with in our self-understanding. But it brings to us a unique contribution in making the element of decision in self-understanding radical and in guarding us against an idealistic or utilitarian interpretation of the ethical imperative. The Old Testament has no heroes, no idealized humanity as the Greeks have, but knows only a man who comes to the realization of the meaning of his life in the midst of historical events, a creature who depends upon God to give his life meaning in time and who does not seek its meaning in a timeless realm. In this understanding of man's existence the Old Testament stands together with the New Testament against the Greek or the humanistic or the idealistic.

But this does not mean that the Old Testament is the word of God for Christians. It remains only law in contrast to the gospel. But Bultmann knows his Old Testament too well to leave that statement unconditioned. He goes on to show that there is also a knowledge of the grace of God in the Old Testament. The giving of the law itself was an act of grace. And it was grace that made Israel a chosen people in covenant with God and sent them prophets and other leaders. They knew also the grace of God's forgiveness. And, if the gospel is the proclamation of God's grace and forgiveness to sinners, then it is

[1] R. Bultmann, " Die Bedeutung des Alten Testaments für den Christlichen Glauben," in *Glauben und Verstehen* I (1954), p. 313.

certainly present in the Old Testament, though not always in its purest form. Thus the church can take over many parts of the Old Testament and make them its own. Finally, there is grace in the eschatological hope of the Old Testament in which God is represented as bringing his salvation to a sinful nation that does not deserve it. God brings the dead to life and makes a new covenant with a people who have hopelessly shattered the old one.

But now, Bultmann makes the strange judgment that this grace in the Old Testament is grace only for Israel. In Christ, God's grace and forgiveness are mediated in a wholly new way. In place of Israel there is a church that has no history as peoples, nations, and cultures have their histories, since it exists solely as the means whereby the gospel is proclaimed. The word of God that is Jesus Christ is so completely new and unique that nothing in the Old Testament can any longer be called the word of God. "For the Christian faith the Old Testament is no longer revelation as it was and is for the Jew. For him who stands in the church the history of Israel is past and done with. Christian preaching cannot and dare not remind the hearers that God delivered their fathers from Egypt, that he led his people into exile, and again returned them to the land of promise. . . . Israel's history is not our history." [2]

Some light is thrown upon this demand for a radical discontinuity by passages in Bultmann's writings in which he pronounces the Old Testament conception of God as creator of the world and Lord of history to be primitive mythology no longer tenable for any thoughtful modern man. We live in a world in which we do not expect either miracles or any other events in which God will act directly. In his recent American publication *Jesus Christ and Mythology*,[3] he says that he is prepared to make the personal affirmation, "God is my creator," but not the cosmic one, that God is the world's creator. In his sermons he does make the cosmic affirmation with considerable emphasis [4] but apparently expects it to be understood in a totally different sense from that which it has in the Old Testament. Also, it is offensive to Bultmann that eschatology in the Old Testament looks for the realization of God's Kingdom

[2] R. Bultmann, *op. cit.,* p. 333.
[3] R. Bultmann, *Jesus Christ and Mythology*, pp. 38, 69.
[4] R. Bultmann, *Marburger Predigten.*

on earth and in a material form. This, to him, is misleading, for the eschatological realm, in which alone man's true life is to be found and which is disclosed in the Word of the cross, transcends the world and history and is accessible only to a faith that surrenders all hope and trust concerning this world. It is peculiar that Bultmann should think it possible for the New Testament to be detached from the Old Testament faith in God as creator and that he should fail to see that in all the concreteness and worldliness of what is expected in Old Testament eschatology the basic hope is for an era in which God's sovereignty in the midst of his people will come to its perfect realization. It is so difficult to find in his writings any adequate reason for his dechristianizing, if not decanonizing, of the Old Testament that one is impelled to ask whether it may not be the consequence of theological presuppositions antithetical to a Biblical faith that have remained hidden even from Bultmann himself. It may have some significance that in his remarkable sermons, delivered during the years of the Hitler regime, in which he sets Christ before his hearers as their only hope for the future, there is rarely a word that makes one conscious that Germans were facing life or death decisions in the realm of political life. While the eschatological realm, in which one is set free from the world to receive his true life and his future as a gift from God, does not remove the Christian from the world, it seems to float beyond the world in which political decisions are made and to have a purely individual realization. There seem to be two realms in which man has his life. The Old Testament doctrine of God as creator of all things and Lord over the events of this world would make impossible any such separation of the two realms.

Kraeling

A viewpoint in some ways similar to that of Bultmann is voiced by an American Old Testament scholar, Emil Kraeling, in *The Old Testament Since the Reformation,* published in 1955. To him so much in the Old Testament is objectionable to the Christian mind and alien to a truly Christian theology that it seems to endanger the church if it continues to be regarded as Christian Scripture. Early in his book he seeks to enlist the support of Luther for his position, making the rather venturesome statement that Luther would have rejected most of the Old Testament if he had not shrunk from doing anything that would seriously detract from the authority of

Scripture. He says: " One definitely feels that if it were not for the use of the Old Testament made in the New Testament, Luther might have veered farther in the Marcionitic direction. If he had realized as clearly as we are able to do today that the Messianic prophecy of the Old Testament does not actually predict the life of Christ or the redemption brought by him in as clear and direct a manner as the New Testament writers and the early fathers believed, the revelation of the Old Testament would probably have shrunk to purely historical significance in his eyes. Human values of a spiritual or moral sort alone would have remained." [5] Having conjured up a hypothetical rather than a historical Luther to support his view, Kraeling goes on to find more legitimate encouragement in Schleier-macher, for whom Christianity, apart from the purely historical relation, had " the same relation to Judaism as to heathenism," so that a " gulf exists between the Hebrew and the Christian consciousness."

An even more sweeping repudiation of the Old Testament is that of Emanuel Hirsch.[6] He finds in it only a negative value, a legalistic antithesis to the New Testament gospel of grace, which is necessary only as a dark background to bring out the brightness of the gospel light. Hirsch tells how from his earliest days as a student he was aware that the Old Testament was not a Christian book, but only when he learned in a parish how easily simple folk could be misled by it into a definitely non-Christian faith did he realize that it imperiled the purity of the faith. To him it is therefore essential to bring fully into the open what seems to be the contradiction between Israelite-Jewish religion and the Christian religion. It is symptomatic of Hirsch's thinking that he was able to bring together both the prophetic faith and Judaism under the one term " legalism " and that the antithesis between Jesus and the Pharisees was interpreted by him as an antithesis between Jesus and the whole Old Testament. He also showed an extreme anxiety to negate the claim of the prophets that their word from God has direct authority over the life of the state, an anxiety that may have been rather directly related to his sympathy with an extreme nationalism in politics. Certainly his attitude must be seen in its social context.

[5] Emil Kraeling, *The Old Testament Since the Reformation,* p. 20.
[6] Emanuel Hirsch, *Das Alte Testament und die Predigt des Evangeliums.*

These three instances are sufficient to show the open challenge that the unity of the Bible must meet today. But in order to see the full complexity of the situation we must balance these denials of unity with several affirmations of unity.

THE AFFIRMATION OF UNITY

Barth

Again, it has been Karl Barth who, more than any other scholar, has insisted upon the inseparableness of the Testaments, that the New Testament cannot be rightly understood apart from the Old Testament or the Old apart from the New. For him, Jesus Christ is the revelatory center of all Scripture. All lines point forward to him and then forward from him. But only in him is the *fullness* of God's self-revelation reality, concrete historical reality, so that what elsewhere is shadowed, obscure, or open to misconstruction, has to be understood from this center. Thus the meaning of the Creation is disclosed not primarily in the Genesis stories of creation but in the union of creator and creation in the person of Jesus Christ, where alone each is revealed in its only true relation to the other. The Genesis stories are then read in the light of this revelation and are found to stand in a most amazing unity with it. Similarly, God's covenant relation with Israel is set in continuity with God's new covenant relation with mankind revealed in the oneness of God and man in Jesus Christ, so that God's eternal will is seen to be a will to community with man, not just with some men but with all men. His covenant with Israel is interpreted then as his giving of himself in love to Israel that, through Israel, he might bind all men to himself, and the new covenant in Jesus Christ as the fulfillment of what remained unfulfilled but nevertheless foreshadowed in Israel. The unity of the Testaments is the presupposition of all Barth's massive volumes on *Dogmatics,* in which the reader stands constantly in wonder — or in abhorrence — at the manner in which he brings widely separated passages of Scripture together to shed light on the others. Whether he goes too far in this we shall consider in the next chapter. Here it is sufficient to say that the exegesis embedded in his *Dogmatics,* which provides both its foundation and structure, presents the strongest case that is to be found anywhere for the conclusion that the Biblical writers in both Testaments, in spite of their wide divergencies, were all of them witnesses, each in his own way, to the reality and saving action of one and the same God.

In many of the Old Testament theologies that have appeared in recent years (Procksch, Eichrodt, Jacob, Vriezen, Knight), it is taken as axiomatic that the Old Testament reaches its goal in Jesus Christ and so has to be understood not as a complete entity in itself but as incomplete and reaching forward toward a completion that is yet to come. But the impression is given too often that, once this is said, a satisfactory recognition of the unity of the Testaments has been achieved, when actually it leaves many of the most important and difficult aspects of the subject undiscussed.

We need to be reminded, perhaps, that more influential than any theologian in forcing this problem to the forefront of attention has been the power with which the Old Testament has spoken in the midst of the dilemmas of the modern church. We have already considered how the German church, confronted with totalitarian Nazism, began to hear from the Old Testament the very words of judgment and promise that were most relevant to its situation. God's first command to Israel, " Thou shalt have no other gods before me," became to some the word of life and to others the word of death. There could be no question but that it was the word of the church's Lord. So also in the American church, confronted by a democratic culture that tends more and more to claim the whole man for itself and to relegate God and religion to a harmless, inner-spiritual or ecclesiastical realm, the Old Testament is beginning to be heard in its robust earthiness, making its uncompromising demand that God's sovereignty should be acknowledged in every part of our human existence. Just because American religion is so permeated by a vague humanistic idealism, the words of the Old Testament, when they are stripped of the coating of sentimental piousness with which they have been overlaid and are heard in their freshness, fall upon the mind and spirit with something of the shock of icy water. We begin to be aware that, beyond this shock and awakening that the Old Testament provides for us, the New Testament takes on a different meaning. Read in the context of the Old Testament, it cuts into the life of the contemporary church with a sharpness that it did not seem to have before. The secret of this is that it has always been easier to find in the New Testament Scripture encouragement for a humanistic, idealistic, spiritualized version of Christianity than in the Old. The Old Testament is like a rude, abrupt, Hebrew guardian of Christian truth who, if we heed it, warns us when we are wandering off into paths of religion and life more congenial though less strenuous. It is because the Old Testament has this power and sharpness today that the question of its relation with the New Testament demands consideration.

An extreme assertion of the unity of the Testaments was made by Wilhelm Vischer in 1935 in his *Witness of the Old Testament to Christ.*[7] He was not content like Procksch and Eichrodt to see in Jesus Christ the goal of the Old Testament but maintained that since Jesus Christ is the Word of God and the Old Testament is in all its parts witness to the Word of God, it should be possible to find direct references to Christ and his church throughout the Old Testament. Therefore, by a liberal use of allegorical and typological interpretations he was able to find such foreshadowing almost everywhere. So offensive has this practice been to many scholars that they fail to recognize the more substantial contributions of Vischer to the discussion of the problem of unity. He must be accorded the honor of being the first among Old Testament scholars to plunge into a subject that was being left severely alone by most of his colleagues, and of being the first to struggle with the problems of the theological exegesis of the Old Testament. Also, his work provoked many other scholars to give their attention to the subject. He saw the problem with clarity, but in his attempt at a solution he fell back too uncritically upon the exegesis of Luther and Calvin. Many of the allegorical and typological interpretations that are found in his writings have their source in the commentaries of the Reformers.

In the English-speaking world, A. G. Hebert's *Throne of David* (1941) and *The Authority of the Old Testament* (1947) were the pioneer attempts to grapple with the problem, but unfortunately they fell in some measure into the same groove as the books of Vischer. Having traced with care the strands of doctrine and life that bind the Testaments into a unity, Hebert proceeded from the premise that the revelation of the Old Testament is Christian in character to the conclusion that Christian truths and realities should be foreshadowed in the text. Typology, or homology as he preferred

[7] Wilhelm Vischer, *The Witness of the Old Testament to Christ.*

to call it, and allegory recommended themselves as ready instruments for the discovery of such foreshadowings, their use in the New Testament seeming to be sufficient vindication of their use today. Hebert and Vischer together have been responsible for the widespread impression that recognition of the unity of the Testaments leads inevitably to a revival of typology.

THE PROBLEM IN THE PAST

In the light of past history it is not surprising, once the question of the relation of the Testaments to each other has come into prominence, to find the answers going to opposite extremes. This is what has been happening ever since New Testament times. The church has never for long found a tenable solution to this problem, periods when the unity has been vigorously affirmed being followed almost directly by some form of equally vigorous denial. The early church affirmed the unity of the Old Testament Scriptures with its gospel, preaching and teaching Christ out of the Old Testament, but, as long as the record of the gospel was in fluid form, a clear distinction was preserved between Scripture and gospel. But when the records of the gospel became canonical New Testament Scripture, united with Old Testament Scripture, the whole came soon to be interpreted as inspired Scripture without distinction. An undifferentiated unity was affirmed, and thereby the problem was created of what to do with elements in the Old Testament that could not readily be harmonized with the New.

Marcion, in the middle of the second century, became the spokesman for those who saw the gospel endangered by the Old Testament. Defenders of the unity of the Testaments might resort to allegory and typology in order to find a Christian meaning in troublesome passages, but to Marcion this was a subterfuge that evaded the real issue. He insisted upon the literal meaning of the text and upon the existence of a radical contradiction in nature between the God of the Old Testament and the God of the New. He was not aware to what an extent it was his Hellenization of the gospel that made the Old Testament so dark and distasteful to him. His realization that the rejection of the Old Testament would carry with it a radical dismemberment also of the New was in its own way a negative witness to the inseparableness of the two. His positive

contribution was in forcing the church to recognize the existence
of the problem, but it was in the distress of the problem that the
church turned so extensively and decisively to allegory and typology in order to retain the Old Testament as an integral part of
Christian Scripture.

Luther and Calvin exposed the problem once more when they
denied the validity of allegory while at the same time asserting the
unity of both Testaments in their witness to Jesus Christ. At many
points in the Old Testament they could find passages in which there
seemed to be a very clear shadowing forth of the ministry, death,
and resurrection of Jesus and of the experiences of his church. But
their difficulties became acute when they applied the Christological
principle to the whole of the Old Testament. Luther had a partial
escape in his selective approach to Scripture while Calvin with his
more comprehensive doctrine of Scripture had to meet the difficulty
in its full dimensions. The most fruitful aspect of Calvin's interpretation lay in his discovery of a very real unity between the word
heard by the prophets and the word that was incarnate in Jesus
Christ, and a continuity of life between the people of God in the
Old Testament and the people of God both in the New Testament
and in the church of the ages. But because Luther and Calvin asserted a unity of the Testaments in which there was no adequate
recognition of the discontinuity between them, their solution was
not able to endure. In the scholastic period that followed, the unity
was asserted in such an undiscriminating way that even the distinctions recognized by the Reformers were ignored and the Old Testament received a direct authority in the church that threatened to
Judaize Christianity. The memory of this Puritan misconstruction
that is still strongly influential, making men react in distrust from
all attempts to reassert the unity of the Old Testament with the
New.

The scholastic assertion of a static and undifferentiated unity was
challenged by the development of historical-critical scholarship in
which there was not so much a direct attack upon the unity as a
totally new approach to the documents in which the unity was dissolved without anyone's being particularly conscious that it was happening. The theory of progressive revelation provided a superficial
pattern of historical unity that kept even scholars from being dis-

turbed by the disappearance of all real theological unity. Unfortunately, in the nineteenth and early twentieth centuries the only spokesmen in our English-speaking world for the theological unity of the Testaments were proponents of a literalistic theory of an inerrant text who were hostile to the whole enterprise of historical and literary research in the Scriptures.

Any new approach to the problem of unity should be attempted in the light of this history. Invariably the attempts to cut the Old Testament apart from the New Testament have accentuated in the church the consciousness and conviction that the Old Testament is Christian Scripture and essential to the life of the church. And invariably the assertion of this unity in any form that verges over into an assertion of uniformity in the witness of Scripture has produced eventually a radical reaction in the direction of a repudiation of the Old Testament. The church in the beginning was actually wiser than it has been in later years, in binding the Testaments together and yet setting a clear line of distinction between them. Unity and yet distinction must both be preserved if a tenable solution to the problem is to be found.

Progressive Revelation as a Tentative Solution

Since there are many quarters in which the theory of progressive revelation is still considered a satisfactory solution, its inadequacies require some attention. Its virtue in the nineteenth century was similar to that of allegory in the second and third centuries — while highly questionable in itself, it has been a very present help in time of trouble, enabling the church to maintain at least the semblance of unity in spite of the difficulties of the situation. But while the church may cling to a plank in time of crisis, it needs a more seaworthy vessel if it is to continue its voyage in a satisfactory manner. The whole concept of a progressive revelation is alive with contradictions. What it usually describes is not a progress in revelation but rather a progressive development of religious ideas and practices, the word " revelation " being used loosely as a synonym for religion. At one time the forms of religion within the Bible were ranged in a neat, ascending order, with primitive, animistic, nomad religion at the bottom representing the Mosaic era and the religion of Jesus at the top representing the apex of religious development. In recent years the reassessment of the Mosaic era and of the whole history of the prophetic movement has shattered that neat formula. We see primitive and highly prophetic forms of religion existing alongside each other and in tension with each other almost continuously. There is also a theological difficulty in speaking of a progress of revelation, if revelation is a name for God's revealing of himself. Progressive revelation suggests a series of revelations of which the earlier ones are quite imperfect and inadequate but which, as time passes, become progressively more perfect and more adequate until the completely perfect and adequate revelation is reached in Jesus Christ. But it becomes very difficult to maintain this pattern when we are asked to indicate the imperfections and inadequacies of revelation in the Twenty-third Psalm, or in the confession of sin and apprehension of forgiveness in the Fifty-first Psalm, or in the praise of God that is offered in the One Hundred and Third Psalm. At what point has Second Isaiah an inadequate knowledge of God in Isa., ch. 40, or in the amazing fifty-third chapter of his book? These examples could be multiplied a thousand times over. The theory of progressive revelation breaks down because it necessitates an artificial structure of progressively higher levels of revelation, a scheme that does not correspond to the realities that confront us in the text of the Old Testament. It must also be said that the theory of progressive revelation has left in many minds the impression that once we have reached the Christian level of revelation the earlier stages are no longer of more than an antiquarian interest. Why should we go back and ascend the steps of revelation painfully with the Hebrews when we can begin on the highest step with Jesus and Paul? This theory, so interpreted, has played a very significant part in encouraging the neglect of the Old Testament. The unity that it seems to establish is no real unity but little more than an intellectual construction to hide a radical disunity.

A Fresh Approach

The first step in a fresh approach to unity should be to ask why the Christian church in its beginnings found the Old Testament necessary to its existence. Harnack[8] a half century ago made the

[8] Adolf Harnack, *Das A. T. in den paulinischen Briefen und in den paulinischen Gemeinden.*

attempt to show that it was only in Jewish churches that Paul made use of the Scriptures (later called the Old Testament) and that in Gentile churches he left them aside as irrelevant for non-Jews, but his argument has very slight support in the evidence and creates far more historical difficulties than it solves. The witness of every part of the New Testament is that in both Jewish and Gentile churches from a very early date the Old Testament was intimately involved both in the preaching and teaching of the gospel and in Christian worship. The Holy Scriptures in the first-century church were simply the Old Testament, not a Jewish sacred book taken over from Judaism without any change in understanding or interpretation, a mere carry-over from the past, but a book transformed in its meaning in the context of the gospel and interpreted in a totally new way by the Christian church.

The Old Testament was essential to the early church because the church understood itself and the gospel of Jesus Christ in which it had its origin as the fulfillment of the age-long purpose of God manifest in the Old Testament. We shall in a later chapter give more careful consideration to the category of promise and fulfillment to show how firmly established it is in the structure of New Testament faith and how reasonable it is to conclude that it was integral to the thinking of Jesus himself. Sometimes it has been represented as invented by the early church in order to justify itself as the true Israel of God in controversy with Judaism, but it belongs at the very heart of the Old Testament faith and was embedded in the earliest credo of Israel.[9] The history of Israel moved from promise to fulfillment, and, as each fulfillment was only partial, it pointed forward to another fulfillment yet to come. Israel lived in its hours of darkness and frustration by faith in a just and gracious purpose of God that was yet to be realized. Jesus, saturated as he was in the Old Testament life and thought, would be thoroughly aware that to speak of fulfillment would at once call promises to mind.

According to Mark, Jesus began his preaching with the announcement, "The time is fulfilled." According to Luke, he followed the reading of Isa. 61:1-3 in the synagogue at Nazareth by saying, "This day is this Scripture fulfilled in your ears." According to Matthew, he countered the fear that he would abolish the Scriptures in favor

[9] W. Zimmerli, "Verheissung und Erfüllung," EvTh (1952).

of his new teaching by asserting that he was come not to destroy the Law and the Prophets but to fulfill them. According to the Gospel of John, it was the word heralded by the prophets that was incarnate in Jesus (John 1:45). The use of the term "new covenant" in the institution of the Lord's Supper is meant to say that what is happening is the fulfillment of Jeremiah's promise of a new covenant. A massive witness to this concept of fulfillment is found also in the frequent quotations of the Old Testament in the New. In some instances these follow a mechanical pattern of interpreting New Testament events as having been predicted in certain verses of the Old Testament, but this must not be allowed to conceal a deeper concern that is evident in many of the quotations. The church's reading of the Old Testament was not primarily a curious search for predictions of the events of the life of Jesus and of the church. This was a secondary development. At the primary level it was a reading of the Old Testament as the promise of what had actually happened to bring the church into being and thus a consciousness of the Old Testament's having been written specifically for the Christian church. The outpouring of the Spirit in Acts, ch. 2, was interpreted as the fulfillment of the promise of the Spirit in Joel. Here, as elsewhere, the concept of fulfillment is eschatological. Christians were conscious that they were living in the Last Days, the days when all God's promises to Israel were to come true. What God had begun in Abraham and Moses, in David, in Elijah, in Isaiah and Jeremiah, he was now bringing to its completion in the new day inaugurated and incarnated in Jesus Christ. As the writer to the Hebrews puts it, the word that God had spoken in many and diverse ways in Israel was present in its completeness in the days of fulfillment.

There is an important distinction between the categories "promise" — "fulfillment" and "prediction" — "fulfillment" that has not always been properly recognized. Promise — fulfillment is a basic Biblical category that is rooted in the prophetic understanding of God's relation to history. God has a purpose for his people that embraces the events of history. The revelation of that purpose is understood by Israel as a promise for the future, but in the promise itself the divine purpose is revealed and is already at work. It is no bare word about a future event, but rather it is a word that contains within it a very real foretaste of that future. Thus the promise to Abraham of a great future (Gen., ch. 12) is not a bare prediction but is a word from God that as it works in Abraham and in those who come after him has in it the power to create that future. Gerhard von Rad, in his *Theologie des Alten Testaments* (1957), points out that the whole of Old Testament history comes to us within a pattern of promise and fulfillment. The Hexateuch in its total scope is a witness to the faithfulness of God. Having promised to the patriarchs a home in Palestine, he eventually brought their offspring to the fulfillment of that promise. So also the historical books represent another kind of fulfillment, God's promise of ruin to an unfaithful Israel being fulfilled in the tragic events of 722, 597, and 586 B.C. Thus when the New Testament church speaks of fulfillment and points to the promises in various parts of the Old Testament, of which Christ and his church are the fulfillment, it is not merely finding predictions of New Testament events in the Old but rather interpreting the whole of the Old Testament as the beginning of a work of God that has its completion in Christ and his church. Thus it is that in order to see the whole of God's purpose, which comes to its fulfillment in Christ and his church, the Old Testament is essential. The promise falls far short of the fulfillment. The mystery of Christ was not made known to men in former generations (Eph. 3:4-5). But it was seen as from afar, and the story of the fulfillment must be held together with the story of the promise and of all the partial fulfillments of the promise, which in their brokenness and incompleteness have ever pointed beyond themselves to the fulfillment yet to come. The Christian gospel, therefore, since it was from the beginning the proclamation not of something totally unheard-of but of the inauguration in Christ of a kingdom and a new covenant and a new Israel promised from of old, took up into itself and used for its primary expression the Scriptures of the Old Testament. So deeply and subtly interwoven is the Old Testament with the writings of the New that no surgery even of the most expert kind can cut the two apart without leaving the New Testament itself in a sadly butchered condition.

It has already been suggested that Jesus himself thought of his mission as the fulfillment of the Old Testament promise. We have not nearly so much evidence for his use of the Old Testament as we have for that of Paul, because he spoke with such directness and never attempted to lend additional authority to his teachings by supporting them in the rabbinic fashion with quotations from the Old Testament. His remarkable independence may well have roused the fear that he was discarding the Scriptures, a fear that he was justly attempting to allay in the words of Matt. 5:17, "Think not that I am come to destroy the law, or the prophets" (i.e., the Old Testament Scriptures). A close examination of Jesus' words and actions brings to light a powerful element of continuity with the Old Testament. He stands in the full stream of the prophetic tradition embodying in himself all their characteristic concerns. He knows himself " sent from God to Israel." We tend to focus so much on his concern with individuals that we miss his character as a prophet of judgment upon his nation who refuses to go beyond or to send his disciples beyond its borders until the nation has heard the call to repent. He is God's spokesman to Israel, but also Israel's intercessor with God. Like all the prophets before him, he expressed in word and action God's special care for the poor and the oppressed and the outcast. Also, like the prophets, he rooted his ethic of justice and mercy and love in the necessity that a people in fellowship with God should be like God in their natures, reflecting his holiness and justice and love. So close did he feel himself to an earlier prophet that he could read Isa., ch. 61, as a description of his own mission and could find in the figure of the Suffering Servant an illumination of his own task and destiny. In his baptism the Voice of God came to him through words that we find in Ps. 2 and Isa., ch. 42, and in his temptations three verses from Deuteronomy clarified for him his Messianic destiny. On the cross the words of Ps. 22 were on his lips. Yet more impressive is the way in which the essential content of the Old Testament is taken up, transformed, and reinterpreted in Jesus' words and actions and in his very being. Thus, when we speak of the Old Testament being fulfilled in Jesus Christ, it is not a formal pattern of promise and fulfillment that is being superimposed upon the materials, but rather it is a recognition that in the most intensely personal way the purpose of God that was at work in Israel through the centuries came to its full revelation and triumph in Jesus Christ. Jesus Christ does not stand alone. Rather, just as he reaches forward and takes his apostles into such intimate oneness with him that the church could hear his voice and know his Spirit only in fellowship with the apostles, so also he reaches backward into Israel and binds himself together with all the servants of God — prophets, priests, and kings — who lived by the word that they heard from God, acknowledging that for any man to be in fellowship with God through them was to be in fellowship with him. There are differences between Jesus and Paul, but no one is likely because of those differences to question Paul's right to say " Christ liveth in me." So also there are differences between Jesus and the various witnesses to God who speak in the Old Testament, but those differences should not prevent us from recognizing the oneness with them that Jesus professed when he called his mission a fulfillment.

There is danger, however, in emphasizing this unity of Jesus with the Old Testament that the radical uniqueness of God's Word and action in Jesus Christ may be forgotten. It is not unknown for students who have entered passionately into the exploration of the Old Testament, have plumbed the heights and depths of the human problem in Genesis and The Psalms, and have learned what it is to wait upon God and to know themselves servants of the Word with Second Isaiah, to be puzzled wherein the New Testament actually goes beyond the Old. The relation begins to seem to them to be merely that between lower and higher peaks in the same mountain range. The wall of separation between Jeremiah or Second Isaiah and Jesus seems very thin. But that is the illusion of the man who stands in the foothills of the mountains and as he looks beyond to the mountaintop is surprised that it seems so near; not until he ventures across the gap between does he realize his mistake. The unity of Jesus with the Old Testament seems shattered when we grasp the dimensions of the claim that the New Testament church made for him (in recognition of the claim that was made, if not by him openly, then in him by the reality of his being). He did not just speak the word of God; he *was* the Word, so that not only his person but also his actions and even the things that happened to him were ultimate manifestations of God's truth. God's Spirit possessed him, not in the broken fashion known by prophets, priests, and others in Israel, but with such fullness and power that there was an identity (in spite of an abiding distinction) between God's Spirit and his own spirit. Others had proclaimed God's holiness and mercy, but in him this holiness was present in such a way that no

man who met him could evade being driven by it either to repentance or to furious self-justification, and this mercy was his gift to
men as he confidently forgave them their sins. God was in him, reconciling the world to himself and creating a new humanity. This
was Paul's testimony, and there is no reason to believe that he invented the interpretation, for it is present in a concealed form in
Jesus' own parables, which reflect his consciousness of what God
was doing for men through him.

There is no incarnation in the Old Testament. Nor is there a
Pentecost, with the Spirit of God taking possession of men and making them his dwelling place on earth. Nor is there a church, whose
members are torn apart from all national, cultural, or even family
relationships to be unconditionally at the service of God that
through them the whole world may be claimed for God's Kingdom. Death is not overcome, nor are life and immortality brought
to light, for the life of God has not yet been made manifest in our
human flesh. In short, the uniqueness of the New Testament gospel
stands or falls by the assertion of John that " the Word was made
flesh, and dwelt among us, . . . full of grace and truth," the Word
that from eternity was with God and yet was God, and whose name
among men was Jesus Christ. The whole Old Testament would
seem to forbid such a claim in its exaltation of God alone and the
hatred of idolatry that made it intolerant of any being alongside
of God. That Jews, saturated in the tradition of monotheism, should
have made such a claim for Jesus of Nazareth and, most shocking
of all, for one who had died a criminal's death, is in itself astonish-
ing. They made it (and here we think particularly of Paul) because to deny that he who met them in Jesus Christ was God was
to deny the God of Israel, the God of their fathers, and to respond
to him in faith and obedience was no idolatry but was to have all
the promises of God fulfilled joyfully in their midst.

The relation of Jesus to the Old Testament is epitomized for us
in the relation of Jesus to John the Baptist. John the Baptist is in a
very full sense an Old Testament prophet of towering stature of
whom the record happens to be preserved in the New Testament.
A report of his work, or a collection of his oracles, if it had been
preserved, could have been taken up into the Old Testament as an
epilogue to the works of the great prophets. In message, in spirit,

and even in outward appearance, he belongs in the Old Testament. And yet he stands at the opening of the New Testament! To him Jesus said both a Yes! and a No! His baptism by John and his words of commendation for John (especially Matt. 11:11) were an affirmation of his oneness with him. And yet Jesus refused to have his message and mission forced into the same pattern as the message and mission of John. Unity but not uniformity! And Jesus justified his difference from John with the words, " Wisdom is vindicated in all her children " (Luke 7:35). Wisdom is a synonym for the Word of God. That which bound John and Jesus together was that each was unconditionally at the service of the Word of God. They differed in their teaching, in their religious practices, and in the general character of their missions, and yet John's word and work was recognized by the Christian church as belonging in close continuity with that of Jesus and as forming the divine preparation for it. It says a great deal that the church set John within each of the Gospels and not somewhere on the outside of them.

Jesus' refusal to let his unity with John be interpreted as requiring a uniformity with him is typical of his relation to the whole Old Testament. It was a shock to the rabbis and to many of the people of his time that he could say a decisive No as well as a decisive Yes to the Old Testament.[10] He said No to the divorce laws set down in Deut. 24:1. He said No to many of the regulations concerning food and the Sabbath. And, if John 8:1-11 contains a valid tradition, he said No to the law that decreed the death penalty for a woman taken in adultery. Many scholars have been misled by Jesus' evident respect for the authority of the Old Testament into equating his attitude to it with that of the contemporary rabbis for whom every word was inspired and authoritative. The evidence indicates that he broke with the rabbinic tradition and that in him the prophetic

---

[10] The placing of Ps. 91:11-12 in the mouth of the devil in Jesus' temptations in Luke 4:10, 11 (Matt. 4:6) involves a repudiation of the surface meaning of the psalm, which seems to promise the believer freedom from all harm, but it does not mean a total rejection of the psalmist's confidence in God's providence. It is interesting that Hirsch quotes this psalm as one of the points at which he first perceived how misleading the Old Testament could be for Christians. Actually, it forms an excellent example of how the New Testament reinterprets the Old Testament. Psalm 91 has to be read by Christians in the light of the cross, and, when so read, engenders a faith in God's providence that has in it no false expectations.

tradition, which had been largely lost in Judaism, came alive again. No prophet ever concerned himself whether or not his message was in exact conformity with the prophets who preceded him. His unity with them was a larger and deeper thing. He was bound into one with all the prophets before him by the unconditional character of his relationship to the word of God, which had found utterance and active power also in them. Therefore, he had freedom to speak his own word in his own time in his own way without any fear that by his differences from the others he would disrupt the goodly fellowship of the prophets. It is this prophetic freedom which comes from the inner binding to the word of God that is characteristic of Jesus and distinguishes him sharply from the rabbis of his time. It is noteworthy that this same freedom is found in Paul, whose intense consciousness of unity with Jesus Christ never led him into any kind of slavish conformity with Jesus. The unity of Jesus and Paul was a reality at such a depth that it required of Paul that he be himself and speak his gospel in freedom in his new situation without attempting at any point to make his words tally exactly with the reported sayings of Jesus. This freedom is evident also in Paul's use of the Old Testament to which, like Jesus, he had to say both a yes and a no, a yes to it as proclaiming the same gospel that he heard in Jesus Christ, a no to it in so far as any part of it could be interpreted as offering salvation by obedience to the law. It was after Paul's time that the church began to confuse unity with uniformity and to expect of the Old Testament that wherever one opened its pages he should be able to hear the Christian gospel.

The unity of the Bible is thus the unity of a multitude of witnesses. Scattered over fourteen centuries and divided from one another in language, in world view, in religious conceptions, and in all the ways that men who live far apart from one another in time are separated, they yet form one unbroken fellowship, because the same God with the same redemptive purpose for humanity was at work in each of them. Their oneness is therefore a oneness in God and can be recognized only when we cease comparing their characters, actions, and ideas and consider each of them from the standpoint of his openness toward God and his service of the word of God in his own peculiar time and situation.

Never in Scripture, however, is there a word of revelation without a people's being called into its service to live a life of obedience to the word of revelation. The word by its nature has not merely to be spoken but has to be embodied and lived out in the difficult circumstances of a concrete human existence. Therefore, the unity of the revelation is reflected in the unity of the people of God who were the bearers of the revelation. The story of Israel in the Old Testament is the story of that costly destiny, and many parts of it that seem to be merely chapters in a secular history are necessary to the story because they show that God in his word claimed the whole of Israel's existence for his service. But that story of God's dealings with Israel and of Israel's response to God did not end with the crucifixion of Israel's Messiah. The story continues in the New Testament as a new Israel comes into being, and the new Israel, the church, reads the story of the Old Israel as its own story in which God gives ever-new understanding and guidance in the problems of his people's life. Here, then, is a second level in the unity of the new with the old, and again a unity in which there is no uniformity. The Israel of Moses is different in its whole way of life from the Israel of Isaiah, and the Israel of Isaiah is radically different from the new Israel of The Acts. And yet the story of the old Israel and the story of the new Israel form one story and not two, and there is one communion of saints in which the church member of today acknowledges himself a member together with Abraham and Moses and David. They without us are not complete (Heb. 11:40), but equally true is it that the Christian church without them would be a different church from what it is. The church is not founded on Christ and the apostles alone, that is, upon the New Testament alone, but also upon the prophets, by which is meant the witness of the Old Testament (Eph. 2:20), and the elimination of any part of that double witness on which the church is founded is certain to endanger the continuity of the present church not only with the church of the Old Testament but also with the church of the New Testament. The preservation of the unity of the Scriptures is therefore no mere academic question but one in which the character of the church is at stake.

The unity of God's purpose in the midst of his people and the unity of those who bore witness to that purpose in widely separated ages came to expression also theologically. Again it must be em-

What is the discontinuity? Is there not discontinuity within the OT?

90   *The Interpretation of Scripture*

phasized that there is a difference between theological unity and theological uniformity. No better example of that could be found than in the first three chapters of Genesis. The J writer and the priestly writer, separated by hundreds of years, are separated also in their approach to the doctrine of God, the Creator. The emphasis falls in a very different place in the two accounts of the Creation, and yet in their essential witness to God as creator of all and to the world and man as God's creatures having their life wholly from him, they stand together in contrast to all other interpretations of the relation between God and the world. There is in both a knowledge of God and of man that is unique, and it is this unique knowledge of God and man, coming to expression in diverse ways throughout both the Old and New Testaments, which gives to the Scriptures their theological unity. H. H. Rowley, in his book *The Unity of the Bible* (1953), makes a great deal of this theological unity and bases his assertion of the Bible's unity largely upon the demonstration of a continuity of theological themes. This is an important element in the unity, but unless it is seen in its proper context it is open to serious misunderstanding. The presence of similar concepts of God, man, sin, and election in both Old and New Testaments, while significant, is not an adequate basis on which to approach the problem of unity. Remarkable similarities in these same concepts can be and have been shown between Jesus and the Judaism of his time, and yet his gospel was intolerable to Judaism. Similarity of concepts does not necessarily mean organic unity. Also, Rowley, while he makes room for the historical diversity of Scripture, seems never to take with sufficient seriousness the discontinuity between the Testaments.

JESUS CHRIST IN THE OLD TESTAMENT

The point, however, at which there seems to be the greatest danger of confusion in the reassertion of the unity of the testaments is in regard to the relation between the word of God to which the Old Testament witnesses bear testimony and the Word of God which was incarnate in Jesus Christ. There is not likely to be much difficulty in identifying the incarnate Word with the word that is to be heard in the witness of the apostles. The tendency in some areas of New Testament scholarship is rather to go too far in assert-

[handwritten margin note: discontinuity again! ?]

ing the continuity of the incarnate Word with the word of the apostles without any adequate recognition of a discontinuity here also. The Christ-event is made to include both Jesus and his church without distinguishing clearly between the unbroken relationship of Jesus Christ with the Father and the always broken and redeemed relationship of the church with God. But the question must also be faced: What is the relation of the incarnate Word to the word of God that sounded in the ears of the prophets? What is the relation of the revelational events of the New Testament to the revelational events of the Old Testament? Do John the Baptist and all his predecessors with him belong to the Christ-event or do they stand outside it and upon a totally different plane from Christ and the apostles? The New Testament church had to face that question, and its answer to it is fairly plain. In John's Gospel the word known to Abraham and Moses is affirmed to have been the same word known to the apostles in Jesus Christ. So also in Paul, as in Hebrews, the doctrine of the pre-existent word is in its intention an identification of the word in Israel with the incarnate Word. It was on the basis of these New Testament assertions that Luther and Calvin established their Christological interpretation of the Old Testament, but they went far beyond the New Testament in their determination to find Christ and his gospel in the Old Testament. The restraint of the New Testament at this point contrasts sharply with the procedure of the Reformers who, upon the basis of the identification of the word of God in the Old Testament with the incarnate Word, assumed that wherever there is revelation in the Old Testament there must be some reference to the ministry or sufferings or death or resurrection of Jesus Christ or to some aspect of his church. And where Christ could not be found in the literal meaning of the text, they resorted to allegorical and typological interpretations in order to discover him and so to reaffirm the unity of the Scriptures in Christ. The example of the author of John's Gospel is a better guide for us. In the Prologue he speaks only of the Word of God when he describes God's coming to man as life and light in preincarnational times, but following the incarnation he speaks only of the man Jesus Christ, in whom God offers himself to the world.

It is an unrestrained Christological approach to the Old Testament that has reappeared in the work of Wilhelm Vischer, A. G.

Hebert, and a number, a disturbingly large number, of other scholars, and also in some measure in the interpretations of Karl Barth. When we are told that Adam and Eve in the second chapter of Genesis represent Christ and his church in their relations with each other and that the deep sleep of Adam in which a rib was removed for the creation of Eve corresponds to the deep sleep of Christ in the tomb that enabled God to bring forth his bride, the church, we have good reason to be alarmed that a new era of allegory and typology is threatening to descend upon us. But it will be most unfortunate if, in our alarm, we react in an undiscriminating way and, in rejecting the allegorical and typological approach, reject also the Christological assertions of the New Testament concerning its unity with the Old. There is no satisfactory answer to Bultmann, Hirsch, and the millions of Christians to whom the Old Testament is no longer Christian Scripture, that falls short of the New Testament affirmation — that the word of God to which the Old Testament bears comprehensive and diverse witness is the same Word to which the apostles are witnesses in the ministry, death, and resurrection of Jesus Christ and in the life of the early church. But if we so state this unity that we conceal in any degree the discontinuity between Old and New Testaments, dealing with Scripture as though there were only one Testament instead of two, we prepare the way again for a reaction that will attempt to subordinate or to exclude the Old Testament.

[IV]

TYPOLOGY, ALLEGORY, AND ANALOGY

THE ASSERTION of the unity of Scripture in any form, but in particular when Jesus Christ is affirmed as the focal center of all Scripture, creates apprehension that this may be the prelude to a revival of allegory and typology. As we have seen, the maintenance of the unity of the Testaments from the second century on produced a lush growth of allegory in which the literal meaning was often lost. Again, in the Reformation, in spite of the unearthing of the living word of Scripture from under a mountain of allegory, the determination to maintain the unity led Calvin into extensive typology, Luther into both typology and a measure of return to allegory, and the post-Reformation church into a much less restrained use of both. Moreover, the strangle hold of allegory and typology upon Biblical interpretation was broken not much more than a century ago by the concentration of historical scholarship upon the literal meaning of the text, was broken only after a long and bitter fight, and in some sections of the church a vigorous rearguard action has been fought to retain it right up to the present moment. The chapter and page headings of the King James Version, embodying as they do both typology and allegory, have given support to this resistance. The apprehension, therefore, has historical grounds, and it is given contemporary justification in both Germany and Great Britain, where theologians who are most insistent upon the unity of Scripture are making use of both typology and allegory in interpretation. But it does them an injustice to assume that they are merely reverting to obsolete interpretations of the past; it is also only fair to consider the possibility that some forms of typology and allegory may have a validation in Scripture that has been overlooked by historical-critical scholarship in its passionate repudiation of all forms of both. The whole matter will bear careful investigation.

The revival of typology

First we must ask what has brought about the revival of typology and allegory among scholars who are completely open and sympathetic to historical-critical investigation and have no intention of reverting to an uncritical and unhistorical viewpoint. No one can suggest that men such as A. G. Hebert and G. W. H. Lampe in England or Wilhelm Vischer and Karl Barth on the Continent are intent upon undoing the achievements of two centuries of historical work. All of them are agreed that the human and historical character of the Scriptures has been amply established. But all of them are equally convinced that certain elements that are essential to the right understanding of both Testaments have been overlooked by historical scholarship.

①

A major factor in the development has been the restudy of the approach to the interpretation of the Old Testament that is found in the books of the New Testament. For a long time it was assumed that, in this respect, the New Testament has nothing to teach us, that, just as Jesus, Paul, and the early church in general took over from Judaism the idea that David wrote the psalms and Moses the Pentateuch, so also they copied their Jewish contemporaries in reading the Old Testament as a book of oracles predicting present events. But a closer comparison of the use of the Old Testament in the New with its use in Judaism brings out some quite unique features that are distinctive of the Christian movement. One of these is the emphasis upon promise and fulfillment, which we have already considered briefly, and closely associated with this is a setting of New Testament events in close correspondence with similar events in the Old Testament, a practice that has been called typology, (whether validly or not has yet to be considered). Allegory, while it is widespread in Judaism, is rare in the New Testament, but correspondences of this kind, which are found in every part of the New Testament records, are not discernible in Judaism anywhere except in the apocalyptic-eschatological literature, which was later to be much more closely associated with Christianity than with Judaism. We shall have to examine these correspondences more carefully in a moment. Here it is sufficient to see that a phenomenon distinctive of the New Testament was calling for consideration.

A second factor, which gave much greater weight to this first one, was the recognition of a pattern of correspondences in events — past, present, and future events — in the Old Testament itself. The activity of God in creation was located not just in the past but also in the present and the future. The deliverance of Israel out of Egypt might be paralleled by a new deliverance of exiles from the four corners of the earth. If this pattern of similar events in various ages is to be called typology, then it would have to be admitted that there is typology in the Old Testament and it would be legitimate to ask whether the phenomenon points to something significant in Israel's understanding of how God works in history and may be the outward expression of an important theological truth. W. A. Irwin [1] speaks with scorn of Walter Eichrodt's articles on typology as though it were unworthy of any Old Testament scholar to write on such a subject. But it is difficult to understand how any element in the phenomena of the Old Testament should be declared outside the bounds of scholarly investigation. If the alleged correspondences actually exist, then they must be understood as part of the total Old Testament picture.

A third factor has been the increasing recognition that a Christian interpretation of the Old Testament must be in some definite way Christological. Some, such as Eichrodt,[2] may stop short at seeing in Jesus Christ the final consummating event in the sequence of revelational events to which the Scriptures bear witness, the final event being the one that makes clear the significance of all the others. Others, such as Vischer, may go to great lengths to demonstrate that the whole of the Old Testament is in some way witness to Jesus Christ. But once the admission is made that there is some form of unity between the revelation of the Old Testament and the revelation of God in Jesus Christ, it is no longer surprising that elements should be found in the Old Testament that are paralleled by elements in the New, and events in the Old that have remarkable similarities to events in the New. Then, if one takes seriously the Johannine and Pauline doctrine of Christ's pre-existence as the Word of God, active not only in creation but in all God's dealings with Israel, so that in essence the word that came to Moses was the same Word

---

[1] W. A. Irwin, JBL (March, 1959), p. 6.
[2] W. Eichrodt, *Theologie des Alten Testaments* I, p. 2.

that was known to the disciples in Jesus Christ, the surprising thing would be to find nothing in the manifestations of the word in the Old Testament that would point forward to the manifestations of the Word in the New Testament.

A fourth factor, which has perhaps been mingled with all the others, has been the renewed interest in the commentaries of Luther and Calvin. A generation parched by the spiritual dryness of a purely historical exegesis had reason to turn to the writings of the Reformers in which the Scriptures are allowed to speak their message to the Christian congregation with theological penetration and pastoral understanding. The Reformers lacked much that the modern commentary is able to supply most competently, but they provided the very elements that have been most lacking in the modern commentary. It was inevitable that their influence should tend to promote a revival of both typology and allegory.

Some Preliminary Questions

It dare not be assumed that the discovery of typology and allegory in the Bible itself justifies their use in the interpretation of Scripture today. The Evangelist Matthew's ignorance of the parallelism of Hebrew poetry, which made him think both an ass and an ass's colt necessary for Jesus' ride into Jerusalem (Matt. 21:5) if it was to fulfill Zech. 9:9, does not obligate us to see more than one ass in the Old Testament verse. And Paul's use of the rabbinic legend that the rock from which water gushed forth to sustain the Israelites in the wilderness followed them miraculously from place to place (I Cor. 10:4) does not validate the reading of legends as though they were history. Jesus' assumptions concerning the authorship of parts of the Old Testament do not settle once and for all the questions of authorship; nor does his reference to Jonah's sojourn in the great fish's belly make that sojourn history rather than parable. Paul cannot be expected to have divested himself of all traces of his Pharisaic training; the remarkable thing is that the influence shows itself in such minor ways in the expression of his thought and that in all the crucial features of his theology he is the antithesis of a Pharisee; [3]

[3] It is difficult to understand W. D. Davies' conclusion, in his excellent study of Paul's relation to Judaism, *Paul and Rabbinic Judaism,* that Paul to his dying day remained a Christian Pharisee. That, like Jesus, he did not repudiate Jewish prac-

yet he does have rabbinic ways of thought in which we are not ob-ligated to follow him. It is a denial of Jesus' humanity to tear him completely out of the context of first-century Judaism as though he would be influenced in no respect by contemporary thoughts and practices. He conformed in many ways to the established customs of Judaism. He followed prophetic practices such as the use of the para-ble. But that does not mean that every Christian preacher and teacher must attempt to communicate his message in parables and must follow Jewish customs where Jesus did. So also, if the evidence should make it clear that Jesus interpreted some passages in the Old Testament typologically or allegorically, that would not place the stamp of validity upon typology and allegory for all time. But it would most certainly make us intent upon understanding why Jesus so interpreted them and whether or not he was seeing something in the Old Testament that is hidden from us.

A second question has to do with whether or not it is wise to use the terms " typology " and " allegory " for the phenomena that meet us in the Scriptures. An answer to that will have to await our closer investigation of examples. Here it needs only to be pointed out that both words are heavily weighted by their past history in the church. Allegory was a method long practiced in the church whereby truths were discovered in verses of Scripture by imposing upon the indi-vidual words meanings that were completely absent from the mind of the original author. It is therefore an unsatisfactory word with which to describe a story such as the fall of Adam and Eve of which the literal meaning is not the intended meaning, the story in its origin pointing to something much more profound than appears on the surface. So also typology through centuries of usage has come to mean a method of interpreting Scripture whereby, for instance, the story of David the king is understood as being in reality the story of Christ the king in a concealed form. But this is decidedly *not* what most scholars who speak of typology today have in mind. Leonhard Goppelt, who has written the most detailed study on this subject,[4] in-sists that typology must not be considered a method of exegesis, " a hermeneutical artifice or technique," also, that there is little or no

---

tices where no principle was at stake ought not to conceal the sharpness of his break with the whole Pharisaic theology.

[4] L. Goppelt, *Typos. Die typologische Deutung des Alten Testaments im Neuen.*

basis in the New Testament for the nineteenth-century typological exegesis that thought to exalt the New Testament event by pointing to Old Testament prophecies — as though the interconnection were a rational proof of the power of God at work in the events. For him the recognition of typological correspondences has its value in enabling us the better to understand the documents in which they occur. But K. J. Woollcombe,[5] in his careful study of typology in the Bible and the early fathers, speaks of it as " an exegetical method," and G. W. H. Lampe,[6] in his essay on " The Reasonableness of Typology," uses the term " the typologist " as though this were a legitimate form of exegesis and the only problem were to determine how to draw the line between legitimate and illegitimate typology. Also, A. G. Hebert,[7] although he insists that typological interpretation is not exegesis, encourages the use of it in preaching as though in preaching a freedom in the use of the text were permissible that would be reprehensible in exegesis, and thus he opens the door to the reintroduction not only of typological but also of allegorical interpretation. All three of the English scholars seem to be aware of the dangers of their procedure, for they attempt, without too much success, to establish criteria to prevent a lush growth of fantastic and extravagant interpretations.

It is doubtful if any safeguard is likely to be effective if the terms " typology " and " allegory " are used for the phenomena under consideration, since, once anything that goes by these names is vindicated, the impression is created that typology and allegory have been at least in some measure validated as exegetical methods.

It is also important to point out that in the various discussions of the subject there is great difficulty in distinguishing between what is typological, what is allegorical, what is predictive, and what is merely the use of Old Testament language to describe the events in which the Christian church came into being. Where, other than in the Old Testament, were Jews to find images with which to express their conviction that a new revelation had taken place and a new deliverance for all mankind had been effected? Lampe defines a type as involving a secret correspondence between two events in history and

[5] G. H. Lampe and K. J. Woollcombe, *Essays in Typology.*
[6] *Ibid.*
[7] A. G. Hebert, *The Authority of the Old Testament.*

then proceeds to illustrate it by the correspondence between Jonah's descent into " the belly of Hades (*sic!*) " followed by his restoration to life in order to bring the message of repentance to Gentiles, and the death and resurrection of Jesus! Hebert uses the term " homology " in preference to " typology " to describe " two corresponding series of earthly events," but when he attempts to distinguish between homology and other illustrative or theological uses of the Old Testament in the New, it is often difficult to see the justice of his distinctions.

That there are phenomena in this area worthy of consideration cannot be doubted. That a considerable measure of confusion exists in the recent discussions of these phenomena is equally evident. Our task, therefore, is to attempt to cut away at least some of the confusion, to bring the Biblical phenomena more clearly into focus, and to assess their significance for our problem of Biblical interpretation.

THE PHENOMENA IN THE OLD TESTAMENT

The Old Testament as it stands today represents the final stage of a long process of reinterpretation in which can be detected the evidences of the earlier stages that have been progressively assimilated and transformed. There can be no question that the remarkable continuity in the life of Israel from the time of the exodus through the ordeal of settlement in Palestine, the pressures of the period of the kingdoms, the catastrophe of national destruction and exile, until at last the nation found itself surviving mainly as a religious entity in its own and other widely separated lands, is directly traceable to the conviction of a special destiny of Israel in relation to God. The miracle of Israel's survival and of the remarkable religious developments that took place within it, not in spite of but rather in consequence of its disasters, is inexplicable apart from the faith that God had chosen it for a purpose of his own and was revealing that purpose in the midst of its history. Any reconstruction of the earlier stages of Israel's development must always be open to challenge, since the assimilation of the earlier to the later stages is so complete that their disentanglement can never be effected with certainty. There are likely always to be differences of opinion as to what belongs to the Mosaic achievement and what was added through the influence of later developments. Fifty years ago the eighth-century prophets were credited with having originated practically everything of permanent significance in Israel's faith, the earlier stages being little different from contemporary pagan developments, while today a much higher estimate is generally made of the earlier periods, and the nucleus of Israel's prophetic faith in God and of their life as a people of God is recognized as already existing in the time of the exodus. The unique destiny of Israel had its decisive formulation through a revelation of God to Moses that was confirmed by the events of the exodus. No serious scholar would be likely to claim that the faith of Israel came into being full-blown in the time of Moses and that all subsequent prophets and priests merely applied its truths and principles to the newly arising situations. None of the prophets is found quoting the records of a previous revelation and merely asking what they have to say to his age (although it is plain that each of them was fully aware of the prophetic heritage that lay behind him, e.g., the influence of Hosea in Jeremiah); but, on the contrary, each is conscious of receiving a revelation of God for the Israel of his own time. Therefore, what took place in Israel was a series of reinterpretations of an original revelation in which it was not necessary to distinguish sharply between past and present, since the God who dealt with Israel in the past was the God who was dealing with Israel in the present. The faithfulness of God, on which everything depended for Israel, was the consistency of his nature in his relation with Israel in past, present, and future. Therefore, the record of God's past dealings with Israel was highly significant for understanding his purposes and intentions in the present and so for interpreting the significance of present events. Eschatology developed as the line of God's action was projected into the future, and the certainty of future events, or perhaps one should say the future outcome of events, was declared upon the basis that God, because he is the sovereign God, must ultimately vindicate his purpose in history.

Here we are at the source of Israel's unique achievement in the recording of history. Because the history is recorded not for its own sake but for its value as a witness to God's purpose in Israel and therefore more as gospel than as history or biography, the fact may be missed, and has often been missed, that this is the birth of history writing in the world. Long before the Greeks made any contribution to history, in Israel there were men wrestling with the meaning of historical events in a profound fashion and preserving a record of such events because of their recognition of the continuity of God's action in past, present, and future. Their belief in God as creator and sovereign of the world made them certain that all things happening in the world must have meaning and purpose not only for God but also for men. Their belief in God's election of Israel made them search specially for evidences of his purposes in the events in the life of Israel. Therefore, we can say that the consciousness of history as a sequence of events with meaning and purpose in them and tending toward some goal was the direct product of Israel's faith in God. In short, history here at its point of origin in the life of mankind is seen to be the product of theology! It is significant that Herodotus and Thucydides, with their purely man-centered approach to history, were indifferent to the problem of meaning in history and had no thought of it as a movement toward a goal. In fact, as R. G. Collingwood points out,[8] the Greek mind located reality so definitely beyond this world of change in an ideal and changeless world of ideas, and so depreciated the possibility of knowledge of the unceasing flux of events in human life, that it was only with the greatest difficulty that any historical consciousness arose among them, and through the operation of the same factors it was speedily dissolved. In contrast to this, the Israelite prophet found the focus of reality in God's relations with Israel, and through Israel with the world, in the concrete events of history. The world of human existence was the stage on which the drama of God's all-encompassing purpose was to unfold.

The consequence of this approach to history was that the story of the past was constantly being recalled, not that the nation might glory in the greatness of its past, though an element of that might be present, but that Israelites might constantly be reminded of the nature of the God with whom they were in covenant. His nature was revealed in his dealings with Israel, his faithfulness and mercy toward those who kept covenant with him, and his severity toward a nation that sought its life elsewhere than in the fulfillment of his will. Therefore all Israel's writing of history falls within a pattern of promise and fulfillment. The covenant bond contained within itself the promise of life and blessing, since the only life worthy of the

[8] R. G. Collingwood, *The Idea of History*. Collingwood does not recognize sufficiently the early contribution of Israel.

name was life in covenant with God. But for the same reason the rupture of the covenant relation bore within it the threat of death and destruction, for outside its relation with God, Israel had no real basis for existence.

Thus in Israel all history is a movement between promise and fulfillment. What God promises he fulfills, and, because the fulfillment is only partial, it contains within it an unfulfilled promise that points forward to a new fulfillment. It is unwise to call this "the rhythm of divine action evident in the history of the past" or "a recurring rhythm in past history," as Lampe [9] does, since that suggests an impersonal rhythm in the events themselves. The history does not proceed in waves. The character of the historical events is determined in part by the character of Israel's relation with God, but, transcending this, by the character of God's purpose for the world, which he may accomplish in spite of, and even eventually through, Israel's resistance to him. But because God is God and cannot change, the expectation is constantly present that what he has been to Israel in the past, he will be to Israel in the future.

It is this which produces a pattern of correspondences throughout the Old Testament. The story of the exodus was retold in each new age to remind Israelites that their God is a God who delivers his people in a marvelous way in spite of every obstacle, and to create the expectation of new deliverances. The recounting of the people's rebelliousness in the desert and of the long wanderings that were the consequence of that rebelliousness was intended to combat a parallel rebelliousness in later ages. Hosea, recalling God's discipline of Israel in the desert in the days of her betrothal to him, looked forward to a new period of discipline in the desert through which Israel would be prepared for a new future. Jeremiah, remembering God's first covenant with Israel and seeing it hopelessly shattered by the nation's spiritual failure, envisaged the making of a new and better covenant through which a new and truer Israel of God would come into being. Second Isaiah shows more clearly than any other this linking of past and future. In a time of dark despair when all hope for the future seemed lost, he looked into the past, and from what he saw there of God's nature and purpose, he became passionately certain of the great future that yet lay ahead for Israel in spite of all obstacles. The God

[9] Lampe and Woollcombe, *op. cit.,* p. 26.

who created the world could and would create a new world. The God who once led a band of slaves out of Egypt, through sea and desert, to the Promised Land to become a nation for him, could and would gather his scattered people from the ends of the earth and give them a new future. The correspondence, therefore, between the events of the past and the anticipated events of the future is no mystic foreshadowing of the future but is simply an expression of the confidence of the prophet that God's faithfulness to his own nature must be vindicated in the events of history, since he is Lord of the world and its history.

Account should also be taken of the fact that, when a prophet undertook to describe any new and as yet unseen action of God, whether of deliverance or of judgment, he naturally drew his imagery from existing descriptions of deliverances and judgments in the past. How could it be otherwise than that a paradise at the end of time should be seen to resemble the paradise that was thought to have stood at the beginning of time? And how could an Israel in exile fail to think of itself as being in a situation similar to the Israelites in Egypt and as awaiting a new exodus? We are in no need of the term " typology " to describe the correspondences that occur; rather, their character tends to be confused by the introduction of any such term.

There are some passages in the Old Testament in which we might say that an elision of past and present takes place, the story that seems on the surface to be the description of a past event being actually intended to act as a mirror to later generations in which they might see themselves in the person of their ancestor. When Israelites read the promise to Abraham in Gen., ch. 12, it was a promise also to them, since they were the children of Abraham and one with him in faith and destiny. God's command to Abraham to yield up to him in sacrifice his only son reminded each new generation of Israelites of God's uncompromising demand for unquestioning allegiance and obedience to him. This was not a homiletic allegorizing of the Abraham stories but rather was the meaning they had within the nation's tradition, just as the story of Adam was in its very origin a representation not of the nature of some isolated individual called Adam but of man as man. It is not difficult to recognize that, in the Jacob-Esau stories, the historical rivalry of the two countries Israel and Edom is reflected and that a humiliating incident narrated concerning Esau was intended to provide embarrassment for the Edomites. At one point it is said specifically that Esau is Edom (Gen. 36:1). Thus, in each of these stories, if one reads it as simply the narration of an incident, he misses the intended meaning of the story. Only in the larger context in which the story takes on a larger meaning is justice done to the text itself. An excellent example of the elision of past, present, and future in a single figure is the Servant in Second Isaiah. He is Israel in its capacity as the servant of God's word in all ages; therefore, not only Abraham and Sarah but all the prophets and priests of all time are comprehended in him. Thus in the description of some actions of the Servant it is possible to see a reference to actions of persons in the past, to actions of the prophet himself or those who stood with him in his own day, or actions that were yet to come in the future. This is not for one moment to be confused with allegory. The passage itself is written in such a way that it has an applicability in different ages.

Prediction in the Old Testament belongs in the context of promise and fulfillment. The prophet's knowledge of the future is not a mystic penetration of future events but a penetration by faith into the secret counsel of God by which future events are determined. " The Lord God does nothing without revealing his secret to his servants the prophets." (Amos 3:7.) The prophet knows what God will do because he knows who God is. God's future action is therefore not a fixed and determined event that nothing can change, but depends in some measure upon the response of Israel to him. Even though disaster has been predicted as judgment upon sin, the repentance of the nation may yet make possible an escape from death into life. A fixed scheme of prediction and fulfillment belongs together with a static conception of history in which from the beginning God has determined all events, a conception totally alien to the dynamic character of the prophetic faith in which history consists of a succession of situations in which the nation is called to choose between the way of life and the way of death.

The Phenomena in the New Testament

Two seemingly contradictory elements are combined in the witness of every part of the New Testament: that the truth of the gospel and the life of the kingdom that came into the world with Jesus were wholly new, unknown to mankind before, and unattainable except through him, and yet that they were foreshadowed and their very lineaments depicted with considerable accuracy long before in the Old Testament Scriptures. Neither of these elements dare be weakened by emphasis upon only one of them. It is possible by emphasis upon the newness and uniqueness of the gospel to lose sight of the extent of its rootedness in the Old Testament, and it is possible by emphasizing how much of the gospel the early church found already present in the Old Testament to lose sight of how wholly new the gospel was. Jesus is reported as saying that he who is least in the Kingdom of God is greater than John the Baptist (Matt. 11:11), and yet all four Gospels are agreed in regarding John as a primary witness to the truth of the gospel and a preparatory herald of the Kingdom. Here is the double witness. The world, for those who through the gospel had entered upon the life of the Kingdom, was a totally new place with totally new meaning, a new creation, and yet they recognized this new world and new life as having been promised to the covenant people of God in the pages of the Old Testament and in the preaching of John.

Because so often in the New Testament an Old Testament quotation is set alongside the account of an incident and the incident is said to have happened as it did " that the Scripture might be fulfilled," the impression is created that the early church's use of the Old Testament was a rather mechanical one — that it searched the Scriptures to find prophecies of known incidents in the life of Jesus and in the life of the church, and in its eagerness sometimes seized upon passages that upon closer examination prove to be quite unsuitable. Also, it seems to have operated with a conception of Scripture as chiefly a compendium of predictions of future events, which is not at all what the original writers of prophecies, psalms, and histories conceived their productions to be.[10] But this impression arises, more than we are aware, from only one level of quotations and also from our familiarity with a modern use of Old Testament predictions as

---

[10] A similar use of Scripture is found in the Qumrân scrolls. The Sectarians, like the Christians, thought themselves to be living in the Last Days, toward which the Old Testament pointed, and so they interpreted passages in the Old Testament as predictions of events happening or about to happen in their midst.

validating the historicity of New Testament events, a viewpoint that certainly was not primary with the New Testament authors.

If we would understand the use of the Old Testament in the New, we must put ourselves imaginatively into the situation of the first Christians. Into their midst had come one in whose spirit and preaching it was as though the whole prophetic tradition that was at the heart of the Old Testament had come to life again. He taught not as the scribes and rabbis but with authority, that is, with the kind of direct authority from God that was characteristic of the great prophets. And yet in so many ways he went beyond anything that was to be found in the Old Testament. He embodied the essence of the Old Testament in his teaching, and yet the life with God into which he called men was of a kind that not even the greatest of the prophets had known. They were living in the dawn of a new world. And as the religious authorities and the nation as a whole rejected Jesus and his gospel, the disciples knew themselves a new Israel, the remnant spoken of by the Old Testament prophets, the only true Israel of God, moving forward to fulfill the function of God's servant-people in the new era. But, as the new Israel, they were conscious of themselves and their story as the one legitimate continuation of the age-long story of Israel. Abraham was *their* father in the faith. Moses was *their* ancestor. *Their* church was founded upon the prophets. The Old Testament was *their* holy Scripture.

We have to think of the disciples, then, even during Jesus' lifetime, reading the Old Testament in a different way from that in which it was read by the rabbis. The assumption has been made too frequently that there was little difference between Jesus and the rabbis in their interpretation of the Old Testament, but the evidence is strongly against this. The rabbis focused their attention upon the law and had little appreciation of the prophets; the opposite, as we would expect, is true of Jesus. The rabbis made wide use of allegory in drawing forth the meanings they desired from Old Testament passages; Jesus makes no use of allegory and it is remarkably rare in the whole of the New Testament. The rabbis used Old Testament Scripture as proof texts to support their doctrines, a practice in which Paul followed them to some extent; Jesus, however, takes up the mind and spirit of many Old Testament passages, and sometimes the very words, into his own teaching, but he gives it forth as his own and never uses quotations as a support for its divine authority. The rabbis in principle acknowledged the authority of every word of Scripture, since all of it was divine (although they might in fact controvert its intention by their teaching), and the challenging of any passage would have seemed to them an offense against God; Jesus, however, could set Scripture against Scripture, denying the present authority of Deut. 24:1, which permitted a man to divorce his wife very simply, and basing the indissolubility of marriage on Gen. 2:24. Jesus' attitude toward the Sabbath shows also a penetration beyond legalistic regulations to the divine intention concerning the Sabbath. It seems reasonable to assume, therefore, that the disciples must have learned from Jesus a different way of reading the Old Testament from what was customary in the synagogue.

C. H. Dodd has made a strong case for the thesis that Jesus directed the minds of his disciples to particular parts of the Old Testament.[11] Dodd examines four blocks of New Testament writings — the Synoptics with The Acts, the Johannine, the Pauline, and Hebrews — each of which came into being in relative independence of the others, and points out that all four make use of the same general portions of the Old Testament. One of them may quote from one part of a psalm and another from another part of the same psalm, but this shows the focus of both upon that one psalm in preference to others. One set of passages has to do with the " day of the Lord " and the intervention of God in history (Joel, chs. 2; 3; Zech., chs. 9 to 14; Dan., chs. 7; 12; Mal. 3:1-6; 4:4-5); another with the possibility of a new Israel (Hosea, Isa. 6:1 to 9:7; 11:1-10; chs. 28; 29; 40; Jer. 7:1-15; 31:10-34; Hab. 2:3-4); another with the Suffering Servant (Isa., chs. 40 to 66; Ps. 22; 31; 34; 69; 118). These, when drawn together, are seen to embody theological implications of great importance: a Christology, a doctrine of the church as the new Israel of God, and a conviction that only through suffering and death is redemption to be effected. The question then has to be faced, Who drew them together? Dodd sees this to have been an intellectual and theological achievement of such magnitude that only Jesus himself could have done it, and that the passages in their cohesion can thus be used to disclose the mind of Jesus about himself, his work of redemption, and his church.

[11] C. H. Dodd, *According to the Scriptures.*

What is most important for us at this point in our consideration, however, is that we see here a way of reading the Old Testament that was to be distinctive of the early church. If Jesus used these passages as Dodd describes, then he was reading in them the story of his own life. He was reading them as " written concerning him " (I Cor. 10:6, 11). They were a revelation not only of what he had to be and to do as the Messiah of Israel but also of the form of the new Israel that was to come into being through his redemptive work. The Old Testament revealed to him a destiny of Israel that was not being realized in the present Israel, a life for man that was unknown even by the most religious and moral men, a world that was the only true world but was hidden from the eyes of men, so that they were blind to the realm in which God intended them to live. But above all he saw in the Old Testament more than hints of what must be the form and destiny of the One through whom the world and mankind would be reclaimed for God. It was all written there to be read by anyone with the mind and heart to understand. He could read it there himself, but it was much more difficult to teach his disciples to see what he could see. Nothing was plainer than that the way of God's servant must be a way of suffering, because God's servant must embody in himself the word of God which cuts across the life of the world like a sharp sword of judgment, and yet at the same time he must bear in his own flesh the burden of the judgment. The word of redemption and the word of judgment could not be separated at any point any more than God's love could be separated from his holiness. And yet even the disciples who were closest to Jesus were blind to this necessity.

It was the death of Jesus upon the cross and his triumph in the resurrection that anchored this way of reading Scripture in the church. We can imagine the awe with which the disciples read Isa., ch. 53, and Ps. 22 in the days following Jesus' death. It was exactly as Jesus had said: not only his death was depicted there but also the meaning of his death as a vicarious offering of himself for sinners and the certainty of his triumph beyond death. Lampe has suggested [12] that the preacher of the early church began to search out correspondences between Old Testament texts and New Testament events in order " to show conclusively that the truth of his message

[12] Lampe and Woollcombe, *op. cit.*, p. 22.

could be proved out of the sacred books recognized by his audience as possessing absolute authority." The primary motive he holds to have been apologetic. We may allow a secondary place perhaps to the apologetic, but surely the primary motive was much simpler and not argumentative at all, an act of recognition by the disciples as they read with amazement in their Old Testament the story of the very events that had just taken place before their eyes. In the light of this experience, is it any wonder that they searched farther afield in the Old Testament to see what else was written there concerning Christ and his church?

Behind this whole manner of reading the Old Testament lay the conviction, first of Jesus, then of the early church, that the events that were taking place were the fulfillment of the promises of God made to Israel from the beginning of its life. We have seen how deeply embedded the pattern of promise-fulfillment is in the Old Testament itself. The whole of eschatology issues from faith in God's sovereignty, the faith that, although his righteous purpose may be hidden in the present moment, God is sovereign in his world and soon will vindicate his righteous sovereignty in outward events. What God has spoken he will do. The word of God cannot fail. It may be delayed by man's sin, but it must eventually triumph. The promise of God in the Old Testament usually takes a material form — settlement in the Promised Land, a numerous progeny, an abundance of food, wealth, security, and peace, an order in society in which not even the animals injure each other — but the material blessedness is always to be understood as the consequence of a right relation between God and his people,[13] so that the essence of the promise is Immanuel, "God with us," the promise of a time when the harmony between God and his people will be reflected in a corresponding harmony in human society. The outpouring of the Spirit upon Israel in the Last Day, as envisaged by Joel, is nothing less than God's own coming to his people to abide with them as their God. So, also, in Second Isaiah it is God's return to his people that makes the desert blossom and creates a paradise on earth. Second Isaiah is not above depicting this time of fulfillment in quite material terms —

---

[13] This is misunderstood by both Bultmann and Baumgärtel (Verheissung, 1952), who deplore the materialism of the Old Testment eschatology and set it in radical contrast to the spirituality of the Christian hope.

Israel triumphing over its enemies and inheriting the wealth of the nations — but he leaves no doubt that it is a time when God's holy will prevails in all the affairs of men.

The testimony of the New Testament as a whole is, then, that the promises of God in the Old Testament are being fulfilled in the events of the New. The only question open to debate is whether this interpretation originated in the early church or with Jesus himself. The whole matter is closely tied together with the question whether or not Jesus considered himself to be the Messiah. His unwillingness to let the title of Messiah be given him has led many scholars to conclude that he refused it. But if he saw in the events of his own ministry the fulfillment of the Old Testament promises, it is difficult to believe that he did not also see in himself the Messiah. In Mark's summary of Jesus' earliest preaching, both the announcement " The time is fulfilled " and the description of the Kingdom as " at hand " point to a conviction that fulfillment is now not only an immediate possibility but also an immediate reality. W. G. Kümmel's argument [14] that " at hand " can mean only " near " for the disciples and others, while it is present reality in Jesus' own person, does not take sufficient account of the fact that the Kingdom is always *both* present and near. The disciples, like Jesus, expel demons by the finger of God. The Kingdom is present for those who by faith have let themselves be laid open to its reality but only near for those who have not yet responded in faith; and even those who have known its presence and power find themselves again and again with it " only near," so that they have to pray for its coming. Thus, in the synagogue at Nazareth, when Jesus said concerning Isa. 61:1-3, " This day is this Scripture fulfilled in your ears," he meant that what was described in those verses was actually happening in his ministry. His works of healing he interpreted as signs that the Kingdom was present with power. (Luke 11:20.) But perhaps more significant than any of these was his possession by the Spirit of God and the outpouring of God's Spirit through him upon the disciples. Both " Spirit " and " Kingdom " express the reality of God's presence. Where the Spirit is, there the Kingdom is. In Judaism no such claim was made to possess the Spirit of God, but rather this was regarded as one of the marks of the ar-

[14] W. G. Kümmel, *Promise and Fulfillment.*

rival of the Last Days.[15] Jesus' baptism with the Spirit was therefore the inauguration of the Last Days. Jesus' identification of himself with the Servant of God, and of his disciples as servants with him, indicates that he saw the hopes of Second Isaiah being fulfilled in himself and them. His taking to himself of the title " Son of Man " shows that he combined with servanthood the expectation of The Book of Daniel. Then, in the Last Supper, his performance of a new ceremony within the setting of the Passover, to be for his followers a memorial of the new deliverance and the new covenant, makes doubly clear that he interpreted his entire ministry as accomplishing finally and decisively the relationship between God and man on which the hopes of the Old Testament were set. This explains also the amazing authority that he claimed for himself implicitly in many of his words and actions (e.g., " You have heard that it hath been said . . . but I say unto you ") and the freedom that he asserted in relation to all religious traditions, not only the rabbinic but also that of John the Baptist. Fulfillment meant the completion in him of the work of God to which the whole of the Old Testament bore witness. That which the fathers had seen and hoped for and tasted from afar was now reality in him and in the new Israel, which as yet had its existence within the old Israel. His gospel was therefore the final reinterpretation of Israel's witness to God. And as fulfillment it stood at every point in closest relation to that of which it was the fulfillment.

We have now to consider the consequences of this relation. First, it confirmed the authority of the Old Testament Scriptures in the new Israel. There was no hiatus between the new gospel and the old Scriptures, for the new gospel could from the beginning be preached out of the old Scriptures. They were not taken over into the Christian church merely because the first Christians were Jews, as has been suggested by some, but because the promises and the fulfillment were inseparable. Secondly, because the gospel was preached out of the Old Testament, the very words with which the events in the life of Jesus were described were colored by the language and by the thought-forms of the Old Testament, so that often where there is no quotation there is nevertheless a strong Old Testament flavor. It is

[15] W. D. Davies, *Paul and Rabbinic Judaism*, pp. 208, 215, 216.

wrong to call this "typology," as Goppelt and others often do, as though it were the result of a deliberate interpretative approach consciously applied. The Old Testament was the treasure house out of which Christians drew the words and images with which to describe their new faith. It is not typology when Jesus speaks of his new covenant in the context of the Passover in which the old covenant was remembered. He was not concerned about interpreting the old or establishing parallels, but with establishing a new relation between God and man in which all the hopes of those who had served God before him would be joyfully fulfilled. It is sufficient, therefore, to recognize that the saving work of Christ in his lifetime and in his church is the completion of a redemption begun in the Old Testament. The first creation is completed by the new creation. The first man, Adam, made in the image of God to reflect God's glory, comes to his true destiny in the new Adam, Jesus Christ. God's image is restored to man in him. God's glory is perfectly reflected and a new humanity is created. The law given by Moses is taken up into a new law given by a new Moses through whom alone men have power to fulfill the law. It is not helpful to speak of this as a creation-typology, an Adam-typology, and a Moses-typology. The passages have their true meaning only within the context of the pattern of promise and fulfillment, which binds the old Israel and the new Israel, and so the Old and the New Testaments, into one, because of the conviction that God's work in creation and covenant is one with his work in the new creation, the redemption, and the consummation.

It was inevitable that in time the pattern of promise-fulfillment should be misinterpreted into a pattern of prediction-fulfillment and parallels sought in the Old Testament to correspond with incidents in the New. Thus Matthew could pair the legend of the descent of the Holy Family into Egypt with Hosea's words concerning Israel, "Out of Egypt have I called my son" (Matt. 2:15), and the settlement in Nazareth with "He shall be called a Nazarene" (Matt. 2:23), which is most likely a mistranslation of Judg. 13:5: "The boy shall be a Nazirite to God from birth." It is this latter development which can be seen as motivated apologetically by the desire to prove the intimate connection between Old Testament Scriptures and New Testament events and so to impress non-Christian Jews with the legitimacy of the claim of the church to be the true continuation of the Israel of God. Perhaps this alone should be called typology, since it is a deliberate practice of finding and establishing correspondences, not with the purpose of witnessing to the continuity of God's action in the midst of his people but rather to impress men with the mysterious connection between Old Testament words and New Testament happenings. It is this quest for impressive parallels that was long followed in the church under the name of typology and that some scholars today seem to be confusing with the necessary recognition of genuine correspondences and so to be in danger of reviving.

the right name?

The claim is made that Paul practiced typology, and what Paul himself calls an allegory in Gal. 4:24 ff. is pronounced typology by Goppelt.[16] The judgment of Paul seems the better of the two, for his use of the figures of Sarah and Hagar to represent the distinction between the two covenants, between the present Jerusalem that is in bondage and the Jerusalem above that is free, is allegory of a kind that was familiar among the rabbis. But it was used to express a truth that had no necessary connection with Sarah and Hagar, that is, it was used illustratively. In Rom. 5:14, Adam is spoken of as " a type of the one who was to come," and here, as has been already noted, the connection is deeper. Jesus Christ is what Adam was intended to be and makes good Adam's failure. But this remains an isolated instance and is no basis for working out a typological network. Goppelt finds an Adam-Christ typology in other parts of the New Testament. Jesus' temptations, he says, are parallel to Adam's temptations in Eden. The note in Mark 1:13 that Jesus was with the beasts in the desert is a reminiscence of Adam's being with the beasts in Eden. That angels ministered to Jesus after his temptations reflects the Midrash on Genesis, according to which angels prepared food for Adam in Eden. It is quite possible that the New Testament story was influenced by such elements from its Old Testament and Jewish background. It would be difficult for Christians for whom Jesus was the very likeness of God not to see a relation between him and Adam, a foreshadowing of him in Adam similar to the foreshadowing of his death in Isa., ch. 53. But there is a long distance between that simple recognition as expressed by Paul and a system of typology as an exegetical approach to the Old Testament.

In I Cor. 10:1-11, Paul interprets the experiences of Israel in the

[16] Goppelt, *op. cit.,* p. 168.

desert as having been set down for the instruction of Christians; and, in order to make his point, he likens their being under the cloud of God's presence and passing through the sea of deliverance to the Christian's entrance upon his new life by baptism in water and the Spirit, and their miraculous preservation through water from the rock and manna from heaven he likens to the Christian Eucharist. Paul emphasizes that in spite of such experiences of God's favor many of the Israelites perished; therefore, Christians should have no false trust through having received baptism and the sacraments, for, unless they resist temptation, they too will perish. The Old Testament story is here a parable in which Christians can read their own situation, and it would be going too far even to call it allegory, much less typology. So also in Rom. 4:23, when the words concerning Abraham " it was reckoned to him as righteousness " are said to have been " written not for his sake alone, but for ours also," this is simply the recognition that when justification by faith is proclaimed in the Old Testament the Christian does right to hear in it his own gospel.

That Paul makes use of rabbinic allegorizations of the Old Testament when they serve his purpose is undeniable. In I Cor. 9:9-10, he specifically denies that the literal sense of the command not to muzzle the ox that treads out the grain can be the intended meaning. God's care is not for oxen but for men. Therefore, the divine intention of the command was to provide for the sustenance of God's ministers. But when R. M. Grant [17] suggests that there was little difference between Paul's approach to the Old Testament and that of the Hellenistic-Jewish allegorizers, and that allegory for Paul was a hermeneutical system, he is forced to strain the evidence and he fails to take sufficient account of the total context within which Paul interpreted the Old Testament. Concerning Paul's reinterpretation of Deut. 30:12-14 in Rom. 10:5-10, Grant uses the term " pure allegorization " when actually all that Paul has done is to identify the word of God with Jesus Christ. This is no more allegory than it is allegory for Christians to identify the servant of God in Isa., ch. 53, with Jesus Christ. Again, he calls the homiletic use of Israel's exodus experiences in I Cor. 10:1-11 " predictive allegory," where there is no indication of any interest of Paul in a predictive element. And the analogy that Paul finds between the relation of husband and wife

[17] R. M. Grant, *The Letter and the Spirit.*

and the relation of Christ to the church (Eph. 5:22-32), which leads him to read Gen. 2:24 as written concerning Christ and his church, is not so much an " allegorization of the marriage of Adam and Eve " as a recognition that in the oneness of the church with Christ the promise that was inherent in the oneness of Adam and Eve came to its fulfillment.

There is no evidence of Paul's searching the Scriptures to find predictions of events in the life of the new Israel as the author of the Gospel of Matthew does. His basic approach is that which we have seen to have been primary in the early church. All the promises of God have been fulfilled in Jesus Christ (II Cor. 1:20). In him God has kept his word and brought salvation to his people. Christians are those " upon whom the end of the ages has come " (I Cor. 10:11). The death and resurrection of Jesus took place in accordance with the Scriptures (I Cor. 15:3-4), inaugurating the new age, and the pouring forth of the Holy Spirit by the risen Lord into the hearts of his people is the guarantee that the Last Days, the time of fulfillment, has actually begun. The Kingdom, long awaited, is now a reality in which those who receive the Spirit have their life, as yet brokenly since sin remains, but with the confidence that soon Christ's perfect Kingdom will be established. God's Spirit alone takes away man's blindness and enables him to read the Scriptures with true understanding, that is, to discern in them the saving Word which is one with Jesus Christ. Therefore, if we are to speak of a hermeneutic principle that belonged to Paul, it is that of seeing in the Old Testament the promises of the Kingdom, of the King, of the church, and of the new creation, promises that were fulfilled in and through Jesus Christ.

TYPOLOGY AMONG OLD TESTAMENT THEOLOGIANS

The term " typology " has been used in recent years by a number of German and Swiss Old Testament scholars who have no interest such as that of Vischer and Hebert in the reintroduction of allegorical and typological interpretations. Articles by Eichrodt, von Rad, Zimmerli, and H. W. Wolff have all dealt with the fact of correspondences within the Old Testament and between Old and New Testaments, and some have called the phenomenon " typology," but all have felt the danger of misunderstanding and have taken pains to limit the use of the word, some expressing doubt whether it is wise to use it at all when it has such a false tradition attached to it.

von Rad

Gerhard von Rad [18] uses typology and analogy as synonyms and recognizes their presence not only in the Old Testament but in all poetry. The Oriental mythological conception of a correspondence between heavenly and earthly things — rivers, cities, and temples being fashioned in accordance with heavenly patterns or models — occurs in the Old Testament only in Ex. 25:9, 40 and in Ezek. 31:8 ff. But in eschatological conceptions there is constantly a pattern of correspondence between what lies behind and what lies ahead: the paradise of Eden, the kingdom of David, the birth years of the covenant relation in the desert. Second Isaiah speaks of a second exodus; Hosea, of a second beginning in the wilderness. In Joshua there is an idealized representation of the conquest of Palestine that has in mind not the past but a future conquest. So the Old Testament itself prepares the way for a New Testament interpretation that will see in the record of past events a foreshadowing of present and future events. On this basis it is legitimate to recognize in Old Testament judgments and redemptions a prefiguring of the New Testament event of Christ. There is no more in this than a faith " that the same God who has revealed himself in Jesus Christ has left his mark also in the history of the Old Testament covenant people, that we have to do with one word of God, on the one hand to the fathers through the prophets, on the other hand to us through Jesus Christ."

Typological exposition thus sees, from the standpoint of the later event, a meaning in the Old Testament text that was not there for the original author. The later action of God in Jesus Christ illuminates the earlier action of God in the Old Testament event. But this dare not be elaborated into a correspondence of details, as has happened so often in the church. Rarely is there an exactness of correspondence. The Israelite's longing for his own land, for rest, and for long life, becomes in the New Testament the longing for eternal salvation. Seeing the Old Testament text from the New Testament vantage point may, far from perverting the exegesis, actually make possible a sounder historical exegesis, the theological meaning lighting up the historical significance of the text. What von Rad is wrestling with is the unity of all Scripture in Jesus Christ, the fact

[18] " Typologische Auslegung des A. T.," EvTh (1952), p. 17.

that " Christ is given to us only in the double witness of the choirs of those who anticipated and those who remembered his coming." He is willing to speak of " a witness to Christ in the Old Testament," since " our knowledge of Christ is imperfect without the witness of the Old Testament." When this is understood as though the truth of Christ were given in the New Testament, and then the Old Testament were to be measured by this truth, violence is done to the Old Testament. The Christ-event is rightly known only when we hear both the Old and the New Testaments bearing their witness each in its own way. He acknowledges the danger that this approach introduces into exposition, since there is no norm by which one can fix the typological meaning of individual texts except the freedom of the Holy Spirit. Yet he is certain the venture must be made.

Von Rad recognizes that the Old Testament, bound together in organic unity with the New Testament, has a meaning that it does not have when read in isolation, and that individual texts appear in a different light when their inner connection with the New Testament event is seen. It is unfortunate, however, that he calls this additional meaning the " typological meaning " in distinction from the historical meaning. The historical meaning of any text is determined by its context, but the context is not to be defined as only the immediate historical situation. Often the meaning of a single historical event is totally obscure until its consequences have worked themselves out in the later history. Often in the life of a man an action early in life is not understood until later actions reveal its significance. On this basis, it can be said that the life, death, and resurrection of Jesus Christ and the birth of the church are the ultimate context of the events of the Old Testament, so that to read an Old Testament text in the light of the New Testament is to see it in its *full* historical setting. There is not historical *and* typological meaning but only different levels of a meaning that is both historical and theological.

H. W. Wolff [19] takes as his starting point the character of the Old Testament text as documents that came into being as Israel responded to God's dealings with them as his people. Directly or indirectly they stood in the service of God's word to Israel. But, if the

Wolff

---

[19] H. W. Wolff, "The Old Testament in Controversy," *Interpretation* (July, 1958), p. 281; "Der grosse Jesreeltag, Hos. 2:1-3," EvTh (1952), p. 78; "Zur Hermeneutik des A. T.," EvTh (1956), p. 337.

God of Israel is God today, the text should still bear witness to God. The problem of interpretation is to enable it to do so. No methodology can extract from the text its witness to God. God himself must speak through it if he is to be known, and our part is to hear. Never does the hearer hear all that lies within the text. This does not mean, however, the surrender of all exact research, as though one had only to wait in simplicity before the text. Historical interpretation by setting the text in its context limits the possible meaning of the words and excludes arbitrary interpretations, but the context must not be defined narrowly. The true context of the Old Testament in its uniqueness as witness to God is not the complex of ancient Oriental religions or the religion of late Judaism and the synagogue, but rather the New Testament as the fulfillment of that which lay at the heart of the Old. " The absolutizing of the law in the synagogue tears it out of the context in which in the Pentateuch it is given in close proximity to God's saving deeds for Israel." [20] In the Old Testament, as in the New, grace is primary rather than law. Also, the rabbinic transformation of the Pentateuch into a literally inspired book in which all the words are equally words of wisdom introduces a principle alien to the Pentateuch. So also the covenant in the Old Testament, though it is for Israel alone, reaches out to draw in all nations and therein points forward to the new covenant in Christ which compasses the whole of mankind. God's action in Jesus stands in continuity with his saving actions in Israel. Jesus is the last paschal lamb, the last king, the last priest of Israel. Therefore, in all these respects Israel was a typological foreshadowing of Christ and the church. The old covenant is to the new as an engagement is to a marriage. There is not an identity between the two, because there are sharp differences, but only an analogy.

In using the word " typology " to express this relation between the Testaments, Wolff recognizes the possible complications, but there seems to him to be no other adequate term. He is as anxious as his critics to avoid eisegesis. To him the achievement of this approach is not to substitute a Christian meaning for the original one in a text but only to deepen the true understanding of the text. The New Testament provides parallel phenomena to illuminate Old Testa-

[20] Wolff, "Zur Hermeneutik," *loc. cit.,* p. 346.

ment material; for instance, the Sermon on the Mount is more useful to clarify the relation between grace and law in the Pentateuch than any contemporary Oriental parallels. Just as in the Old Testament itself older traditions are being constantly reinterpreted to bring out their true meaning, so the New Testament may be regarded as a final reinterpretation in which meanings formerly obscure emerge into the open. Why he must call this typology is not clear when it is no more than a recognition of the total organic context of the Old Testament.

The danger inherent in speaking of a " typological interpretation " becomes evident when Wolff goes beyond a statement of principle to examples of hermeneutic method. Because the Old Testament is only a foreshadowing of the truth and not the truth itself, it cannot by itself proclaim God's word to Christians. Something must be added from the New Testament to make it Christian. Continuity with the Old Testament cannot be direct for Christians. Because we belong to Christ and his church we must read our Old Testament with him. This has in it a very real truth, but for Wolff it means that, in preaching on an Old Testament text, we must set alongside it a New Testament passage concerned with the same theme and interpret the two together, the New Testament one illuminating and correcting the earlier one. In a sermon on Gen. 15:1-6, Abraham's destiny should be compared with that of Christ and his church, Abraham's objection that he has no son being seen as parallel with Simon Peter's denial of Jesus Christ.

Certainly there are New Testament parallels that throw light on dark places in the Old Testament. But, apart from the complications of the suggested method and the fanciful parallels that many men are likely to find (with the help of earlier exegetes), the presupposition on which it is based seems defective. It implies that the Old Testament is not really Christian Scripture. The word of God at the heart of it is not really the word that was to be incarnate in Jesus Christ, but something less. Its revelation is a deficient revelation. We cannot preach on a text from Amos without bringing in Paul to correct and complete what Amos says. Not only is this clumsy in practice but it is without basis in the New Testament. According to Paul, when God has set his Spirit, the Spirit of the Lord, in our hearts, he has given us the key to the Old Testament

and freedom to hear the witness borne to him in its text. Because
the Spirit of the Lord Jesus Christ is the same Spirit in whose power
Amos spoke, the words of Amos fall upon our ears not just as the
words of an isolated prophet of the eighth century B.C. but as the
words of an Amos who belongs in a oneness with Jesus Christ similar to, though not identical with, that in which Paul stood. The
word of Amos does not have to be *made* Christian, for it has already
been taken up into the word of Jesus Christ and confirmed by him.
Amos as a prophet has therefore an authority for us similar to that
which Paul has as an apostle. The one came before and the other
after Jesus Christ, but both belong together with him. Amos is not
Jesus Christ any more than Paul is Jesus Christ, but his relation
with him is such that through the hearing of Amos' words we are
called into the fellowship of the prophets and the apostles, which has
its living center in Jesus Christ. It is sufficient, then, for us to let
Amos speak with the utmost clearness and decisiveness in the Christian congregation and in the world of our day, and we need have no
fear but that the voice that is heard, if it is truly that of Amos, will
be recognized as the same voice that is heard calling men and claiming them wholly for himself in Jesus Christ.

Friedrich Baumgärtel has written extensively in criticism of the
tendencies of von Rad and Wolff [21] and particularly against any revival of typology. His fear seems to be that theological exegesis,
by bringing the Old Testament into too direct and unified a relation with the New, will intrude a New Testament meaning into
the text and no longer permit it to speak with its own pre-Christian
and unchristian distinctiveness. Therefore, he emphasizes the various respects in which the Old Testament religion is not the Christian religion: the relation of God is primarily to the nation and not
to the individual; the Old Testament congregation is a political
and cultic community in one; the Hebrew has no hope of life after
death, so that his relation with God is limited to his earthly life;
his hope for the future is intensely material, contrasted with the
spiritual hope of the Christian. In short, the Old Testament man had
a different self-understanding and a different life relationship with

[21] F. Baumgärtel, *Verheissung: Zur Frage des evangelischen Verständnisses des
A. T.* "Das Hermeneutische Problem des A. T.," TLZ, No. 4 (1954), p. 199.
"Ohne Schlüssel vor der Tür des Wortes Gottes," EvTh (1953), p. 413.

God from that of the New Testament believer. Therefore, since we cannot share his faith, we are in principle shut out from understanding even such passages as Isa., ch. 6, and Ps. 51 as he understood them. Baumgärtel's concern in thus sharpening the antithesis between the Testaments is to let the Old Testament be the *Old* Testament. There has to be a *Christian* understanding of the Old Testament, since a Christian is excluded by the nature of his faith from a Hebrew understanding of it. In this the Christian hears from the Old Testament only the word that can be for him the word of Jesus Christ. All else falls away: all psalms in which the believer expresses confidence in his own self-righteousness, all passages in which God is pleased with bloody-handed servants, all hopes for material power and glory. It is particularly disturbing to Baumgärtel that the Old Testament theologians question the ability of historical research to disclose the ultimate meaning of the Old Testament text and speak of the scholar's having to wait upon the Holy Spirit to reveal the meaning. It seems to him altogether too easy for the Holy Spirit to become an excuse for eisegesis and for all sound scholarly methods to be undermined. Yet here the basic issue is laid open: whether the historian is able with such confidence to declare the ultimate meaning of the text and whether he can be quite so sure that the authors of Ps. 51 and Rom., ch. 5, belong in separate congregations. Perhaps in spite of differences of self-understanding God is able to draw them both, and us with them, into one communion of the saints.

Walther Zimmerli [22] does not find it necessary to speak of typology as he demonstrates how the Old Testament is bound together within itself and then with the New Testament by an incessant movement of life from promise to fulfillment. Not only was this category of understanding basic to the traditions of Israel from the earliest and simplest credo to the latest formulation of the Pentateuch and the Deuteronomic history, but also the prophets as heralds of coming events saw Israel's history always as moving toward a judgment or deliverance that was promised the nation in God's word. Never was the future a fixed event that could be exactly predicted, because God's relation with his people in history was a per-

[22] W. Zimmerli, "Verheissung und Erfüllung," EvTh (1952); *Das Alte Testament als Anrede* (1956).

sonal one, judgment and deliverance being simply the death of separation from him and the life of reconciliation with him. For this reason, it is false to make judgment stand alone in early prophecies and promise or deliverance stand alone in later prophecies. Both are essential to prophecy, since they predict not an impersonal something but a confrontation with a personal God who kills and makes alive. Zimmerli brings out forcefully the theological significance of this way of thinking, first, as a reflection of the nature of God: his forethought for his people, his purposes that compass all their life, and his faithfulness that makes his word to them to be trusted unconditionally; and then, as the recognition of history as the stage on which God lets the drama of his purposes unfold. Jesus Christ as fulfillment brings the Old Testament to an end, but in doing so he brings it to its highest honor and gives it abiding validity, since Christ as fulfillment can never be rightly known apart from the promise that he fulfills. A quotation of Dietrich Bonhoeffer's, given by H. W. Wolff,[23] helps us to see why this is so: " He who desires to think and feel in terms of the New Testament too quickly and too directly is in my opinion no Christian." The Christian today has to move from promise to fulfillment just as Israel did. Neither in Israel nor in us does God accomplish his purpose in a moment. Jesus Christ both then and now comes only to those who are willing to wait for him in faith, living by hope and not by sight. Therefore, again and again we find our true situation before God mirrored in the Old Testament, and in our darkness we are saved from despair, first by knowing that one *can* live in the darkness by trusting in the promise of God's word, and secondly by hearing in the story of Israel that in the fullness of time Christ came with his deliverance to those who hoped.

Walther Eichrodt,[24] when he speaks of typology, is thinking primarily of the way in which the New Testament church found the Old Testament to be a book about its own life and experiences. In doing this the New Testament authors at times placed an interpretation on texts that they will not bear, so that we cannot adopt the New Testament interpretations of the Old Testament uncriti-

[23] H. W. Wolff, "The Old Testament in Controversy," *loc. cit.*

[24] Walther Eichrodt, "Ist die Typologische Exegese sachgemässe Exegese? " ThZ (Nov., 1956), p. 642.

cally. But, when full allowance has been made for these, there remain many remarkable correspondences between persons, institutions, and events in the Old Testament and the New Testament in which the Old seems to be a divine prefiguring of the New. No exact correspondence of details is to be looked for but only a striking analogy between the two as between Moses and Jesus and between Adam and Jesus. The Old Testament types are not mere shadows but are real historical events and persons in which God was at work. Typology is distinguished from allegory by the fact that it fastens onto the historical reality of the event where allegory disregards the historical reality and draws out a contemporary meaning that has nothing to do with the original event. It is also distinguished from prediction, since in the Old Testament passage there is no consciousness whatsoever of the future New Testament meaning. The Old Testament event is seen as a type only from the vantage point of the New Testament. Eichrodt's concern is only to establish the fact that these correspondences exist and must be taken into account in interpretation. They point for him to the unity of the revelation of the two Testaments, that it is one God who is dealing with men in both. He has no use for typological or Christological or pneumatic exegesis. Our reading of the Old Testament does not need to be the same, and in fact cannot be the same, as that of the New Testament authors or the Reformers. But we must begin and carry through our exegesis with a frank recognition that our life is rooted in the salvation that is possible for us only through Jesus Christ. We must make no apologies for the fact that we are *Christian* exegetes.

These Old Testament scholars have been reviewed in such detail in order to show that they give no encouragement to a typological exegesis that reads New Testament meanings into the text of the Old Testament, even though they use the term " typology." Their use of it would seem to be both unnecessary and unfortunate, unnecessary because the term " correspondences " is quite adequate to describe the phenomena with which they are concerned, and unfortunate because in the minds of their readers the very use of the term lends encouragement to the revival of typological interpretation of the patristic and Reformation order.

A New Testament scholar who has recently written of typology is Paul Minear in *Horizons of Christian Community* (1959). When

Mmear

the New Testament links Jesus with Adam, Isaac, Joseph, Moses, Aaron, David, Elijah, and Jeremiah, these are "typological links" to Minear, and when it calls Christians "sons of Adam" or "sons of Abraham" or envisages the new Israel of the church as twelve tribes ruled by the twelve apostles, these are "typological correspondences." "Typology is an analogical form of thinking and speaking which focuses attention upon two or more pivotal realities (e.g., Adam and Christ) and in so doing apprehends the hidden connection between those realities and their common source. It thereby simultaneously apprehends the connection, also hidden, between those realities and other earthly phenomena" (p. 65). "The later event is conceived as present in some sense with the earlier, and the interpreter who views them both becomes contemporaneous with both" (p. 67). "The two-point analogy becomes a three-point analogy, 'Adam, Christ, ourselves.'" "Authentic typology indicates an action of the Holy Spirit in the storyteller, an action which relates both prophet and audience to the God who was at work in Jerusalem" (p. 68). But does it really help to call this typology or does it introduce needless confusion? The New Testament links Jesus Christ and Christians with the Old Testament figures and events because the gospel fulfills what was present in promise in those figures and events, and we who share in the fulfillment through Jesus Christ find ourselves present also in Adam and Abraham and all the others, laying hold upon the promise and reaching out in expectation toward the fulfillment. Our life moves ever from promise to fulfillment and therefore from the Old Testament to the New. But it is not just where types are to be found that the Old Testament has this significance for us. The whole of the Old Testament was "written for our sakes," that in our companying with Israel on its long and tortured journey we might find ourselves again and again on the road that can have no other destination than Bethlehem and Calvary. Minear's concern seems mainly to be to recognize the continuity between Old Testament, New Testament, and church, that the Christian of today may discover his own history in the Biblical history, there revealed in its true significance in relation to God. The question is whether the use of the term "typology" forwards or obstructs this purpose. Is it gain or loss when it is left aside?

THE PRINCIPLE OF ANALOGY

Karl Barth has made wide use of a principle that he calls the analogy of faith in his interpretation of Scripture. At times it is difficult to distinguish from typology, and there can be no question that it has given strong encouragement to others in their use of typology. But it has in it deeper and more valid elements than are found in Vischer and is in part responsible for some of Barth's profoundest insights into Scripture, so that here we are confronted with the task of disentangling two forms of interpretation that are contained within the one word " analogy."

At many points Barth simply draws out for us the implications of the unity of Scripture. He is not blind to the discontinuity of the Testaments, but he proceeds with his exegesis on the basis that the God who dealt with Israel throughout its history was the God and Father of Jesus Christ, and that his revelation of himself in Jesus Christ is the light in which we can see more clearly the meaning of his words and deeds in Israel. Thus, in Jesus Christ as the Son of God it is revealed to us that, within the Godhead, God the Father is not willing to be alone. There must be a " Thou " to his " I." This throws light upon the duality of male and female in the nature of humanity: in order to reflect God's nature, man and woman are so created that they can be themselves only in an " I-Thou " relation. It throws light also upon the covenant relation first with Israel and then with the church, for the people of God is the earthly " Thou " to the divine " I " and the joy both of God and of his people is in the richness of God's self-giving and of man's response within the covenant. The source of the analogies between events on earth lies in the fact that all historical events have their origin in God's own life within the Godhead in eternity. Eternity is not endless time but rather a different kind of time from ours, God's time in which past, present, and future are all contained at once. Since the inner life of the Godhead is revealed to us in Jesus Christ alone, in him alone do we understand God's works and ways with men. Applying this to the story of creation, Barth asserts that God's creation of the world has its only analogy in God's begetting of the Son (*Dogmatik* III, 1, p. 13). Therefore, our primary understanding of the Creator, the Creation, and man must be drawn not from Gen., chs. 1 to 3, but from the Word made flesh.

As a consequence of this approach, Barth has eyes to see many things in the text of Gen., chs. 1 to 3, that were hidden from an exegesis that read the chapters in a narrower context. He also brings light from the larger Old Testament context. Therefore, thus far the issue is simply whether chapters such as these are to be interpreted only in their immediate historical context or in their *total* historical context as well.

The difficulty arises when the principle of analogy is applied to details. Heaven and earth in Gen. 1:1 correspond to the heavenly and earthly elements in Jesus Christ and also in man. (*Dogmatik* III, 1, p. 18.) The waters in Gen. 1:2 are to be understood in the light of perilous waters in various parts of Scripture: the waters that wiped out the world of man in the Flood, the waters of the Red Sea that blocked Israel's way in the exodus, the waters of the Sea of Galilee that endangered the lives of the disciples in a storm. To this he relates the fact that Israel never became a seafaring nation and that Jonah's attempt to cross the sea ended in disaster! Solomon's building of ships was a Messianic characteristic of this direct son of David, pointing forward to Jesus' sovereignty over the sea, shown in his stilling of it and walking upon it! The author of The Acts tells the story of Paul's journey on the Mediterranean and his shipwreck because he understands " the sign of the sea " and wants to indicate that God's conquest of the dangerous sea is a fulfillment of Old Testament prophecy. Thus, in Rev. 21:1 the sea is abolished. This seems fantastic until one learns that for Barth the sea, like the darkness, is a Biblical symbol of the chaos, the " Nothing," which is a " metaphysical peril " ever threatening the life of man. He may well be right in interpreting the chaos in Gen. 1:2 as a representation of the emptiness and meaninglessness of an existence cut apart from God's creative word, but when, by analogy, water everywhere in Scripture takes on this same meaning, sound exegesis is endangered. An instance of where this method can lead is shown in the interpretation of the firmament of heaven that holds back the water above the earth. Since the waters represent the " metaphysical peril," the firmament symbolizes God's provision of a bulwark to hold back this fearful evil from above, and the opening of the heavens in the New Testament has the effect of rendering the chaos harmless.

Why was it not sufficient to say on the basis of other texts that God does not leave man defenseless before the world's evil and that in Jesus Christ God robs evil of its power over man? The truth for which Barth elsewhere witnesses so powerfully is endangered when he resorts to exegesis of this kind

Again, in the interpretation of the stories of Adam and Eve he is on sound historical and theological ground when he sets the stories against the background of the covenant relation between God and Israel. Man's relation to God in Gen., ch. 2, has behind it Israel's relation to God. The relation was not just intellectually conceived by the Yahwist; it was actually lived by Israel. Therefore, the riddle of Israel is the " final subjective content of the text " (*Dogmatik* III, 1, p. 270), and this riddle points beyond itself to the Messiah of Israel, Jesus Christ. But now the analogy changes from God-Adam, Eve//God-Israel, to God-Israel//Adam-Eve, which is something quite different. The marriage relation of Adam and Eve is said to be like the marriage of Hosea and Gomer, an earthly reflection of God's marriage with Israel. Both point forward to the perfect realization of the relation in Christ and his bride, the church (Eph. 5:32). And now on the basis of these analogies an interpretation is given of the details of Gen., ch. 2 (*Dogmatik* III, 1, pp. 367 ff.). Man could not be alone because Christ needed his helpmate in the church. Man had to fall into a deep sleep to let woman come into being because the church had to have its origin in Christ's sleep of death and to stand before him complete in his resurrection. Adam's rib was given to make the woman because Jesus Christ's death was his giving of himself for the church. In return, he receives the church's flesh, i.e., its weakness, as Adam received Eve. A man leaves his father and his mother to cleave to his wife because Jesus left the glory of his father for the sake of his bride that he might unite her with him. Adam and Eve were naked and yet not ashamed because Jesus and his people are utterly humbled before each other and yet are not ashamed. Interpretation of this kind is similar to the typology of Calvin by which he was able to interpret the story of King David as a foreshadowing of the career of King Jesus.

Barth's exegesis of the parable of the prodigal (*Dogmatik* IV, 2, pp. 21 f.) illustrates a rather different use of analogy. He begins with the admission that it cannot be given a directly Christological interpretation. Directly, it speaks of man's sin and the death that threatens him in consequence of his sin, of repentance and return to God, and of the grace with which God receives the returning sinner. In the immediate context the prodigal is identified with the publicans and sinners, and the elder son with the scribes and Pharisees. Luke, however, is said to have widened the context of the parable with his universal interest and to have intended, in his retelling of the story, that the younger son should represent the Gentile world and the older son the Jewish people. On this basis an interpretation is validated that strictly is not present in the original use of the parable. This suggests to Barth a possible validation of the Christological interpretation. In contrast to Harnack, who used the parable as evidence that there is room in the gospel of Jesus only for the Father in his goodness and mercy toward man, he favors the view of Gollwitzer that the context of the parable is Jesus' own love for and acceptance of the publicans and sinners. Therefore, Jesus himself is present in the parable in the father's running to meet the son, and is hidden in the kiss that the father gives the son. But Barth is not wholly satisfied with this. He therefore proceeds to identify the central figure of the parable, the younger son, with Jesus Christ. He sees an analogy between the descent of the son into the far country and the descent of the Son of God into the world, and between the return of the son to his father and the return of the Son of God to the Father in heaven. The prodigal's journey into a profligate life is not the journey of Jesus of itself but only in so far as he identifies himself with fallen man. So also his return to the father is not Jesus' return but only a weak imitation of his rise out of humiliation into the glory that is his at the right hand of the Father. There is thus an analogy between the movement of Jesus down into the darkness of human sin and misery that he may return triumphant to God and the movement of man away from the Father into the world of sin and death and back to the Father's home. The possibility of man's return depends upon the reality of Christ's return. And the elder brother rejects this whole scheme of sin and forgiveness, disowning both the God who is the God of the lost son and the man who is lost and found.

One asks why Barth has to superimpose upon the parable an interpretation of this kind in order to understand it as Christological.

Why is he not content to find Christ present where Gollwitzer finds him so validly and so meaningfully? Does he not endanger the whole Christological interpretation of Scripture by an excess of this nature? It is important to recognize (as so few interpreters have done) that a parable such as that of the prodigal belonged originally in the context of Jesus' redemptive mission and was an instrument of that mission. The sinner who by the hearing of the parable came to himself and to God found not only the Father but also Jesus Christ himself as the One in whom the searching love of the Father met him concretely. Separated from the person and mission of Jesus, the parable ceases to have its true meaning. It is Christological when Jesus Christ uses it either then or now as the opening of a door whereby through him men return to the Father. But to make the prodigal into an analogy of Christ himself in his relation to the Father is likely to produce only confusion. What Barth tries to make the parable say is already said elsewhere in Scripture much more clearly and need not be forced into the words of Jesus.

This feature of Barth's use of analogy is puzzling, because the solid body of his exegesis of Scripture is of a very different nature. He has the most remarkable ability to light up the dark places of Scripture, largely because of his use of one passage to interpret another and his faculty of penetrating to the underlying presuppositions of Scripture itself. He lets it stand in its own light. It would misrepresent him if the impression were given that the examples of eisegesis cited above are found with frequency in his writings. They are not; and moreover, where they occur, they could be removed without affecting materially the structure of Barth's doctrine. They are not essential to his thought. But when others copy his method, they seem to become fascinated with this element of analogy or typology, and it grows like a weed in their interpretations, concealing the text of Scripture from sight.

Conclusions

There seems, then, to be no basis in the New Testament for validating either a typological or an allegorical form of exegesis. Paul, as a consequence of his rabbinical training, uses allegory occasionally but more as a homiletical aid than as an essential part of his theology. The removal of all instances of allegory from his writings would not change the structure of his theology. This surely is the decisive test. Some of Jesus' parables may verge over into allegory, but there is no trace of allegory in his use of the Old Testament. That which is essential to both Jesus and Paul is the recognition of a unity between the central concern of the Old Testament and the central concern of the gospel, so intimate that in many parts of the Old Testament we hear what is almost but not quite a proclamation of the gospel. John's Gospel puts into the mouth of Jesus an assertion that he who truly responded in faith to the word of Moses would also respond in faith to the word of Jesus (John 5:39, 46), and again that " your father Abraham rejoiced that he was to see my day; he saw it and was glad " (ch. 8:56), thereby claiming that Abraham, in receiving the promise of that which was to come, already had a glimpse, or foretaste, of the fulfillment. This is not allegory or typology but something much more profound, which we cannot ignore in our interpretation of Scripture without taking leave of the central discernment of faith throughout the whole New Testament, the indissoluble bond between the promises embodied in Israel in the Old Testament and the fulfillment of those promises in Jesus Christ and his church. The new Israel was the *true* Israel, which received in Jesus Christ the final revelation of God's will and purpose in the light of which it reinterpreted all that had gone before and took up into itself the whole of Israel's inheritance of faith. Because of this direct continuity of the Old Israel with the New, and the unity of the revelation in which the promises were given with the revelation in which their fulfillment was effected, the church both in the first century and in the twentieth can preach its gospel out of the Old Testament, but always out of an Old Testament whose full meaning and intention is revealed by the Spirit of the Lord.

A final word needs to be said about the viewpoint expressed by both Hebert and Lampe that, although the allegorizing of Scripture may have to be held within severe limitations in exegesis, a much freer rein may be given to it in preaching. A similar sentiment is voiced by two Scottish theologians. Ronald Wallace resorts to allegory in his expositions of the stories of Elijah and Elisha.[25]

[25] Ronald S. Wallace, *Elijah and Elisha: Expositions from the Book of Kings* (1957).

Elijah's residence at Cherith and then at Zarephath is said to be symbolic of the Christian's residence in two worlds, the kingdom of this world and the eschatological kingdom. If he stays too long at Cherith, the brook dries up. " This may surely be interpreted as if it were an allegory," says the author (p. 14). In his preface he states his intention " to avoid exaggerated allegorical interpretations especially where the passage, viewed historically, had another obvious meaning," but then goes on to make the degree of allegory to be permitted dependent upon the mind of the congregation rather than upon what is actually meant by the text. " Some will be able to find inspiration and instruction and profit in an allegorical interpretation which others will reject. In this matter the expositor will be guided by the attitude of the congregation to whom he is preaching." G. S. Hendry, in an article on " The Exposition of Holy Scripture," [26] after having established securely the necessity that theologians should take seriously the Bible's own claim to be the vehicle through which God speaks his living word to us, asks the question how these writings out of an ancient world can be this living word today unless they are interpreted allegorically. " It is impossible to resist the conclusion that the exposition of Holy Scripture must be allegorical; for its aim is not the elucidation of what actually happened long ago when Israel came out of Egypt or when the apostles gazed into the empty tomb, but the endeavor to find what the Spirit is saying to the church in and through these words." This is something quite different from Wallace's allegorization of Scripture. Hendry's concern is simply that God may speak through Scripture into our present life situation, that the exodus may not remain an incident in the life of Israel but may proclaim what God can and will do in the midst of his people today, and that Jesus' forgiveness of men's sins may be present reality and not just something reported in a series of New Testament narratives. But surely there is no need to use the term " allegorization " for this securing of a contemporary relevance. Our plight would be sad if no Scripture could speak to us with a present urgency until it was allegorized.

Hebert, in a similar fashion, confuses spiritual interpretation, symbolic meanings, allegorization, and the finding in Scripture of

[26] G. S. Hendry, " The Exposition of Holy Scripture," *Scottish Journal of Theology* (1948), p. 29.

meaning that is applicable to the contemporary situation. It is a "spiritual" interpretation of circumcision when Deut. 10:16 calls for a circumcision of the foreskin of the heart, and of sacrifices when in Ps. 51:17 and Isa. 66:2-3, a humble and contrite heart is described as the only offering that God is willing to accept. But Hebert makes the material circumcision and sacrifice the symbols of the spiritual whereas, for the prophet certainly and perhaps also for the psalmist (if the final verse is a later addition), the material sacrifice was being declared useless and the spiritual alone acceptable. Toward the patristic allegories Hebert takes a lenient view, seeing value in some of them, even though they are not legitimate exegesis of the text. Recognizing how fantastic allegorical interpretations can become, he seeks a rule to control them and formulates it in this fashion: when meanings are based upon a text that are not the original and proper meaning of the text, or a legitimate development and fulfillment of it, they should be sanctioned as long as they are "soundly based on the general sense of Scripture." It is hard to see how this rule can exercise any restraint, since each allegorist is likely to be certain that his theology is soundly based on the general sense of Scripture. R. A. Marcus[27] takes much the same view. He equates typological with spiritual exegesis and considers that "there may be a legitimate place for such use of Scripture, even if it cannot always claim to be exegesis — particularly for homiletic purposes. Much of the fathers' spiritual exegesis falls under this heading." In the body of his article it is evident that his concern is to read the Old Testament as a Christian and not as a Jew, to approach the Old Testament in the light of the revelation that has been received in Jesus Christ, and to maintain the unity of the two as the early church did, but he is convinced that this is impossible without resorting to allegorical and typological interpretations.

Implicit in this viewpoint is the denial of the very truth it means to affirm, the unity of revelation in Old and New Testaments. Allegory is a means of fastening upon a text a meaning that is not actually present. Therefore, if the Christian gospel cannot be found in the Old Testament without allegory, this is tantamount to a confession that *it is not there* but has to be inserted from without. The

[27] R. A. Marcus, "Presuppositions of the Typological Approach to Scripture," CQR (Oct.–Dec., 1957), p. 442.

conviction of Jesus, of Paul, and of the early church was that the gospel *is* there, though as yet partially concealed and not fully present. The Spirit does not insert the gospel into the Old Testament, thereby validating all manner of eisegesis, but rather opens the blind eyes of men to see it there and to respond to it in faith and obedience.

What is needed, then, in interpretation and preaching is not a return to allegory and typology but a faithful exegesis and exposition of Scripture that will wrestle with the words of these ancient witnesses until the walls of the centuries become thin and they tell us in *our* day what they knew so well in *their* day. They knew God, and the goal of our exegesis must be, not to foist upon their words spiritual meanings that we in our ignorance think to be the general sense of Scripture, but to let each of them speak to us in his own way until through his words he becomes our elder brother in the faith, sharing with us his knowledge of God and of that life that is possible only in the knowledge of God.

a better term

[V]

THE PROBLEMS ILLUSTRATED

THERE IS PERHAPS no better way of giving concreteness to the problems discussed thus far than to take some one concept that is important in both Testaments, has theological significance, and is easily traceable through various ages in the church. The term " image of God " as a description of man's nature or destiny does not occur with any frequency in the Old Testament, but it can be shown to be more basic to Old Testament thought than these few references would suggest. It acquires more prominence in the New Testament, and then in the church becomes one of the key concepts of theology. It serves our present purposes admirably.

THE VARIETIES OF INTERPRETATION

An examination of commentaries and of theological books that deal with the nature of man reveals a wide disparity in the answers given to the question of how to define the meaning of "image" and "likeness" in Gen. 1:26-27. J. J. Stamm, in an essay in the volume *Antwort*,[1] has a valuable summary of the definitions given by scholars. He points out that since 1940 there has come to be general agreement among Old Testament scholars that the image in its essence has to do with a likeness in form and cannot be given a purely spiritual reference. This does not mean that it does not include man's spiritual nature. In fact, the Hebrew way of thinking of man was to make no separation between body and spirit but to think of man as a whole self. Therefore, an exclusion of the physical from the image would be false just as any confining of it to the physical would be false. Before 1940 there were four widely held

[1] E. Wolf, *et al.*, eds., *Antwort: Karl Barth zum siebzigsten Geburtstag.*

134

views of the image among historical scholars. First, it was defined as a spiritual quality in man: by Delitzsch as self-possession, by Dillman as the sense for the eternal, true, and good, by König as man's self-consciousness, rationality, and immortality, by Heinisch as reason, by Procksch and Sellin as personality, and by Eichrodt as man's spiritual superiority. Holzinger, Köhler, and Hempel equated it with man's dominion over all the other creatures. Gunkel insisted that it referred to man's bodily form while not excluding his spiritual nature, and he was followed in this by several others. Vischer interpreted it as an expression of the immediate relationship between God and man, denying that it was a quality possessed by man in himself and asserting that it was only lent to man in his relation with God.

The work of Humbert, in *Etudes sur le récit du paradis et de la chute,* 1940, has been widely influential in producing a change in view. He defines *säläm* ("image") as the outer likeness, the plastic form, and shows that it was used of a hewn or cast image or of a statue. *Demut* ("likeness") he finds in the majority of cases to be an object that is not identical with the original but has a strong resemblance to it. He regards the second word as having been added to the first in order to prevent *säläm* from being given too literal a meaning. Köhler more recently has taken "image" to refer to man's erect posture. Von Rad and Galling recognize the presence of the physical element but warn against any separation of the physical and the spiritual, since it was the whole man that was created in the image of God. Vriezen interprets the imprinting of God's image upon man as signifying that, because man has been called by God and stands in communion with him, he is, in spite of all that he shares with the animal creation, a different being from them. One point at which there is general agreement among scholars is that no conception of a loss of the image at the time of man's fall from grace is present in Genesis. This, which was a basic tenet of Reformation theology, has no support in the text, since in Gen., chs. 5 and 9, man in spite of his sinfulness is still described as being in the image of God.

Nothing is added to this picture when we examine commentaries in the English language. Driver spiritualizes the image completely. He acknowledges that *säläm* suggests more the idea of material resemblance and *demut* an immaterial resemblance but does not think the distinction can be pressed in this instance, since here both words clearly refer to spiritual resemblance alone. The image must be something that forms the basis of man's entire pre-eminence over the animals, something that could be transmitted to his descendants and therefore belongs to man in general and not just to man in a state of primitive innocence, also something that relates to his immaterial nature. Driver's conclusion is that it can be nothing but the gift of self-conscious reason, man's creative and originative power, his ability to conceive intellectual and moral ideals, and that element in him which makes him able to pass beyond himself and enter into relations of love and sympathy with his fellow men. Here, as in so many of the German definitions, the image is identified with a spiritual quality or power in man that he possesses inalienably. Skinner disagrees with Driver, emphasizing that the image denotes primarily the bodily form, but agrees with him in including within it man's distinctive spiritual attributes. Reinhold Niebuhr, in his *Nature and Destiny of Man,* identifies the image with man's power of self-transcendence, which is really an enlarged conception of reason. Cuthbert Simpson, in *The Interpreter's Bible* (Vol. I), sees in it a parallel to the Babylonian conception of the physical likeness between gods and men, but finds that it also signifies man's powers of thought, communication, and self-transcendence. What one misses among English-speaking interpreters is the view expressed by Vriezen and Vischer, that the image refers primarily not to a quality or power in man but rather to something that belongs to him in his relation with God. This viewpoint remains thus far unrepresented.

We have reviewed by no means all existing views. Those of Barth and Brunner have been deliberately omitted since they are to be considered later. But the sampling that has been made has been sufficiently wide to show the variations among competent scholars in their interpretation of a single concept in Scripture. Why should there be such wide variations? It would be difficult to find two more balanced and highly skilled exegetes than Driver and Gunkel, and yet, in spite of a number of points on which they are agreed, their basic interpretations are at opposite extremes. It is clear that neither has succeeded in separating the two questions: What was the image of God in the mind of the priestly writer? and What is the image of God in man as we know him now? They intend to practice only historical exegesis, but theological exposition has exerted a strong determining influence upon their exegesis.

THE IMAGE OF GOD IN THE OLD TESTAMENT

It may be assumed that wherever the priestly writer speaks of man's being in the image of God, the same concept is present. It appears three times: in Gen. 1:26-27; 5:1-3; and 9:6. In the first instance, in the story of the Creation, it is clearly intended to signify the unique status of man in the midst of the Creation. He is creature, created the same day as the animals and dependent like them upon the plants for his sustenance, but he is separated from them by being made in God's likeness and in being given the responsibility of rule over all else in the Creation. Likenesses could have been found and noted between man and the animals, but the significant thing for man and his future was not his likeness to the animals but his likeness to the God who made him. How this likeness is to be conceived is the problem. That to the ancient thinker it meant a similarity in person between man and God seems incontestable. Abstractions are alien to the Hebrew mind. When the Hebrew thought of God, he thought of a person, and a person for him possessed eyes to see with, ears to hear with, arms and hands with which to strike or to bless. This is true not just of primitive levels in the literature but also of the most advanced. No prophet thought more profoundly concerning God than Second Isaiah, and yet, when he envisioned God coming in judgment, he saw him as a mighty warrior trampling on his enemies until his garments were dyed red with their blood. God remains God, however, for the Hebrew prophet. He may picture him like a man in appearance, but he never thinks of him as other than the God of justice, holiness, and truth. He is all that man is not; he is never, as in Babylonia, Egypt, and Greece, merely man written large and endowed with supernatural powers. Therefore, there is nothing crude or pagan in the conception of a resemblance in person between God and man. It becomes crude and pagan only when it is denied that there was

anything more present in the priestly mind than the physical likeness, and few interpreters would any longer support such a view.
The wholeness of man's nature which was present in the Hebrew
mind no matter what part of man he mentioned would suggest that
it is the whole man who is made in God's likeness. Therefore, we
have hardly begun to suggest wherein the likeness consists when we
have admitted its physical reference.

This application to the whole man is supported by Gen. 5:1-3,
where Adam begets a son in his own likeness and image just as God
had created Adam in his likeness and image. The fact that both
terms are used this second time shows that the author was conscious of the parallel and intended to emphasize it. It is not just
Adam who bears this image but also Seth and all who come forth
from the loins of Adam. In ch. 5:2, this universality of the image
is indicated when God names the man and woman who bear it
" man," which in this instance means " mankind." Again, in ch. 9:6,
the reason given for God's protection of the life of Cain, the murderer, is that he is a man made in the image of God. Not even his
evil act in murdering his brother can make him other than what
God has made him.

There is an important parallel that comes out clearly in these
verses but has never been sufficiently noticed. For Seth and Cain to
be sons of Adam is for them to be in the image and likeness of
Adam. Does it not follow that for Adam to be in the image and
likeness of God is for him to be the son of God? That this is *not*
said is most likely because of the pagan connotations of the idea of
a man's being the son of the deity. This was a familiar conception
among the nations of the Near East. As in other parts of the Creation story, so here the pagan element has been carefully excised, but
there remains the suggestion of an intimate personal relationship
like that of a father with a son. This was how Hosea and others
conceived the relation of God to Israel, and it may well have been
in the mind of the priestly writer. That a son should be like his
father was an expectation that became an idiom in Hebrew, " son
of a dog " meaning having a character like that of a dog, and " sons
of Belial " indicating a kind of conduct fitting for those who stand
in an intimate relation to Belial.

The important distinction that here emerges is that it is in man's

relation with God as a son to a father that man is in the likeness
of God. That Cain becomes a murderer does not cancel this relation.
The sin of Cain could bring a tragic and unhappy order into the relation, but he still remained one who was created to reflect the nature of God as a son reflects the nature of his father. This location
of the image not in some quality or power residing in man as man
but in the relation between man and God receives further support
from the context of the Creation story. Because it comes first in
Genesis and the story of the covenant follows it in ch. 12, the fact
is concealed that the story of the Creation belongs within the context of the story of the covenant. In the growth of the tradition the
covenant came first. God chose Israel to be a people in covenant
with him, that is, to be a people in the most intimate kind of personal relation with him. In love he chose Israel, delivered them out of
the bondage of Egypt and bound them to him during the years in
the desert. In return he asked not just that his commandments be
obeyed but that this people respond to his love with love, with all
the heart and mind and soul. It belongs to the essence of such a personal relation that its maintenance is possible only when there is a
likeness of nature and character. Therefore, God's demand upon
Israel is that there should be in them a holiness that will correspond
to his own holiness. " Ye shall be holy; for I am holy." (Lev. 11:44.)
" Be ye holy: for I am Yahweh your God . . . which sanctifieth
you." (Lev. 20:7, 8.) As Israel's horizon widened, the God of the
covenant was seen to be the God of the whole earth, the Creator of
all things. One of the remarkable features of both creation stories is
their completely universal outlook. The man who is created is not
a Hebrew but simply man, the ancestor of all mankind. Because of
this universalism we may lose sight of the fact that the God who
creates the heavens and the earth is the covenant God who has
chosen Israel to be his own servant people, that through them he
may accomplish his purpose for the whole world. Therefore, since
creation is within the context of covenant, it is quite in order to
read the story of the Creation of man against the background of the
covenant purpose of God. God created man to be such in his nature
that he could enter into the covenant relation, responding to his
love with love and reflecting the very holiness of God's own nature.
To be created in God's image is therefore to be created for this rela-

tion, and to be such in his nature that the fulfillment of the relation is possible.

Edmond Jacob, in his *Theology of the Old Testament* (1958), has a different approach to the question of the image, which, however, tends in this same direction. He takes as his starting point the evidence that in the ancient East the purpose and function of an image was to represent someone. The image or statue of a god represented the presence of the god, so that prayers might be addressed to it, and its destruction was equivalent to the destruction of the god. The image of a king was set up in regions that he could not personally visit in order to give an indication of his authority. In Egypt the king was spoken of as the image of the god Amon, and in one instance men are described as images coming out of the flesh of the god. For this reason, Jacob asserts that the conception of man as an image of God first occurs in Egypt, " where humanity is supposed to have originated by way of generation from the divine world." Therefore, when it was taken up into the Hebrew story of the Creation, its primary intention was to express man's place in the universe as the representative of God on earth, and it follows naturally in Gen. 1:28 that through him God exercises his rule over the Creation. Man is the intermediary between God and the Creation. Jacob goes on then to show that this involved no claim of divine powers for man, since " the *imago Dei* means for man a relationship with, and dependence upon, the one for whom he is only the representative. To wish to be like God, the temptation suggested by the serpent, is to desire to abandon the role of image. . . . To remain an image, man must maintain his relationship with God, he must remember that he is only an ambassador and his dominion over creation will be effective only in proportion as that relationship becomes more real."

Jacob then draws into relation with the conception of the image the closely associated conception of the imitation of God as the principle of the moral and spiritual life. What God is in his nature is to determine what Israel shall be. Because God is holy, Israel must be holy. Because God is righteous and just, Israel must be righteous and just. Because truth is God's nature, truth must be the inmost quality of Israel's life. This correspondence of nature is particularly clear in Hosea, where the word *hesed* is used at one and the same time for the attitude of God to man, of man to God, and of man to his fellow. Jacob suggests that the command to love one's neighbor as oneself applies in the human realm God's own attitude " who, by creating man in his image and clothing him with a dignity like his own, loved him as himself." The issue of Jacob's interpretation, it can be seen, is therefore to find the essence of the image not in something that man possesses in himself and of himself but in something that belongs to his nature only as a consequence of his relation with God. He has perhaps pressed too far the element of representation, for this is hard to sustain in Adam's begetting of Seth " in his own image and likeness " and in Cain's possession of the image.

Jacob's association of the image of God with the principle of the imitation of God points to phenomena that have not been taken into account sufficiently in the interpretation of the image. It has been customary to assume that this highly important conception of man as being created in God's image was introduced only in the priestly strand of the Creation story and failed to show itself in any other portion of the Old Testament, appearing later, however, in several places in the Apocrypha and in the New Testament. This strange absence of it has often been noted.[2] But the absence has to do only with the *words* " image " and " likeness." The conception, when once it has been understood as the reflection of God's nature in man that is essential to man's intimate personal relation with him, far from being absent from the rest of the Old Testament is seen to be the very foundation of the teaching of the prophets. Man is truly man only when he reflects in his whole being and conduct the characteristics of God's nature. He cannot do this if he is far from God and pursuing his own ways. But even in his most flagrant desertion of God and surrender to evil he remains a man who was created for something else, and the prophet appeals to him, not to rise to some new height of virtue, but to return to the covenant relation and to the life within it for which he was created.

If one had asked a prophet why man should be just and faithful, he would have answered not with some demonstration of the practical value of justice and faithfulness but with the simple statement,

[2] G. von Rad, TWNT, Vol. II, p. 378, assumes that absence of the term involves absence of the concept.

" Because our God is just and faithful." Israelites were bidden to be kind to strangers because their God was kind to them when they were strangers in Egypt (Ex. 23:9). The prophets called for mercy toward the poor, the hungry, the naked, the prisoner, because Israelites were the people of a God whose nature it was to have mercy. The failure of Israel to reflect the nature of God was always understood by the prophets as an indication that the covenant relation between Israel and God had been broken. For Amos, to abide in the covenant relation was to live, and to forsake it was to die, not just spiritually in a figurative sense but actually as a nation. It can be seen, then, that basic to all the prophets is the assumption that man is truly alive only in a relation with God in which he is so responding to him that God's nature is reflected or imaged in him. Perhaps their reason for not using the specific term " image " was that it was known among their hearers in its pagan connotation. In the Apocrypha and the New Testament it could be used more freely, since the possibility of any such misunderstanding was no longer present.

An important aspect of this interpretation is that it explains how Cain could be said to bear God's image even though he was a murderer. One of the great difficulties that has been felt concerning the image in Genesis is that it seems to belong to man as man, as something inalienable from his nature, whereas in the New Testament the image belongs to man only in redemption. This difficulty arises directly from the individualistic approach that has determined the impressions of so many scholars, an approach completely alien to the Old Testament writer. For prophetic and priestly writers alike it was instinctive to think of man-in-relation and not of man as an isolated individual. The one thing that man is incapable of doing is to isolate himself from any relation to God or to his fellow man. Therefore, it is man-in-relation-to-God who is in the image and likeness of God. He may pervert this relation as Cain did, so that it becomes one in which he knows God's anger, but he cannot escape from the relation itself. In short, he cannot make himself anything other than a man who was created to reflect God's nature. Even in his most self-destructive sin that shuts him out from the face of God, this remains the structure of his being. To put it in slightly different and more familiar terms, he may be a son who has rebelled against his father and has wasted his substance in riotous living in a far country, but he remains a son of his father. And just as Cain, the murderer, still bore the marks of the image, so also the son in the far country still was a son of his father, and the Creator-Father did not cease to care what was happening to his son.

It is striking that Ps. 8 — which is so distinctly reminiscent of, or at least related to, the priestly Creation story and focuses upon the power and majesty of man, made a little lower than the heavenly beings and appointed to rule over the Creation — makes no specific reference to the image or likeness. The omission is deliberate and must be for a definite reason, most likely the one we have suggested for the prophetic avoidance of the term — its pagan associations. But where we would expect a reference to the image we have the phrase "Thou hast made him a little lower than 'Elohim,'" which may here be translated "heavenly beings." This cannot, for the Hebrew psalmist, be taken to mean "Thou hast made him in some measure divine," since there is no trace in the Old Testament of any smudging of the distinction between God and man. God is God and man is man, even in Ps. 8. "A little lower than" the heavenly beings (or even "than God") means "not divine" but so far above all the rest of the Creation as to come into the neighborhood of God and to belong in the company of God, receiving from God commissions as his representative. The psalmist first of all is impressed with man's smallness and insignificance when he sees him in the midst of God's majestic creation; he is so tiny and weak that he seems to be a mere infant. But when he contemplates the destiny to which God has called man and the purpose for which he has created him, he stands in amazement that such a poor weak creature should have a place of such power in God's creation. A word has been placed in the mouth of this mere infant through which God's enemies shall be conquered, and as God's viceroy he is to rule over all things. Again it is clear that it is not anything in man of himself that raises him to such an eminence or endows him with these powers. It is in the nearness of his relation to God, in his representation of God on earth, that his glory and honor consist. It is not his own word but the word of God in his mouth that endows him with power. Since the author of Ps. 8 may well have been familiar with the priestly tradition concerning the Creation, we may understand this as his translation of " made in the image and likeness of God."

The Image of God in the New Testament

It is only in the Pauline letters and in Hebrews that the term " image " is used in the New Testament. This might be taken to mean that it was not present in the mind or speech of Jesus but was imported from the Old Testament by Paul and the author of Hebrews as they elaborated their Christology against an Old Testament background. But we are warned by our experience in the Old Testament not to assume that the absence of the term signifies the absence of the conception. When we examine the teaching of Jesus we find it directly in line with that of the prophets in this respect. In Matt. 5:44-48, the disciples are commanded to love their enemies and to pray for those who persecute them. The reason given is that this is how God deals with his enemies, making his sun rise upon the just and the unjust and sending his rain on both alike. But most significant is Jesus' statement that they are to do as God does " that you may be sons of your Father." We have already shown that in Genesis and elsewhere in the Old Testament " to be sons of " and " to be like " are synonymous. Thus the perfection for which Jesus calls in v. 48 is the fulfillment by the disciples of their human destiny as sons of God, to reflect in their being and conduct the very nature of God himself. Not until they are in God's likeness will they truly be what they were created to be. Often this verse is read with the emphasis upon the word " perfect," as though God were demanding of man a perfection that is impossible. The emphasis rather is upon " Be like God," the perfection of his nature being exemplified in his love for his enemies, and man being called to imitate him even in this. This imitation of God, however, is not set forth by Jesus as an isolated code of conduct. It belongs in the context of vs. 1–16 of the same chapter, where the intimate personal relation between the disciple and God is described. It is the disciple whose vision of God has made him aware of his own poverty of spirit, who has learned the meekness of those who are utterly humbled under the hand of God, who has received God's mercy and so has become merciful, in short, the disciple who through the new Moses has entered into the new convenant with God, who is called upon to love his enemies and so be like God.

This same mirroring of God's nature as the basis for human conduct is evident in Jesus' teaching concerning forgiveness. He breaks through all preceding conceptions of forgiveness when he expects his disciples to forgive as God forgives, not setting limitations upon the forgiveness but forgiving seventy times seven, by which he means not 490 times but an infinite number of times (Matt. 18:21 ff.). Peter did not understand this kind of forgiveness. It seemed to him, as it does to all men, that a person who forgives an offender seven times has been very merciful. But forgiveness that is limited in frequency will be limited also in regard to what persons are to be counted worthy of forgiveness and what offenses are to be considered forgivable. It is a limited forgiveness, which is something totally different both in kind and in consequences from God's unlimited forgiveness. Because God's love is primarily focused upon overcoming the offense and conquering the evil that makes man an offender, and forgiveness is his way of reaching past the offense to the offender to give him new standing ground, to make him hate his offense and so to recover him for life, there can be no end to God's forgiveness. Therefore, for those who are God's witnesses in the world, to exercise a limited forgiveness instead of an infinite forgiveness like God's is no less than to misrepresent God and to conceal his nature from men. The Christian must forgive as God forgives, because this is the nature of a true child of God who know's God's forgiveness.

Jesus' use of the terms " Father " and "child " for the relation between God and man expresses the same basic truth. To be a child of the Father is to be like the Father. Here again the difficulty arises that in some passages all men seem to be regarded as children of God while in others only those who have received the Spirit of God are children of God, a difficulty that we already encountered in Genesis where all men seem to bear God's image while to be truly in God's image means to reflect his nature in a relation of intimacy and faithfulness. But the contradiction is only on the surface. All *are* children of God, but all do not know they are children of God and all are not living as children with a Father in heaven. All *are* created in God's image, but all do not know that this is their only true nature and destiny and all are not living in a relationship with God in which his likeness can be clearly seen in them.

Two uses are made of the conception of the image by Paul: on the one hand, to describe the perfection of the nature of Jesus Christ, and on the other, to define the destiny of man in Jesus Christ. Twice Paul speaks of Christ as "the image of God" (II Cor. 4:4; Col. 1:15), but in neither instance does he enlarge upon it. It is simply another way for him to say that the fullness of the divine nature was manifest in Jesus Christ. The author of Hebrews uses a different word, meaning the express image as of a seal (Heb. 1:3), to indicate the identity of nature between the Father and the Son. Perhaps the infrequent use of the term "image" in the New Testament is due to the fact that the same truth was expressed in the universal practice of calling Jesus the Son of God or the Son of the Father. For the Hebrew mind, this would signify before all else the conception of "likeness." But equally universal was the practice of calling Christians "sons of God" or "children of God." In Eph. 1:5, our destiny is to be sons of God through Jesus Christ. In Rom. 8:29, the same destiny is described as "to be conformed to the image of his Son, in order that he might be the first-born among many brethren." To be a brother of God's Son is here to be made like him in nature and so to reflect the nature of God. In II Cor. 3:18, the sanctification of the Christian is described as a transformation that takes place in him as he "beholds the glory of the Lord," that is, as God is revealed to him in Jesus Christ, so that he is "changed into his likeness from one degree of glory to another." The image of God which is the nature of Jesus Christ is formed in the Christian through faith. In Col. 3:10, the new nature, which is born in the Christian through his dying and rising with Christ, is not at once complete but "is being renewed in knowledge after the image of its creator." Here quite clearly the image of God, far from being a natural possession of every man, is the goal of his redemption.

The Johannine literature gives even stronger support to the equation of sonship with likeness. In I John 3:2, Christians "are God's children now," and their hope for the future is that in the day of consummation they will be like him, for they will see him as he is. Clearly, to be God's children is to be like him in some measure, with the promise of a more perfect likeness in the future. The impression of other passages in the letter is that the likeness is already far advanced for any who are truly Christians. They " walk in the light, as he is in the light." If they walk in darkness, it is an indication that they have no fellowship with him. It is in fellowship with God that the Christian reflects his nature. The likeness is never something that he possesses in himself apart from this relation. The love of God dwells in him as a response to the love with which " he first loved us " (I John 4:19). In fellowship with God sin is overcome, so that the purity of God is reflected in the nature of the Christian (chs. 1:7; 3:6, 9; etc.).

In John's Gospel, Jesus is not only in his nature but also in his works the image on earth of the Father in heaven. " He who has seen me has seen the Father " (John 14:9). The identity could not be more complete. " Of myself I do nothing," Jesus constantly repeats (ch. 8:28; etc.). His words are not his own, but are the words of Him who sent him (ch. 12:49, 50). He is God's representative on earth both in judgment and redemption (chs. 5:22; 6:37; 13:3). He can do nothing on earth except what he sees his Father doing in heaven (ch. 5:19). In his very being, in his words, and in his works, he is the perfect reflection of the nature, words, and works of the Father. But the relation of Jesus to the Father is to be reproduced in the relation of the disciples to Jesus. As God the Father has sent him into the world, so does he send them (chs. 17:18; 20:21). They have life from him as he has life from the Father (ch. 6:57). They know what he is doing just as he knows what the Father is doing, so that, as his works reflect the Father's, they are to be in turn reflected in the works of the disciples (ch. 15:15), which will be even greater than those of Christ himself (ch. 14:12). So also their words are to be his words, just as his word was not his own but the word he heard from God (ch. 15:7; cf. ch. 12:49, 50). And their love is to be his love, the very love of God that dwelt in all its fullness in him. To these riches of his nature which he communicated to his disciples we can add his peace (ch. 14:27), his joy (chs. 15:11; 17:13), and even his glory (ch. 17:22). As his nature was the image of the Father's nature, so the natures of his disciples were to be the image of his nature, and thus the revelation of it to the world. To put on this new nature revealed in him is to be born of the Spirit or to be born of God and so to be children of God (chs. 1:12, 13; 3:3, 5, 6).

We would conclude, therefore, that, in spite of the infrequency of the term " image " in the New Testament, the conception that underlies it plays a large part in the thought of the church, and this in turn points back to the part that it had in the teaching of Jesus himself.

The Image in the History of the Church [3]

There seems to have been no consciousness in the New Testament authors of any contradiction between the Old Testament and the Christian gospel in their references to the image of God. It might be alleged that, since the likeness to God is now the goal of redemption, we may assume that in the New Testament church in general man as man was considered to have lost the image through sin. The fall of Adam being the beginning of sin, and that fall being conceived as a historical event, the loss of the image would be located in the Fall as one of its consequences, and the parousia, being a return of paradise, would see the restoration of the image. This is the way in which we find the church fathers thinking in the second century A.D., but, rather remarkably, there is no evidence of it in the New Testament documents. Paul, in tracing the origin of sin and death to Adam, makes no mention of any loss of the image. On the contrary, the way in which throughout the New Testament all mankind is assumed to belong to God and to be by rights his children suggests that there is good reason for the absence of any mention of the loss of the image. In a Jewish church, or at least for writers who were saturated in the Old Testament, the likeness to God was understood within the context of the covenant relation, so that, while the restoration of the covenant would be the restoration of man into the likeness of God, the breach of the covenant would not obliterate all signs that man had been created in God's likeness to have his only true life and destiny in covenant with him. But as the gospel passed into a Gentile world that was accustomed to a more individualistic way of thinking and Gentile minds interpreted the Old and New Testaments, it seemed only logical to assume that, if it were neces-

[3] David Cairns, *The Image of God in Man,* is a valuable guide to the history in the church and has been used extensively in tracing the history of the church's interpretation, though at a number of important points I see it differently from Cairns.

sary for the image to be restored in Jesus Christ, it must have been lost at some earlier time.

Irenaeus, in the middle of the second century A.D., worked out an elaborate doctrine of the image that was to be widely influential in the church of his own time and in later centuries. He was anxious to do justice in his conception of man both to the distinctive nature of the Christian man as witnessed by the New Testament and to the admirable rational and moral qualities that were to be found among non-Christians. He was accustomed from his Greek philosophy to think of mind and virtue as godlike characteristics in man, the human mind being considered to be nothing less than a fragment of the divine Mind. Therefore, he could not bring himself to regard intelligent and virtuous pagans as being totally without any likeness to God. Yet at the same time he was aware of a crucial lack in the intelligent and virtuous pagan's humanity. What he lacked was that which Christ came to bestow upon men, the Spirit of God that calls man's spirit into life. It is this Spirit which is the bearer of the divine likeness and restores it to man. To be born of the Spirit is to be fashioned into the divine likeness, which has to do with the reflection of the divine nature in man.

What, then, of the pagan's likeness to God in rationality and virtue? Irenaeus met this problem by distinguishing between the likeness and the image. The fact that Gen. 1:26-27 uses two words instead of one he took to indicate that there are two aspects to man's reflection of God's nature: one the image, and the other the likeness. The image of God in man, which he defined as that in man which makes him capable of rational thought and virtuous action, was implanted in man in such a way that it is inalienable from his nature and universal in its presence. It has never been lost and cannot be lost. But the " likeness," into which man is transformed by the Spirit of God indwelling his nature, was lost at the Fall and is only restored through the redemptive work of Christ and the receiving of the Holy Spirit. Irenaeus divided man into body, soul, and spirit. Unregenerate man consists of only body and soul, but through regeneration he becomes body, soul, and spirit. As body and soul he is in the image of God, but through the receiving of the Spirit he comes to possess both the image and the likeness. This doctrine became the foundation of Roman Catholicism's union of the natural and the supernatural in its theology. Because the natural man is in God's image he possesses through his reason a certain measure of genuine knowledge of God and of God's law. This in itself is incomplete but not false and needs only to be completed by the Christian revelation and by the work of grace through Jesus Christ. The far-reaching influence of this structure not only in Roman Catholicism but also in Protestantism shows what may follow from a misinterpretation of Scripture. Irenaeus approached the text with the individualistic assumption that whatever image and likeness meant, they must signify some quality or reality residing in man, something that in both Christian and pagan was capable of psychological description. It is this assumption which through the centuries has confused the interpretation.

Athanasius, early in the fourth century, produced two quite different interpretations. In *Contra gentes,* pursuing a mystical-philosophical view, he conceived salvation as being attained through reflection upon the word of God. By this process of reflection upon God's truth man was gradually to free himself from the things of sense until his soul, cleansed and polished like a mirror, should reflect the very face of God. Man would thus become himself a reflection of God and so a creature in the image and likeness of God. Here Athanasius seized the relational nature of the image, that it belonged to man not in himself but in his relation with God and as a reflection of the nature of God, but he made its attainment the goal of a mystic and philosophical discipline rather than of the saving and sanctifying work of the Spirit of God in and through Jesus Christ. In a second work, however, *De incarnatione,* which was written about the same time, Athanasius propounded the view that was to become the traditional view of later times: that man in the innocency of Eden was perfectly in God's image, that the fall of Adam and the entrance of sin into the life of man effaced the image until in the fullness of time it was restored in Jesus Christ.

Augustine attempted to define the image psychologically, approaching it as something that must belong to the intrinsic nature of man. To be a reflection of the divine nature it would have to have a threefold quality to correspond to the triune nature of God. He tried various approaches and finally settled upon the triad in man of memory, understanding, and will. The rationality of the soul comprehended all three and constituted a capacity in man to behold and to understand God. These were his uniquely human characteristics which made it possible for him to know God and respond to him. Even though few have followed Augustine in his search for a triad in man, many have accepted without questioning his assumption that the image should be psychologically identifiable.

In Luther, as in Irenaeus, we find a double conception of the image and for much the same reason: to explain how unregenerate men who have not had God's image restored to them through Jesus Christ can nevertheless be capable of maintaining order in human society, framing laws for the benefit of all, acting in a rational manner, and in general maintaining a visible superiority over the animal creation. He did not, however, accept Irenaeus' distinction between the image and the likeness. Rather, he chose to speak of a " public image " and a " private image." The public image consisted of those vestiges of God's image which remain in man in spite of the corruption of sin in order to distinguish him from the animals, to endow him with a measure of reason and understanding, and to preserve his status as governor over nature. All men, even though they know nothing of Jesus Christ, have received through the Logos (John 1:4) these capacities. They are not in any way sufficient for salvation, but they remain in spite of the ravages of sin. The private image was that likeness to God which Adam possessed in his innocency, an original righteousness, but which was lost in the Fall and can be restored only in Jesus Christ. Goodness, justice, and love, in which the Christian reflects God's nature, are the characteristics of the private image.

Similar as this pattern may seem to that of Irenaeus, nevertheless at another point Luther undercut the whole Roman Catholic structure of natural theology. In criticism of Irenaeus and Augustine, he insisted that the vestiges of the image in the unregenerate, although sufficient to preserve an order in society, provide no basis for any confidence that man can in a measure know God and achieve virtue apart from Jesus Christ. The natural will and the natural intellect in sinful men are subject not to God but to the devil. There is no uncorrupted reason exempt from the power of sin that a man can trust to lead him in the direction of God. He has to put his trust in Jesus Christ alone. It is clear that Luther in his initial definition failed to break with the psychological approach of the earlier fathers. He was trying to take account of powers in man that made him capable of certain achievements in life. But his conviction of the power of sin to corrupt the whole man and of the power of Christ alone to redeem and enlighten the whole man cut across the traditional pattern and made him at least try to guard himself against its abuses. His doctrine of a double image remained, however, to give trouble to his followers in later times. The demand for a natural theology as a recognition of the capabilities of man apart from Christ was likely always to base itself upon the " public image."

Calvin's approach to the question was strictly Christological. According to his view, we can know nothing of what the image means except from its restoration in Jesus Christ. Since the image has been corrupted by sin in all other men, no true knowledge of its nature can be inferred from what we know in human experience in general. Starting from Christ, then, we define the image as the reflection of God's nature in a man's nature as in a mirror. The whole of nature, including human nature, is meant to reflect God's glory and to give God praise. It was created for this before all else. And man in particular as the crown of creation can fulfill his destiny only by reflecting God's glory, mirroring his nature, and responding to him in faith and obedience. Calvin, like Luther, falls back into the psychological approach when he declares that the image was lost in the fall of man and wavers between saying that it was completely lost and that some vestiges remained. He agrees with Luther that nothing in man remains uncorrupted by sin and that man has no possibility of knowing God apart from Jesus Christ. But the necessity of explaining the admirable gifts of pagan lawgivers and philosophers and the diversity of human skills and accomplishments seemed to call for the recognition of some powers remaining in sinful man that must have their source in God. This concession, however, did not relax in any way Calvin's conviction that a saving knowledge of God is possible only through Jesus Christ. Thus Calvin, although he saw the relational character of the image in his likening of it to an image in a mirror, tumbled eventually into the traditional error of conceiving it as something residing in man.

BARTH AND BRUNNER

It is impossible to follow through all the variations of interpretation in Protestantism since the Reformation, but it may serve our purpose to look carefully at those of Karl Barth and Emil Brunner, these two men representing two forms of a revival of Reformation theology in the present day. It should be kept in mind, however, that in the nineteenth and early twentieth centuries the term " image of God " became practically a monopoly of liberal theology in its optimistic emphasis upon the divine powers residing in man whereby he is able to know God and respond to him. " Man in the image of God " came to mean " man's natural kinship with God." Genesis 1:26-27 and Ps. 8 became favorite proof texts for the justification of natural theology. If man is in God's image, then he must be capable of knowing God. This conception of man, which was in conscious antithesis to the Reformers' doctrine of the total corruption of the natural man by sin, seemed to receive strong Biblical confirmation from the findings of historical-critical scholarship. First was the general agreement of scholars that the priestly author of Gen., chs. 1; 5; and 9, had no conception of a loss of the image in man but on the contrary taught that it belonged to mankind universally, which seemed to negate the traditional conception of the absence of the image in unredeemed humanity. To this was added the agreement of most scholars in seeking the image in some quality or power residing in man, although in the absence of evidence it was very diversely defined.

The first " agreement " is open to question as soon as one gives up thinking of the priestly document as a completely independent document and regards it as a reinterpretation of an existing tradition that consciously took up the older tradition into the new. Yet, even if that were not so, we have to think of the final edition of the Creation stories as reflecting the mind of the editor and determining their impact upon the readers, so that, even though there is no word in Genesis of a destruction of the image, the distortion of man's relation with God through sin as described in Gen., ch. 3, cannot be held in isolation from the description of man's nature and destiny in Gen., ch. 1. Even if the priestly document once existed as a separate document, it was not so read in Israel from the time of its incorporation with J, E, and D. The second " agreement " has already been set in question as representing a psychological approach that was alien to the original Hebrew writer and originated only when the Bible was read by a non-Hebrew individualistic mind. There is no evidence anywhere in Scripture on the basis of which the image can be identified with man's reason, creative capacity, or any such aspect of his nature.

Brunner's whole approach to the problem is determined by his positing a radical difference between the Old Testament and the New Testament in their conceptions of the image: that in the Old Testament it is universally a possession of man (as also in James 3:9), that which makes him man and not an animal, while in the New Testament it defines the new nature of man that becomes his only through redemption. Brunner finds in these two conceptions two necessary elements in a Christian doctrine of man, the recognition of something in man simply as man that makes him capable of responding to God, and at the same time the recognition that only through Jesus Christ does he attain to his true nature as a child of God. Like Irenaeus and Luther, he is anxious to do justice to all those elements of rationality and creativeness which have been evident in the human race quite apart from the Christian faith. It is not surprising, therefore, that he follows Luther and Irenaeus in elaborating a double doctrine of the image. Seeing dangers in Luther's recognition of vestiges of the image remaining in spite of sin, since it suggests a part of our natures undamaged by sin, he avoids this conception and speaks instead of a formal and a material image.

The formal image expresses " man's inalienable standing before God as a responsible being and his inalienable confrontation with his fellow men and responsibility for them." It is universal and signifies that man's relation with God is not annihilated but only perverted by sin, so that even in his sin he remains responsible. The material image is identical with man's new nature in Jesus Christ. It is destroyed totally by sin and is restored only in Christ. Brunner tries to incorporate the concern of the Reformers to make man's salvation wholly dependent upon Jesus Christ by insisting upon the totality of the perversion of man's nature by sin and upon the impossibility of making the formal image a transitional stage to the material image. And yet it is more than the desire to do justice to man as man that makes Brunner assert the formal image. This becomes evident as he bases upon it his doctrine of the " *Anknüpfungs-punkt* " or " point of connection " with God. The formal image is that " something " in man which makes him capable of hearing God's word and responding to God. What Brunner is concerned about here is that in spite of sin there should still remain a relation between man and God that makes communication possible, a quite legitimate concern. But why he should doubt God's power to sustain this relation in spite of man's rupture of it and should find it essential to assert a formal likeness to God in man as a kind of bridgehead for God in his coming to man is not at all clear. Also, it is hard to take seriously that the formal image is only formal; it must have content or it cannot serve the purpose on which Brunner is intent. David Cairns follows Brunner closely in his conception of the twofold image, and it is significant that he defines the image in one place (p. 51) as " a character or quality of man's existence." Here we have the individualistic, psychological approach again, and it is this which lies behind Brunner's conception of the formal image. He has failed to break free from that tradition and to see the image in the context of relation.

The aspect of Barth's doctrine of the image that has captured most attention and received most criticism is his location of the image in the " I-Thou " relation of man and woman. One of the most important elements in Barth's anthropology is his recognition that God has created mankind in such a way that male and female are essential to each other in the fulfillment of their human destiny, a truly human life being impossible for any human being as an isolated individual. Also it is basic for him that the union of man and woman is used in the Old Testament as an analogy of the relation of God to Israel and in the New Testament as an analogy of the relation between Christ and his church. Therefore, he attributes a major significance to the fact that in Gen. 1:27 the account of the creation of mankind in God's image is followed directly by the explanatory note " male and female created he them." We must recognize that if the second half of the verse is in parallelism with the first, repeating its thought in a slightly different way, then " created in the image of God " and " created male and female " would stand in an extremely close relation to each other and Barth's proposal must be taken seriously by exegetes. To Barth, this existence of mankind in an " I-Thou " relationship is the reflection or image of the " I-Thou " relation in the nature of God himself. The plural pronouns in " Let *us* make man in *our* image " he interprets as referring to a plurality of persons in the Godhead.[4]

There are a number of difficulties in this novel interpretation of the image. It necessitates a complete disassociation of the reference to the image in Gen. 5:1-3 from the use in Gen. 1:26-27, since in Gen., ch. 5, the image does not denote an " I-Thou " relation. It also attributes to the priestly writer a conception of separate persons in the Godhead, for which there is no evidence elsewhere in P, or, for that matter, anywhere in the Old Testament. We ought not, however, to dismiss too quickly the suggestion that the *relation* of man and woman may have been intended to have some bearing upon the nature of the image, even if it does not contain its primary meaning.

Much more valuable, however, than this novel interpretation is Barth's setting of the Creation within the context of the covenant and his insistence that God's purpose to have a people in covenant with him must be understood as the very ground plan of the Creation. The covenant was not an afterthought with God when the Creation failed to turn out right. A people in covenant with God is a people in communion with God, responding to his love with love and fulfilling his joy, and it was for this that the world came into being. Man was created, therefore, to be a " Thou " to God's " I," to be able to speak a word in answer to the word addressed to him by God. Thus man is in the image of God when he is fulfilling his destiny as God's " partner " (*Gegenüber*), reflecting in his nature not only God's glory but also his holiness, righteousness, and love. What Barth has grasped firmly here is that the image has no meaning except in a relation between God and man in which man has his very existence in responding to God. This relation came into being by God's initiative and is sustained in being by God. Man may destroy the relation from his side by his sin and rebellion against God, but he has no power at all over God's side of the relation. It is here that Barth disagrees most radically with Brunner. The lines of communication are always open between God and man *from God's side*. God is always free to speak and act in relation to man, no mat-

---

[4] So also G. A. F. Knight, in *A Christian Theology of the Old Testament.*

ter how drastically man has cut himself off from him. Man in his sin remains God's creature, made for fellowship with him, and unable to be truly a man in isolation from him. Not only is there no need to posit some species of image in man as he is by nature in order to make him capable of receiving God's word, but, from Barth's standpoint, even the most formal image as man's natural possession is the thin end of a wedge that makes man something less than *wholly* dependent upon Jesus Christ for his knowledge of God and for his being made in the likeness of God. In place of Brunner's formal and material images, Barth might be said to substitute the image that is known only in and through Christ, which alone can be called the image of God. The *mark* of the image remains in man even when his sin has made him wholly unlike God. The mark is not a vestige of the image but rather what might be called the aching vacancy in man caused by the absence of the image. Barth's great contribution, then, is in leaving behind all attempts to define the image psychologically and in setting it in the context of the divine-human relation.

Smartis own conclusions

IMPLICATIONS FOR BIBLICAL INTERPRETATION

It will be seen that almost all the problems of interpretation that we have discussed in preceding chapters are illustrated in some way in this complicated history of the exegesis of Gen. 1:26-27. Bold would be the interpreter who would claim that his exegesis is completely objective and uninfluenced by any theological presuppositions. In each of the instances we have studied, the exegesis of these verses bears a very definite relation to the anthropology and theology of the exegete. What he sees in the verses is deeply influenced by the theological standpoint from which he reads them. And the exegetes of the late nineteenth and early twentieth centuries who were most certain of their scientific objectivity were as deeply influenced by their theological standpoint as any, a standpoint that was, not only here but frequently, in antithesis to the Hebraic. They form excellent examples of the impossibility of attaining a historical exegesis that is completely separate from a theological exposition, that is, of separating the two questions: what the text meant *originally* and what it means *for us now*. The identification of the image with some faculty of the human person was a project in which the text gave them no help whatsoever, for the simple reason that it never occurred to the Hebrew writer to make any such identification; but because the exegete was accustomed to think in those terms, he had to do this in order to find meaning in the words.

What hope, then, is there of arriving at an interpretation that is not unconscious eisegesis, and that we can offer with confidence as the meaning of the text? If we wish to be able to say that we have arrived at the final and absolute meaning of the text, then the outlook for us is not a hopeful one; but would not that be a presumptuous demand for us to make of Scripture, indicating that we had no awareness of the depth of the truth that meets us in Scripture? If the ultimate content of this text, as of others, is the mystery of God's revelation of himself to man in which he reveals to us also who we are and what is the meaning of our life, then we ought not to be troubled by our inability to settle the meaning of the text once and for all. But this is not an abandonment of the attempt to get at the real meaning of the text. Rather, as we have seen, our subjective misconceptions are overcome as we let the text speak to us in its own way. The recognition that the author thinks in terms of the whole man, physical and spiritual alike, overcomes our false spiritualizing of the image. The recognition that he thinks, not individualistically and psychologically but relationally, puts an end to our attempts to find something in man as man that we can call the image. False interpretations are cut away as we eliminate from our thinking everything that is without a basis in the text itself. It has to be read first in its immediate context in the priestly document, then in the wider context of the final redaction of Genesis, then in the context of the Old Testament as a whole. All that we can do is to submit our thinking as completely as possible to the text itself. In short, there has to be a dialogue between the text of Scripture and the interpreter in which the interpreter is emancipated from his misconceptions and so is laid open to both the original and the present meaning of the text.

What influence, we may ask, has the New Testament had upon our interpretation of Gen. 1:26-27? Has our attention to it made us eisegetes? The simple fact is that no Christian interpreter as he approaches Gen. 1:26-27 can forget that there is a New Testament doctrine of the image. He may look away from that doctrine in order to let the Old Testament speak in its own way, but he always knows that it is there. It is perhaps the determination *not* to be guilty of reading the New Testament doctrine into Genesis that has led scholars so to define the image in Genesis that it is practically the antithesis to the image in the New Testament. But when the image is understood within the context of the covenant relation, this antithesis disappears and the New Testament conception becomes a direct and logical though wholly unexpected development of what is found in the Old Testament. Man in covenant with God reflects God's nature. The destruction of the covenant relation, and not just the fall of Adam, brings with it the clouding of the image, but, just as God maintains the covenant relation from his side so that Israel in spite of its sin remains the people of the covenant, so man in spite of his sin remains the man whom God made in his own image, and this remembrance contains within it the promise of what man may yet be. When Jesus comes to restore and renew the covenant relation and embodies that new relation with God in his own person, what was more natural to a Hebrew than to call him the Son of God or the very image of God? or to describe the goal of redemption as a restoration of man to the likeness and image of God? The unity of Old Testament and New could not be better exemplified, and yet at the same time the difference between them is apparent. The Old Testament is promise and the New fulfillment. In the Old Testament there is the hope of what man may be, based securely upon the knowledge of God's nature, but it is a constantly broken and frustrated hope. It has always to be a kind of hoping in spite of the darkness. But in the New Testament there is certainty as the true nature and destiny of man are revealed in Jesus Christ. The priestly writer dare not be made to speak as though he knew what was coming five hundred years after his time. He speaks with a certain brokenness and vagueness because he does not know. But neither dare he be made to speak as though his vision of God and man were a vision of a different God and man from that revealed in Jesus Christ. The Old Testament remains Old and the New Testament New, but both become Christian Scripture when the New is recognized as bringing the completion of what was unfinished and unfulfilled in the Old.

[VI]

THE INSPIRATION OF THE BIBLE

THE MYSTERY of Scripture points to its origin in God and raises the subject of inspiration, one of the most contentious subjects with which the church has had to deal. Much confusion has been caused by the variety of meanings that may be placed upon the word " inspiration." It has been used freely since ancient times concerning the work of poets, philosophers, and creative workers of various kinds who feel themselves seized and uplifted by a spirit other than their own, so that they themselves are amazed at what they achieve. Sometimes this " other " spirit is identified with the deity, sometimes with the muses or with a private daemon (Socrates), but more often it is recognized as merely an intensified and rarefied form of one's own spirit. In a number of religions, sacred writings have been called inspired to signify that they are of no human origin but proceed from the deity himself, so that their words are the very words of the god. Sometimes their validity as divine words is conceived as guaranteed by miraculous divine interposition, as in Allah's dictation of the Koran to Mohammed, or Aristeas' story of the preservation of the Septuagint translation from error, each of the seventy-two translators miraculously producing an identical copy. Such meanings as these being widely current, it is necessary to make very clear what is intended when the Bible is described as " inspired." What is needed is that we should be specially on our guard against drawing our definition of inspiration from some other source than the Bible itself, or, within the Bible, from passages on the periphery rather than at the very center.

We cannot do better than to approach the question of inspiration Christologically. Jesus Christ is the center of Scripture. The inspira-

The nature of Jesus's inspiration

tion of Jesus Christ is our surest guide to the meaning of the inspiration of Scripture. But when we ask concerning his inspiration we ask concerning the source of his words, his actions, and his whole person. The witness of the Gospels is that Jesus had his source with absolute uniqueness in God. When Luke says that he was conceived by the Holy Spirit, he is not so much concerned with the manner of Jesus' physical generation as with the origin of his whole being in God. Then, the fact that at the beginning of Jesus' ministry, in his baptism, the Holy Spirit is revealed as resting upon him signifies that it is not to be through powers and talents that he possesses in himself that he will fulfill his ministry but through the power of God's Spirit. When he preaches and teaches, when he heals, when he casts out demons, it is the Spirit of God who makes his words and actions effective. His words are the very words of God, and in his actions God acts. John's Gospel emphasizes this identity in saying that Jesus says and does nothing on earth except what he has seen and heard the Father saying and doing in heaven: yet, in this, John's witness is essentially no different from that of the Synoptics. For Jesus, then, to be inspired meant for him to be indwelt and possessed by God's Spirit so completely that in his being he was one with God, and in his person, his words, and the events of his life God himself was revealed. But the witness of the New Testament is also that this oneness of Jesus with God was realized without the dissolution of his humanity. He was not only born of the Holy Spirit, he was also born of Mary, a helpless babe within the limitations of a human life like our own in which he had to grow " in wisdom and in stature, and in favor with God and man." So complete was his humanity that his oneness with God could be maintained only in a personal relation in which the existing Scriptures and private prayer played a most important part. He was subject to all the temptations that befall humanity, and he finally died and was buried as all men must die and be buried. It is evident that to the New Testament authors there was no contradiction in asserting both the divinity and the humanity of Jesus' words, deeds, and being.

The two errors into which the church has constantly fallen in understanding the inspiration of Jesus have proceeded from a failure to preserve the New Testament unity of the divine and the human. On the one hand have been those who have been willing to grant that Jesus was inspired in his words and actions, more inspired than any poet or philosopher or religious teacher who ever lived, but who refuse to see any difference except one of quality or quantity between his inspiration and that of Plato or Goethe or Shakespeare. The spirit that possessed him is a spirit generally available to all men, and it makes little difference whether one conceives it theologically as a divine Spirit or humanistically as denoting merely the higher reaches of the human spirit. The prophets and psalmists and apostles were also inspired men, seeing farther into the truth of things and experiencing more intensely the meaning of life than other men, so that their writings have a permanent value and may be called inspired as long as we remember that it is the authors and not the words that were inspired, and that their status as inspired men in their own time does not necessarily give their judgments authority in other ages. On this basis, the New Testament claim that Jesus' words and actions have an identity with the words and actions of God becomes an exaggeration of the degree of his inspiration through the blindness of an enthusiastic faith.

At the opposite extreme, however, have been those for whom the assertion of this identity necessitates the denial of Jesus' humanity, at least in part. If in his words, actions, and being he was one with God, then he was so completely God that his humanity was swallowed up in his divinity. He was at each moment of his life omniscient, knowing not only the future events of his own life but all that had happened or ever would happen in the lives of others. He was also omnipotent, so that at any moment he might have broken through the seeming limitations of his humanity. He could have come down from the cross if he had chosen to do so. To many Christians it seems a denial of his divinity to challenge these assertions, although it does not occur to them to claim that Jesus in his earthly life was omnipresent (though this too has been asserted by theologians in the past). There is no difference in principle between a limitation as to presence and a limitation as to knowledge or power. Already in the Gospels there are perceptible indications of the tendency to attribute to Jesus in his earthly life both omniscience and omnipotence (e.g., his power over waves and storms and his ability to tell the Samaritan woman the story of her marriages), but the unanimous testimony of all parts of the New Testament and of the church of the first three centuries was that Jesus was wholly human in his oneness with God. The divinity of his words and actions and of his very being, which constitute his inspiration, was not static but dynamic, being preserved by the indwelling of the Holy Spirit in his person.

It is essential also to understand that the inspiration of Jesus' words and actions did not lend to them an " inspired " quality that made their divinity evident to every onlooker or hearer. The results of the inspiration were not externally observable; nor was the fact of the inspiration something that could be proved to men's reason then or at any later time. His words of themselves were simply so many human words, and his actions were those of a traveling preacher and healer from Galilee. Even the disciples did not recognize their true import until after the resurrection. The voice and action of God were *hidden* in them. To Simon the Pharisee the words and actions of Jesus at supper in his home (Luke 7:36 ff.) were the words and actions of an impertinent upstart of a religious teacher who had gained a following for himself by a lax attitude toward sinners, while for the woman from the street the love and mercy of God met her in his every word and gesture and created for her a new world. The presence and power of the Holy Spirit in Jesus was evident only to faith, that is, only where there was an openness to the same Spirit of God that possessed him; from all other persons, however intelligent or religious they might be, it was hidden, and Jesus' inspiration could be nothing more to them than the presence of certain moral and spiritual qualities in him that commanded their respect — or perhaps their resentment.

This unique character of Jesus' inspiration is our key to the understanding of inspiration in Scripture as a whole. It would be false to say that no other conception is found in any part of Scripture. Moses is represented as receiving the commandments at the express dictation of God. The author of the book of Revelation pictures himself as receiving his messages to the churches directly from the Lord in an ecstatic vision. But when we examine the phenomena of Scripture as a whole, we find at its center the same double witness that the New Testament bears to Jesus Christ. Constantly the claim is made by different parts of Scripture that they embody the very word of God himself; yet in every part they confess also their human character and make plain that it is in the words and lives of men like ourselves that this word of God is found. The Biblical writings are a human witness to a divine word, and because they are human, they bear upon them the marks of their authors' human involvement, each in the life of his own age.

The church's misunderstanding of Scripture has followed the same pattern as its repeated misunderstanding of Jesus Christ. The emphasis upon the divinity of Scripture has tended for long periods to obscure its humanity. If the words of the Bible are God's own words, men said, then they must be wholly divine, a truth so perfect as to be above all the shifting patterns of human thought. The suggestion of the presence of any human frailty or error at any point in the record of Scripture was thought to constitute a denial of its divinity. Combined with this has often been a tendency to externalize the divinity of Scripture as though its inspiration should be immediately evident to every reader or can be established by rational arguments convincing to any open-minded person.

In reaction against this divinizing of the words of Scripture the achievement of historical criticism has been to demonstrate their humanity. The spotlight of scholarship has been turned on the human character of the authors and on the human situation in which their work and words were set until every line and blemish upon their faces and even the slightest stutter in their voices is evident. But, from the true observation that they were wholly human in all they said and did, the false conclusion was frequently drawn that their writings could no longer be considered inspired in more than a purely human sense and that to speak of the Bible as a whole as the word of God was no longer realistic. The choice seemed to be between a divine book in which the human element was on the point of vanishing so that it became irrelevant for man's world, and a human book in which the divine element was on the point of vanishing so that it was little more than man's nobler thoughts concerning himself and his problems. Both views were the product of a failure to understand the Bible on its own terms and on the basis of its own definition of inspiration, that is, as a book in which God, really God, the Lord of heaven and earth, speaks to man with a human voice and comes to men in human flesh, so concealing himself in his human manifestation that he cannot be recognized and known as God except by a faith that is willing to receive him now as the Lord of life.

The situation has been further confused by the widespread failure of scholars in general to distinguish between two concepts of inspiration that, while they have certain similarities of expression, are radically different from each other in intention and character. When it is said of any portion of Scripture that it is " inspired by the Holy Spirit " (Matt. 22:43) or *theopneustos:* " God-breathed " (II Tim. 3:16) or that the words are the very words of God himself (John Calvin), it is assumed that the speaker holds to a static literalistic concept of inspiration. Thus Jesus and Paul are classified with the rabbis as agreeing with them that the text of Old Testament Scripture is in every detail divine revelation, and both John Calvin and Martin Luther are consigned to the ranks of the literalists. William Sanday, writing on " Inspiration " [1] in 1893, and strongly desiring to establish a concept other than what he called the " traditional " one, nevertheless conceded that the static literalism of the nineteenth century that was so distasteful to him was essentially the same view as prevailed in the church in 200 A.D. and was already present earlier than that in the canonization of the Old Testament. Thus Benjamin Warfield [2] in 1894 could use quotations from critical scholars such as Sanday, Schultz, and others to support his contention that, from the time of Jesus until the rise of historical criticism, his own literalistic concept of Scripture had been " the settled faith of the universal church of God," " the assured persuasion of the people of God from the first planting of the church until today." Warfield's case is further strengthened by interpreters of Luther and Calvin who fall into the same confusion and think that when the Reformers insist that God himself speaks through the words of Scripture they have identified themselves unequivocally with literalism.

There can be no health in the discussion of inspiration until this confusion is dispersed. The literalist is impregnably reinforced in

[1] William Sanday, *Inspiration.* It is puzzling that S. Mowinckel, in his valuable popular treatment of the subject, *The Old Testament as Word of God* (Eng. tr., 1959), begins by attributing to the apostles a conception of inspiration as " heavenly dictation " but later shows a very different conception to be intrinsic to both Old and New Testaments.

[2] Benjamin B. Warfield, *Revelation and Inspiration,* p. 52.

his view by the confidence that he is in direct line with Jesus, Paul, the early church fathers, the Reformers, and practically the whole church until 1750. And the critical scholar is uncomfortably concerned to establish a concept of inspiration that will do justice to the Scriptures while breaking free from most elements in what seems to him a mistaken tradition. Thus, Sanday hoped to see " a transition from the traditional conception to one which is more strictly accurate and scientific." [3] Starting with the prophets whose integrity gives one confidence that their " words from God " are a genuine revelation and not an illusion, he wished to establish a criterion within Scripture by which inspired words could be distinguished from uninspired ones, and he finally arrived at a definition of revelation as " a number of concrete truths contained in written books on the subject of God and religion. And they are truths because these books are the work of inspired men, so that even through the printed page there speaks the Spirit of God." [4] C. H. Dodd, wrestling with the same problem at a much later date,[5] fell back on the completely unbiblical concept of religious genius to account for the inspiration of the authors of Scripture. Critical scholars on the whole have been inhibited from taking seriously the Biblical concept of " inspired by the Holy Spirit " because of their identification of it with static literalism, even though it has been before their very eyes constantly that Biblical authors in both Testaments combined belief in Spirit-inspiration with a remarkably free attitude toward sacred writings of the past.[6]

This chapter will attempt to clear a road through this confusion. First, it must be shown that the Old Testament writings embody a concept of inspiration that is dynamic and not static and that has only superficial resemblances to the static concept. Secondly, the source of the static concept must be traced to its true place of origin in Greece, whence it flowed into Judaism in the postexilic period to displace the original dynamic inspiration that was at the heart of the entire earlier development in Israel. Then, we must see how in

[3] Sanday, *op. cit.,* p. 424.

[4] Sanday, *op. cit.,* p. 426.

[5] C. H. Dodd, *The Authority of the Bible.*

[6] Note the freedom of the priestly writer in relation to the Yahwist, of the Chronicler in relation to the Deuteronomist historian, of Luke and Matthew in relation to Mark, and of John in relation to the traditions that came to him.

Jesus and Paul what may be called the prophetic tradition was reborn and the dynamic of prophetic inspiration was recaptured, only to be submerged again, not wholly but in a large degree, in the second- and third-century church because of the combined influence of Judaistic and Hellenistic ways of thinking of sacred Scriptures. In the Reformation there was again a rebirth and recapturing of the secret of prophetic inspiration by Luther and Calvin [7] that liberated the power of the gospel, but they made use of the language and remained involved in the thought-forms of the church from which they came to such an extent that it was very easy for succeeding generations to lose the liberating insight and slip back into a static literalism. If this interpretation is valid, then the so-called "traditional" concept is recognized as an intruder from the pagan world who more than once closed the ears of the church to the voice of God in Scripture. And the task of critical scholarship is not to construct a modern concept of inspiration to replace a Biblical and traditional one but to comprehend and bring to adequate expression an understanding of inspiration that is intrinsic to the Scriptures themselves.

It may be worth noting at this point that missionaries are often in a dilemma because new Christians seem to take most readily to a naïve literalistic view of Scripture, so that the missionaries are afraid to introduce them to the modern historical-critical approach lest it undermine their confidence in the Scriptures themselves. It seems to the missionary that he would be setting a modern scholarly view against the simple Biblical view. But this thinking is fallacious. The Bible itself in its detailed character is the enemy of literalism. Its many parallel but differing documents are as obstacles thrown in the way by Providence to make literalism as difficult as possible for the Bible reader. A literalistic view can be maintained only by

---

[7] J. K. S. Reid, *The Authority of Scripture*, has provided a careful study of the Reformation and post-Reformation periods as background for our modern problem and has distinguished the doctrine of Scripture in Luther and Calvin both from the Roman doctrine and from that of Protestant scholasticism. He challenges the frequently expressed idea that one concept of inspiration persisted uninterruptedly in the church from the second century A.D. to the eighteenth. He has perhaps failed to take sufficient account of the extent to which the literalism of the pre-Reformation church influenced both Luther and Calvin in spite of their new and revolutionary insights.

shutting the eyes to many of the plainly visible features of Scripture or by concocting lame apologies to explain away the contradictions. New Christians do not find their naïve literalism in Scripture but rather bring it with them from their pagan background, as so many early Gentile Christians did. It is the pagan religionist, and not the prophet or apostle, who assumes that sacred Scriptures in which God speaks to man must be in every detail infallible. Unfortunately, too often new Christians have been encouraged in this concept from their earliest contact with the church and have had no opportunity to learn anything different. What is needed is not to set them before a choice between a supposedly Biblical view and the view of modern scholars but to let them discover in the Old and New Testaments how inspiration was understood. The choice is between a dynamic Biblical view that is fully in keeping with a recognition of the human historical character of the documents and a static Greek-rabbinic view that creates endless problems and obstacles that are needless for the reader of Scripture.

INSPIRATION AND REVELATION IN THE OLD TESTAMENT

It is notable that in the history of interpretation as sketched by H. P. Smith, R. M. Grant, E. C. Blackman, and James D. Wood [8] interpretation is regarded as having its beginning with the rabbis or with the New Testament. It is assumed that first there was Scripture and then there was interpretation. The fallacy in this approach is that everywhere in Scripture we find a combination of event and interpretation, and in many instances we can trace in the text a process of reinterpretation whereby a single element in the tradition is incorporated into ever-larger contexts. An excellent illustration of this is the strange story of Abraham's duplicity concerning his wife preserved in Gen., ch. 12. The fact that the same story appears in two other versions (Gen. 20:1 ff.; 26:6 ff.), with Isaac as the central character in the third instance, and the evident satisfaction of the storyteller that with his God's support Abraham should by his trickery have despoiled the Pharaoh of Egypt of

[8] H. P. Smith, *Essays in Biblical Interpretation,* and E. C. Blackman, *Biblical Interpretation,* both begin with the rabbinic period. R. M. Grant, *The Bible in the Church,* and J. D. Wood, *The Interpretation of the Bible,* begin with the New Testament interpretation of the Old Testament. None of the four examines the Old Testament for principles of interpretation.

Smart uses the work of the BK group to illustrate the presence of interpretation in origin and process of tradition.

The Inspiration of the Bible 169

some of his wealth, shows that it was at one time a favorite folk tale among the people. But, incorporated by the Yahwist into his cycle of patriarchal stories at a point directly following the narration of God's call to Abraham to be the father of a chosen race through whom great blessing would come to the whole world, it takes on a new meaning. Abraham, in whom Israel is intended to see reflected its own nature and destiny, is now represented as risking his whole future in order to protect his own life in the midst of the perils of Egypt. Only God's protecting care keeps Sarah, the mother of a people yet to be born, from being taken into the harem of the Egyptian monarch. Thus, in the Yahwist's reinterpretation of the story in a larger context, it begins to have theological significance, God's promise to Israel being followed by a warning against betraying its destiny through fear or greed.

Zimmerli, building upon the work of von Rad and Alt, gives a masterly example of this process of reinterpretation in an essay on "The Separate Story and the Total History in the Old Testment." [9] First the story of the exodus was told, not as a bare account of a historical event but, like the New Testament Gospels, as a people's witness to what God had done for them in certain events of history, so that it embodied the faith of Israel. The nucleus of the tradition was a confession of faith, a credo, which declared God's nature: "I am Yahweh . . . who led thee out of the house of bondage in Egypt" (Ex. 20:2; cf. Hos. 12:10). The plagues became multiplied in the tradition in order to emphasize the theme of God's will to deliver. The whole story of the exodus from its beginning in Egypt to its termination on the borders of Palestine was an explication of the original credo, gathering up into itself lesser traditions such as Ex., chs. 19 to 24, which may orginally have been the liturgy of a festival of the covenant. Then, the patriarchal stories, which had their origin as separate traditions preserved at Palestinian shrines, were prefixed to the exodus story in such a way as to widen the scope of God's will to deliver, the exodus thereby becoming the fulfillment of the promises made to the fathers. This larger story was then in turn set in a universal context when Gen., chs. 1 to 11, was built in to show that God's saving purpose in Israel was the purpose with which he brought the whole world and mankind into being.

[9] W. Zimmerli, *Das Alte Testament als Anrede.*

By the Deuteronomist this early tradition was then combined with the history of Israel in Palestine in which the central theme of God's faithfulness to the covenant issued not in the fulfillment of blessing but in the negative fulfillment of the curse. Finally, the priestly school gave its reinterpretation to the tradition. Zimmerli points beyond this stage to the incorporation of the Old Testament story with the New Testament as the final step in the process, each step bringing with it a new interpretation of the materials embodied in the tradition. He likens the process to that which we see in the growth of the Gospel traditions.

What concerns us, however, is to discern whether there is a specific conception of inspiration implicit in this process of reinterpretation. Was there a consistent attitude among prophets and priests alike in their handling of the traditions concerning their faith? Two things stand out above all else: first, a respect for traditional material that kept them from revising it in order to make it conform in every respect to their own ideas, and secondly, the remarkable freedom with which they reinterpreted it by building it into a different context.

Both these characteristics are evident in the early chapters of Genesis. We dare not think of the final text of Genesis as a scissors-and-paste job performed by a neutral editor who had before him the various documents, J, E, and P, and merely pieced them together rather imperfectly to form a continuous story. The priestly writer must be conceived as himself prefixing his account of the Creation in Gen., ch. 1, to that of J in Gen., ch. 2. Had he been satisfied with J's account, there would have been no need for him to add anything. It is likely that J's extremely anthropomorphic description of God's dealings with man, shaping him from clay with his own hands, operating upon him to remove a rib from which to form Eve, and going looking for him in the Garden of Eden in the evening, gave P some distress. He himself preferred to represent God as creating through his Word and Spirit. But fortunately he was able to see in the J account a genuine witness to God in creation and restrained his hand from tampering with the tradition. The contradictions in detail between his own account and that of J did not disturb him in the least. It was not necessary to have a verbally exact account of creation! What was important was not the detail of the process

but the truth of the activity of God in the Creation and in relation
to man. But the fact that he prefixed Gen., ch. 1, to Gen., ch. 2, indicates that he thought it necessary that there should be a reinterpretation of the Creation in the light of the faith as he understood it.
Surely a distinctive view of revelation and inspiration is evident
here. The J story of the Creation is for P a sacred document of revelation, but its sacredness lies not simply in its words but in its revelation of God as the Creator and of man as God's creature. The
details are significant only in so far as they serve the essential revelation. In the retelling of the story of the Creation the details may
be changed without fear in order to make even clearer what it
means that God is the world's Creator and that man is God's creature with a very special destiny. The priestly writer quite plainly
knows nothing of an infallible record of God's revelation to which
he himself is adding more infallible words.

This same principle is seen at work in the legal traditions of
Israel. The whole body of law at the close of the Old Testament
period was called the law of Moses, and it was described as though
every word of it came from the mouth of Moses. But upon examination it shows itself to be a complex of laws that bear upon them
marks of their origin in different ages. Some belong to desert life,
some to a primitive agricultural society, some to a highly organized
kingdom, some to a nation scattered through foreign lands, some
to a restored Palestinian community. All are called the laws of
Moses because they are adaptations in new situations of the constitu-
tion that Israel's life received at the hands of Moses. Scholars differ
as to the definition of the Mosaic nucleus of the law. Many now
would find it in the Decalogue with its confessional preface rather
than in the ritual law. But clearly a basic law underwent a series of
necessary revisions, and this mobility, which would have been impossible if at any stage the tradition had become a static and infallible code, was one of its distinctive characteristics. When it finally
became a static and infallible code for rabbinic Judaism, it was
necessary to institute an oral tradition to provide adaptations of the
law to new situations. In the Old Testament itself the inspiration of
the law is of a nature that provides for mobility and adaptability,
there being a will of God and a relationship with God in the midst
of the laws that have to be understood ever afresh.

There has been much emphasis in recent years upon the way in which the revelation of God in Scripture is primarily in events. God's word is his action, the root *dâbâr* signifying action as well as speech. God revealed himself to Israel by his act of deliverance in the exodus. God's decisive revelation in Jesus Christ was in the events of the cross and resurrection. The Scriptures, therefore, are the story of God's acts in history, the events in which he has revealed himself. The gospel is essentially the narration of what God has done for man's salvation. This emphasis is in conscious antithesis to the representation of God's revelation as a body of religious truths or propositions that have been communicated to man by means of the Scriptures, and it is a healthy reaction in so far as it points to the inseparableness of the revelation from concrete historical events and to the character of the word of God in Scripture as a word that cannot be known unless in it God acts upon the hearer and himself comes to him. Sometimes, however, in this emphasis upon event, the fact is lost from sight that in both Testaments the event is always an interpreted event. Event in history and interpretation are inseparable, so that the event without the interpretation would not be a revelation to anyone. The impending events of Amos' time were God's acts of judgment upon an unfaithful nation, events that would lay bare how things stood between God and Israel. But what God was doing in the historical event he revealed to his people through the prophet (Amos 3:7-8). Otherwise, the disasters of 734 B.C. and 722 B.C. might have been for the Israelites merely the political misfortunes of a small nation caught in the net of a powerful empire, or an indication that the Assyrian gods were mightier than Yahweh. The coming disaster was seen by Amos in a special context: in the light of Israel's unique destiny as a people in covenant with God, in the light of his faith that Israel's God was the Lord of all nations and of the whole earth, and in the light of his conviction that Israel cut apart from God could have no future but in covenant with God would fulfill a glorious destiny in God's service in spite of every human obstacle. The event was interpreted by Amos against the background of what he knew of God's nature and purpose from the traditions of the past and from his own immediate awareness of God's presence. The revelation resided in event and interpretation together.

G. E. Wright, in *God Who Acts: Old Testament Theology as Recital* (1952), makes a significant contribution at this point but overstates his case by isolating the revelation in the event, so that he equates history with revelation. "The primary and irreducible assumption of Biblical theology is that history is the revelation of God" (p. 50). There are theological inferences from this revelation in history: "Israel inferred from the exodus event that God had chosen her" (p. 54). "The being and attributes of God are inferences from events" (p. 57). Here the revelation seems to be located in the event, and theological truth is "inferred" from it. It is not clear whether "inference" signifies a process of rational deduction or a secondary revelation. The inference is called "an interpretation of the event which to Israel became an integral part of the event and which thus could be used for the comprehension of subsequent events" (p. 50). Again, it is said, however, that "God reveals himself and his will in various ways to the inner consciousness of man, as in other religions" (p. 55), where the last four words seem to suggest that the inner revelation does not share the uniqueness of "revelation in events." This tendency to equate revelation with the historical events fails to take account of the fact that, everywhere in Scripture, the revelation, which is the inmost meaning of the event, is hidden until it is revealed by the Spirit of God to the faith of man. The event itself is capable of receiving other interpretations. The cross to the indifferent onlooker was merely an unfortunate miscarriage of justice. The revelation of its meaning is nowhere described as a human inference from a divine event but as a direct revelation of God to man of what he is doing. So also the election of Israel, like the election of Isaiah or of Paul, is a call of God which is communicated in an immediate personal relation. Revelation in outward event and the interpretation through the inner subjective revelation in God's word belong together as the two halves of a single reality.

We may for the moment look beyond the Old Testament to the New to take account of a similar viewpoint that is found in C. H. Dodd's *Apostolic Preaching*. He distinguishes between a kerygma, which is a recital of "the facts" concerning Jesus' death and resurrection, and a didache, in which the apostles "expound and defend the implications of the gospel rather than proclaim it" (p. 9). The apostles are " witnesses to the facts," and the saving power resides in their recital of them rather than in their teaching, which is " based upon them." Dodd continually uses the term " saving facts." Since these alone are kerygma, even the collections of Jesus' teachings are classified as didache, so that in them no proclamation of the saving gospel is to be expected! But when one examines the " facts " of the so-called kerygema, as described by Dodd, one finds them to be a mixture of event and interpretation: the age of fulfillment has dawned in the ministry, death, and resurrection of Jesus; Jesus is Lord; the Holy Spirit signifies Christ's present power and glory; the consummation of all things is soon to come in the return of Christ; all men must repent. But these are not facts in the ordinary sense of the word. Rather, they constitute a confession of faith concerning the inner meaning of events, and the confession can be made only by men to whom this hidden meaning has been revealed. The apostle Paul did not preach the " fact " of the cross when he preached " Christ crucified, . . . the wisdom of God, and the power of God "; rather, he bore witness to how Jesus in his death had struck the blindness from men's eyes and broken open their hearts to the presence of God himself in his truth and sovereignty. But what would the cross have been to Paul or to anyone else if beforehand there had been no ministry of Jesus, no teaching of Jesus, no living impact of the person of Jesus upon the lives of men and afterward no church to spell out the meaning of it all?

The revelation of God in Jesus through his ministry and teaching is of one piece with the revelation of God in his death and resurrection, and of one piece also with the revelation of God through the Spirit in the church. Therefore, a concept of kerygma is highly suspect that tears apart elements that in the New Testament are recognized as inseparable segments of one vast work of God. There would be less possibility of misunderstanding if we used Jesus' own term " gospel " instead of " kerygma." It then would be impossible to demote Jesus' teaching and preaching to the level of " didache " (Dodd) or mere preparation for the saving kerygma (Bultmann), and much of the apostolic teaching to the level of theological explanations of the kerygma (Bultmann). Jesus preached and taught the gospel of God's gracious and sovereign coming to man for his salvation, and all that he said and did was related to that coming of

God to man and of man to God. That God's coming and man's response were concrete event and reality in his own person could not be proclaimed openly by him but was known to others only by the insight of faith, and even then only brokenly. It was the death and resurrection of Jesus that opened the eyes of the disciples to know what God was doing for man in him, and so made possible and necessary the proclamation of the gospel in a wholly new form as the good news of God's action for man's salvation in the life, death, and resurrection of Jesus Christ. But, however great the difference between the church's preaching and teaching and that of Jesus himself, we have to recognize the continuity and the essential unity of the two. Both have their center in the same divine event. Both live in the strength and joy of the reality of God's sovereign presence not only with but in our humanity in Jesus Christ. In both instances the divine event and the human words in which the event is spoken of and interpreted to men are inseparable and together constitute the gospel.

So also in the Old Testament, event and interpretation are both essential to God's self-revelation in Israel. He is the living God, Creator of heaven and earth and Lord of history. All things are in his hand. He is known in Israel by what he has done, both his acts of deliverance and his judgments upon the nation's sin. But neither his mercy that brings deliverance nor his wrath that brings judgment would be recognized and understood had he not chosen and called Israel to be a people in covenant with him and had he not revealed the secret of this election and vocation in intimate converse with individuals within Israel such as Moses, Elijah, Amos, and Jeremiah. The election and call of each prophet is in nucleus the election and call of Israel,[10] and the knowledge of God that becomes a personal reality in this direct " I-Thou" relation is the source of the prophet's understanding of what God is doing in history. The God known in the events of the outer world and the God revealed to the prophet in his inmost mind and heart are affirmed as one God. Therefore, these two aspects of the revelation cannot be separated. The Word heard by the prophet as morning by morning he opens his inner ear to God, or has it opened for him (Isa. 50:4), is the same Word by which the events of the past have been

[10] H. H. Rowley, *The Biblical Doctrine of Election.*

shaped and the events of the future are to be shaped (Isa. 55:11).

The prophet does not stand alone, however, as he interprets the divine action in his time, depending upon a sudden illumination to be received by him without relation to what has gone before. He stands within a tradition in which a remembrance is preserved of God's words and actions in the past. Yet never is this tradition merely repeated by him as though of itself it were an adequate revelation of God in the present. Each prophet speaks both in remarkable unity with those who preceded him but also in remarkable independence of them, never quoting them in order to validate his own authority, and quite untroubled that at some points his word may be different from theirs. A literal conception of the relation of the divine inspiration to the words of the sacred tradition would have made impossible this freedom and independence that is so thoroughly characteristic of the Biblical authors. The unity of each witness with his fellow witnesses in Israel was not secured superficially by making his words and ideas agree with those of his predecessors but much more profoundly by the fact that all alike were witnesses to the same God. Thus it happens that books of a radically divergent character are found together within the one canon of Scripture. Any theory of Scripture that endeavors to make each part of the Old Testament speak in perfect agreement factually and theologically with every other part is forced to do violence to the text and to the thought.

It is this very lack of unity on the surface which forces us below the surface to ask the question, In what way is this writing witness to the God of Israel? Ecclesiastes and Second Isaiah cannot be lightly harmonized; yet each in his own situation and in his own unique way speaks a word for God and against the darkness of unbelief, a word that is essential to the life of the people of God. Plainly, what mattered was not a neat and unified system of theology in which every detail would fit perfectly with every other detail and so provide man with an intellectually satisfying statement of truth, but rather that there should be in Israel a knowledge of God in which the total life of the nation would be laid open ever afresh before the presence of God himself, his justice exposing every injustice, his love calling for a like love in return, and Israel being reminded at every step what it means to live in covenant with God.

Through many channels God kept Israel aware of his presence —
prophets, priestly guidance, psalmists, historians, teachers of wisdom
— human channels, all of them, that show the marks of their time,
but show also the marks of the divine Spirit, which spoke through
them to Israel.

THE RABBINIC CONCEPT OF INSPIRATION

The period between the fifth and the second centuries B.C. is one
in which great changes took place in the life of the Jewish people
and Judaism assumed a character that in spite of many changes and
developments it was to retain for many centuries. The great succession of the prophets that had been the dynamic of the earlier period ceased, although a lone voice such as that of the anonymous
author of The Book of Jonah shows that their spirit was not wholly
dead. It is not true to say that the written word of Scripture took
the place that had been occupied by the spoken word of the prophets, for there was already a body of sacred writings by the late sixth
century and Second Isaiah could base his faith on the word of God
that lay at the heart of this sacred tradition (Isa. 40:6-8) without
seeing any necessity that the living prophet should disappear. Nothing could replace the ministry of the prophet. The weaknesses and
false developments of Judaism were largely the consequence of the
absence of a prophetic ministry, and, later, many of the differences
between Christianity and Judaism were to be the result of the restoration through John the Baptist and Jesus Christ of a prophetic
character to the ministry. The priestly element became dominant in
Judaism, the priest becoming more completely preoccupied with the
ritual of the Temple, and his function of giving torah, or religious
guidance, to the people devolving upon the rabbis. Faithfulness to
the covenant was interpreted in legalistic terms to mean the scrupulous observance of all commandments of God to be found in
Scripture, ritual, religious, and ethical laws being all alike binding
and the fulfillment of God's glorious promises of blessing being
dependent upon the exact keeping of them. This being the dominant concern of religion, the task of the rabbi as a Biblical interpreter became that of the expert in law, who could make clear in
doubtful cases what the law of God required. Since new situations
constantly arose that were not covered by any Biblical law, the rabbi

had also to frame new laws upon the basis of the Biblical ones with the result that gradually there grew up a new body of oral laws to supplement those of Scripture. Being based on the Mosaic law of Scripture, they were regarded as equally authoritative, and the theory was evolved that they represented an oral tradition originating with Moses that had been transmitted alongside the written laws of Scripture.

This brief and wholly inadequate description at least makes clear the radical difference between the prophetic and the later priestly faith as they are reflected in the Old Testament documents on the one hand and the traditions of Judaism on the other. The centuries of transition are sparsely documented, so that we catch only glimpses of the Palestinian community and see still less of the Babylonian and Egyptian Jewish communities. We are not able to observe the changes closely or to account for them exactly. We are able to trace an apocalyptic strain in Judaism that keeps alive the prophetic confidence in God's ultimate victory and creates a literature of its own, but whether it existed alongside the legalistic faith as a separate movement, or was in some measure fused with it, is difficult to discern. But one thing is plain: that in Judaism, although the exact boundaries of Scripture were not yet fixed with exactness, sacred Scripture was regarded as divinely inspired in every part, every word containing in some way a revelation of God. There were degrees of sacredness and inspiration, the Pentateuch being primary, the prophetic books as applications of the Mosaic law to later centuries being secondary, and the Writings being subordinate to both. But inspiration in any degree meant divinely given and divinely preserved from error. To challenge the validity of any word of Scripture was blasphemy: " He who says the Torah is not from God, or even if he says, The whole Torah is from God with the exception of this or that verse which not God but Moses spoke from his own mouth — that soul shall be rooted up " (Sanhedrin 99a). Here the divine origin of Scripture means its direct dictation by God, so that Moses' human personality is obliterated in the process. Also the revelation is equated with the written Torah in such a way that the text is held to contain the whole mind of God: " Say not that another Moses shall arise and bring another law from heaven; there is no law left in heaven " (Commentary on

Deut. 30:2). Every detail of the text being held to contain revelation, meanings were deduced from the smallest peculiarities. In Gen. 2:7, the verb " create " contains two yodhs where there should be only one; this was interpreted as pointing to the fact that man is composed of two elements, the earthly and the heavenly. In Deut. 10:20, " Thou shalt fear Yahweh thy God," the word " Yahweh " is preceded by " eth," the sign of the accusative, but, because " eth " may also be the preposition " with," Rabbi Akiba translated the sentence, " Thou shalt fear the doctors of the law along with Yahweh." Allegorical interpretations were used freely and become characteristic of the rabbis.

It is not difficult to recognize that this whole approach to Scripture represents a new development. It cannot be explained, as it sometimes is, as an inevitable consequence of the consolidation of the nation's religious traditions into a written Scripture. It was no more necessary then than it is now that a written Scripture should lead to a static view of inspiration and to the use of allegory. Under what influence, then, did this change take place if not through the influence of the Scriptures themselves? We know that, from the fourth century B.c. on, the Jews were exposed to the influence of Greek culture, not only in Asia Minor and Egypt but also in Palestine. The resistance in Palestine might be stronger, but such influences have a way of getting past even the most vigorous defenses. Men are unconsciously molded by the forces that they resist. We know also that the Greeks claimed to have an inspired literature which in every part contained divine truth and moreover to have oracles that had been received directly from the mouth of their gods. In defense of the honor and prestige of their own Scriptures, what was more likely to happen than that the Jews would claim for them an inspiration and God-givenness similar but superior to that of the Greeks?

The idea of divinely inspired sacred writings occurs early in Greece. Homer may not have been the first, but at least he set the pattern among the poets of claiming more than a human origin for their words.[11] The Muses spoke through the poet. Hesiod claimed a

[11] R. M. Grant, *The Letter and the Spirit*. The description of the development of allegorical exegesis in Greece draws heavily from Grant's account, but I see the implications for Biblical interpretation very differently from him.

dream encounter with the Muses, and Parmenides that he had journeyed to heaven itself in order to learn the truth. Pindar attributed to the Muses both the form and the content of his odes. The philosopher Democritus, in the fifth century B.C., defined the poet's inspiration as coming from outside himself while his rational faculties were in a state of suspension, although he seems to have left some place for human creativity in the process. Plato moved from a view similar to that of Democritus toward an elevation of the inspiration of the philosopher far beyond that of the poet. What is significant for us, however, is that from an early period in Greece and persisting into later ages there was a deeply entrenched conception of inspired sacred traditions that, because they proceeded directly from the gods, must be divine truth in every detail.

Xenophanes and Pythagoras are the first Greek thinkers to exercise a theological critique upon these traditions. They accused the poets of telling lies about the gods in attributing to them conduct that would be disreputable among men. The progress of a rational interpretation of the world and life made it increasingly difficult to reconcile the treasured sacred writings with what men recognized as truth. In the tension of this situation the inspiration of the poets could be maintained only by finding in their words a meaning other than that which appeared on the surface. The truth was regarded as concealed behind their words in such a way that it had to be elicited by a process of allegorization, which meant attaching to words and actions a significance other than what they normally bore. By this means the philosophers were able to " discover " their truths and principles already present in the writings of the most ancient and venerable poets. The Stoics became specially expert in this practice, thus lending the authority of the divinely inspired poets to their own expositions of Stoic philosophy. The Epicureans denounced the whole process of allegorization, but the union of sacred poetry with rational philosophy had an irresistible appeal.

The prevalence of a similar approach to sacred writings among Jews in Alexandria is not difficult to demonstrate. Aristobulus, at the end of the second century B.C., was using the Stoic method of allegorization to show the presence of philosophical ideas in the Old Testament and to escape the distress of the anthropomorphic references to God which were an embarrassment to his Greek mind. Aristeas in the same period combined a Greek conception of Scripture as literally inspired with the use of allegory. Philo, a century later, held Scripture to have been dictated by the divine spirit, the reason of the authors withdrawing to leave God completely free. Even the Greek translation of the Old Testament was inspired (as with Aristeas), so that every detail of the text was divine. In spite of his free use of allegory, Philo laid emphasis upon the reliability of the historical narratives and maintained the inerrancy of the text in every detail. Josephus, whose viewpoint in some respects shows a Palestinian rather than an Alexandrian influence, had the same conception of inspiration and explained the ability of the prophets to predict future events by their possession of inspiration, its genuineness being proved by the events happening. The Palestinian rabbis did not have the Alexandrian interest in finding a philosophy in Scripture, remaining loyal to their more legalistic form of religion, but their conception of inspiration and their resort to allegory were typically Greek.

What made a transition from the one concept of inspiration to the other, that is, from the Hebrew to the Greek, particularly easy for the rabbinic interpreters, was the similarity in the terms used to describe them. The prophet was possessed by the Spirit of God, and so completely did he identify his words with the words of Yahweh that the " I " of his discourse was Yahweh himself. It would be difficult to distinguish between this and the Greek identification of the words of the Delphic oracle with the very words of Apollo, or of the words of the Homeric poems with the words of the Muses. It requires even today close examination of the context of each to discern that what seem to be almost identical in conception are actually two completely different complexes of thought.

The Hebrew mind is dominated by an intensely personal conception of the relation between God and man, so that possession by the Spirit of God as referred to by the great prophets signifies always a personal relation between the prophet and God in which God speaks and the prophet hears and responds; then, in full consciousness of what he is doing, he declares what he has heard to Israel. Inspiration takes place in this personal relation, so that the prophet retains all his faculties in the discharge of his office. He may even, like Jeremiah, rebel against the word that God commits to him. The Greek mind, in antithesis to this, conceives inspiration in more impersonal terms, the deity or muse obliterating the reason, consciousness, or personality of the recipient of the revelation, perhaps not totally but at least in a considerable degree. The creative powers and talents of the poet may be left some scope, but the relation between the deity and the human recipient is not conceived as one of personal and fully conscious communion. This appears most clearly in the instance of the Delphic oracle, but it is present also in the philosophical theory of later times. If reference is made to the ecstatic phenomena of the cult prophets in Israel in which possession by the Spirit of God seems impersonal in character and such that it blots out the normal consciousness of the prophet, it must be admitted that prophetic ecstasy at certain levels in Israel is indistinguishable from other Near Eastern forms of ecstatic divination. But this cannot be held to have become normative in the prophetic tradition. In fact, by the seventh century it had become the mark of the false prophet. There may be ecstasy in some of the major prophets such as Amos and Ezekiel, just as there was ecstasy in Paul's communion with God, but it is of a different kind and does not belong within an impersonal or purely passive relation with God.

There is no reason to hold that the Hebrew understanding of inspiration was completely displaced by the Greek. The two were confused, and the Greek became dominant, but the Old Testament itself would continue to create a certain measure of understanding of its own unique manner of thinking and speaking. The fact that Judaism incorporated into the sacred Scriptures books that in their details contradicted earlier books, as the books of Chronicles did the books of Samuel-Kings, shows something of a nonliteralistic view. But the dominant viewpoint became that of a Scripture divinely inspired in its minutest details.

It is important to note that the immediate effect of a theory of literal inspiration was not to reinforce the authority of God's word in Scripture as a word in which man must ever afresh seek guidance in the affairs of life but rather to make the Scriptures useful as the divine validation of a system of doctrine and practice. The infallibility attributed to the Scriptures was transferred directly to the doctrines and practices that were considered to be founded on Scripture, with the consequence that a static religious order came into being. Allegory was used freely to show that the doctrines and practices were those prescribed specifically by God himself in the Scriptures. Literal inspiration and its companion, allegorical interpretation, were therefore, as with the Stoics in Greece, devices by means of which a sacred literature could be made the vehicle of a later religious or philosophical system, even those who accommodated the one to the other remaining unconscious of what they were doing. But the system, once established, made it very difficult for any word to be heard from Scripture that might set in question the established order of doctrine and practice. In short, it was a method of interpretation that robbed the revelation of Scripture of its freedom. God was no longer free to contradict the established religious order. The doctrine of the infallible inspiration of Scripture had the same effect later in Roman Catholicism, making the Scripture the bastion of an infallible church and denying any possibility that the word of Scripture might seriously set in question the order of the church. So also in scholastic Protestantism it was used to validate the established Protestant doctrine and order and to claim for it an infallibility similar to that claimed by the Roman Church. Doctrines and practices soundly based on an infallible Scripture could not be subject to any essential change. There could be no error in them. Thus has man in different ages used Scripture to establish his own or his own human church's authority over men. One can appreciate Cocceius' sarcastic remark in the seventeenth century to some of the exegetes of his time in Holland: "You would not be pleased to find your doctrine contradicted by the word of Scripture." The theory of literal infallibility, far from being an expression of genuine respect for Scripture, is open to the accusation of being a means whereby, subtly, under a semblance of extreme respect, an established order of religion makes use of Scripture for its own purposes and subordinates it to itself, thereby removing from God's word in Scripture its power to revolutionize the existing order.

INSPIRATION IN THE NEW TESTAMENT

There is a widespread tendency today among New Testament scholars to see very close affinities between Judaism and the early church. B. H. Branscomb [12] states: " The two religious communities used the same Scriptures, had the same conception of God, and possessed in general the same ethical ideals. Thanks to the work of such scholars as Bacher, Abrahams, Montefiore, Moore, Strack-Billerbeck, and others, the similarity in ethical outlook of early Christianity and Judaism has been placed more and more beyond dispute." He acknowledges that the evidence concerning Jesus' attitude to the Old Testament points in divergent directions. "One can construct a sort of chromatic scale made of sayings of Jesus in which all the notes are struck from the complete rejection of the law to its complete affirmation," but his basic conception of Jesus as a " loyal Pharisaic Jew " makes him consider the affirmation as primary, and from the evidence of Jesus' Jewishness, such as his regular attendance in synagogue and his use on several occasions of a rabbinic form of argument (Mark 12:26, 36), he concludes not only that he accepted the oral law but also that " he quotes law, prophet, or ' writing ' as the final authority in matters of religion, regarding in rabbinic fashion the wording of the text as literally inspired " (p. 121). R. M. Grant [13] uses the term " inspired " regarding Jesus' conception of Scripture as though for Jesus it meant essentially the same as it did for the Greeks and for the rabbis. " Belief in the fulfillment of prophecy implies belief in the inspiration of the prophets. And it is plain from Jesus' message as a whole that he accepted the inspiration of the Old Testament. The psalms were obviously inspired, since David spoke ' in the Holy Spirit ' (Mark 12:36). But Jesus himself was inspired by the Spirit (Mark 3:29-30), and because of his authority he could make distinctions within the law delivered by Moses." Inspiration has thus only one meaning. Jesus' freedom in relation to the Old Testament arose from his claim to possess in his own words the same inspiration that he and the rabbis alike attributed to Holy Scripture.

There can be no question but that for Jesus the Old Testament was authoritative, that he himself heard in it the very word of God himself, and that he regarded its authors as speaking through the

---

[12] B. H. Branscomb, *Jesus and the Law of Moses.*

[13] R. M. Grant, *The Letter and the Spirit,* p. 41. In his earlier book, *The Bible in the Church,* he seemed to discern a greater difference between Jesus and the rabbis in their approach to Scripture.

inspiration of the Holy Spirit. But, as we have already seen, this does not necessarily mean that his conception of inspiration was the same as that of the rabbis. The same terminology can express a very different content. Scholars have too often been misled by parallel terminology in rabbinic literature and in the New Testament to conclude an identity of meaning. Similarities in their language concerning God do not mean, as Branscomb alleges, that they have " the same concept of God." To reach such a conclusion it is necessary to ignore the significance of Christology in the early church for the definition of what Christians meant by the word " God." The total context of the terms must be taken into account. Also, parallels in ethical instructions can be deceptive, since the theological context of the ethic may give it a very different meaning. The parallels between the rabbinic summary of the law in the two great commandments and Jesus' identical summary, or between Hillel's version of the Golden Rule and Jesus' version, are completely misunderstood unless the context of each is kept in view. For the rabbis the context is a complex legal system in which the keeping of the two great laws must be accompanied by the keeping of all the lesser laws and regulations; for Jesus and Paul, to love God with all one's heart and soul and to love one's neighbor as himself is in itself the fulfillment of the law, setting one free from the minutiae of the Jewish legal system. So also the use of parallel terms concerning inspiration does not signify an identity of meaning.

Basic to the understanding of the New Testament in this matter is the recognition that in Jesus and in the Christian movement there took place a rebirth of the prophetic tradition of the Old Testament. It is perhaps too narrow to call it " prophetic," since it permeates the priestly writings of the Old Testament as well. It may be better to say that the movement of the Spirit of God in Israel that brought the Old Testament into being burst forth with new power in Jesus Christ and his church. It is difficult to see how anyone can be misled by parallels in detail to miss the radical difference in character between the ministry of Jesus and the ministry of the rabbis or between the collections of Christian literature in the New Testament and the collections of rabbinic literature in the Targums and Talmud. That there are parallels and points of contact is undeniable. After all, Jesus *was* a Jew of his time who loved his nation with all his heart and did not lightly offend against its hallowed laws and customs. So also was Paul. They differed with the established order only where they were compelled to differ in allegiance to the gospel of God, which claimed their primary loyalty. Both differed sufficiently to be accused of overthrowing the whole order established by Moses. Matthew 5:17, which is often quoted to prove Jesus' rabbinic literalism, actually implies that his attitude was felt by his contemporaries to be so revolutionary that the Scriptures themselves were in danger of being abolished by him. He met this by affirming that his mission would fulfill the word of Scripture and so establish its authority.

It has already been noted that, like the prophets before him, Jesus did not make a practice of quoting Scripture. This in itself could give the impression that he was abandoning Scripture, especially when it was compared with the practice of the rabbis, who quoted Scripture constantly as the authority for their doctrine. The relation of the Old Testament to Jesus' teaching is like the relation of the J tradition to Amos, or of the books of Amos, Hosea, and Isaiah to Jeremiah. Their content is incorporated in the teaching but not in any superficial verbal fashion. Quotations from the Old Testament are rare in Jesus' teaching, but the content of the Old Testament is powerfully present. That the meek inherit the earth (Matt. 5:5) was known by the psalmist (Ps. 37:11), and in Jesus' beatitude meekness has its true meaning only when understood with the psalmist as the utter humbling of man before God. That only those who feed the hungry and clothe the naked can be among the true people of God and be ultimately acceptable to him (Matt. 25:31 ff.) was a truth that belonged at the very heart of Second Isaiah's gospel (Isa. 58:6 ff.). Also in Second Isaiah, Jesus found a heralding of the nearness of the Kingdom, a hope of its coming which brought new life and strength to men in the midst of despair, and the very name " gospel " for the good news of the herald. There and elsewhere in the Old Testament he traced the figure of the Servant that was to be so important for his own ministry. From the prophets he took over and perfected a type of parable in which he broke through the defenses of men's souls to reveal them to themselves (compare II Sam. 12:1 ff. with Luke 10:25 ff.). He absorbed into himself and his teaching the favorite prophetic likeness of the shepherd of the sheep. His whole use of Scripture is in direct line with the prophets and represents an abrupt break with the rabbinic tradition. The revelation of God is not something that has been completed in the past and is embodied in its completeness in a written Scripture; on the contrary, there is a revelation of God and of God's Kingdom taking place now that not even John the Baptist knew. God's greatest works are yet to come. The Spirit, whose inspiration and power Jesus claims for himself, is to possess also his disciples so that they will live and work and speak as God's children in the power of his Spirit.

This concept of Jesus' relation to the Old Testament is anchored in his conviction that in him and in the events of his ministry the promises of God and the purposes of God manifest in the Old Testament are coming to their fulfillment. Enough has been said concerning this in a preceding chapter. Here we need only emphasize that this approach to the Old Testament is unknown in rabbinic Judaism. But it pervades every strand of the Christian tradition and most likely had its origin in the New Testament with Jesus himself, although it is firmly based upon a way of thinking of God's action in history that is central in the Old Testament.

In spite of Paul's deeper involvement in rabbinic ways of thinking (e.g., his use of allegory and his quoting of Old Testament passages as support for his own doctrines), he maintains the same two-sided approach to the Old Testament that we have seen in Jesus: an assertion of its authority as the word of God and a remarkable freedom in the reinterpretation of it. Like Jesus, he refused to let it be made the basis for any kind of legalism. The word of God in the Old Testament was the gospel of God's gracious purpose for man. Not only the events of Jesus' ministry, in particular his death and resurrection, but also the power and wisdom of God manifest in the church's word and action, were the fulfillment of the Old Testament. Christians were living in the days of fulfillment, and by the light of God's Spirit they could read their own story in the pages of Scripture. The Spirit that took away men's blindness to the meaning of Scripture was the Spirit of the Lord Jesus Christ himself (II Cor. 3:15-17). At this point as at so many others Paul followed directly in the footsteps of Jesus, and his freedom in relation to the Old Testament was as offensive to Judaism as the corresponding freedom of Jesus had been.

It is notable that Paul's relation to the letter of Jesus' teaching is similar to Jesus' relation to the Old Testament and the relation of Old Testament prophets to each other. The fact has often been noted that Paul rarely quotes directly the words of Jesus and that he uses a quite different terminology from that of Jesus in his proclamation of the gospel, so different that he has sometimes been accused of preaching a different gospel. His unity with Jesus is a unity in the Word and Spirit that not only gives him freedom to speak in his own way to his own situation without fear of betraying the gospel but compels him to do so. Had he merely parroted Jesus' gospel, he would have been no apostle. The inspiration of the Old Testament and of Jesus is an inspiration that Paul himself shares, since he is possessed by the same Spirit of God and is a witness to the same grace and truth of God. But his relation with the Spirit of God as an apostle is wholly subordinate to and dependent upon God's revelation of grace and truth in Jesus Christ.

It is clear from the New Testament that there were two strands of development in the Jerusalem church of very different character, one of them much closer to the legalism of contemporary Judaism than the other. The Greek-speaking church of which Stephen was a martyr seems to have preserved the more radical and revolutionary features of Jesus' ministry, as Paul was later to do. Stephen was accused of speaking blasphemous words against Moses and God. (Acts 6:11.) We hear of no such accusation against the Judaistic church. The equation of Scripture (Moses) and God indicates the literalism that had been challenged by Jesus' whole outlook and was challenged afresh by Stephen. But there was most likely a less radical form of Biblical interpretation in the more orthodox section of the Jerusalem church that the non-Christian Jewish community regarded as inoffensive, heretical perhaps from a rabbinic standpoint but not sufficiently dangerous to require its elimination. The Judaizing Christians who were later to be so bitter against Paul and were to draw upon themselves his rebuke for trying to coerce Christians back into the slavery of a legalistic religion would undoubtedly maintain an approach more like that of rabbinic literalism. There is every reason to posit a very close relation between their viewpoint and that of rabbinic Judaism. Because the Pauline interpretation was in time vindicated and pervades the New Testament, we tend to underestimate the strength and influence that this other viewpoint possessed throughout the length and breadth of the church. Those who condemned the freedom with which Paul both preached to the Gentiles the gospel of justification by faith alone and swept aside for Gentile Christians the whole complex structure of Jewish religious laws would condemn equally the freedom with which he interpreted the Old Testament. But they themselves would represent a mingling of the rabbinic and the prophetic concepts, distasteful to orthodox Jews because of its prophetic elements and unacceptable in non-Jewish circles because of its rabbinic elements, so that it is not surprising that it faded into the background as the church moved from a Jewish into a Gentile context. Only here and there in the New Testament do vestiges of it remain. We detect it in Matthew, where the pattern of promise-fulfillment verges over into a pattern of prediction-fulfillment, and words attributed to Jesus to the effect that "not one jot or tittle of the law will pass away until all is fulfilled" are preserved in the midst of a chapter in which it is emphasized that Jesus' words transcend the law of Moses.

The New Testament as a whole, however, is dominated by the Old Testament attitude to sacred documents. The church was plainly untroubled by differences of detail in parallel traditions. The author of John's Gospel claimed for himself a very high degree of freedom in reinterpreting the traditions concerning Jesus in order to bring out clearly what he knew to be the truth of the gospel. A church in the bondage of literalism could never have admitted John's Gospel alongside the three earlier ones that tell their story so differently. The lateness of its general recognition was most likely a consequence of the difficulties its character provided for those in the church who could not endure contradictions in sacred Scripture.

By the close of the first century the church had passed largely into a Greek world, where it would feel the pressure of Greek thought in which it was taken for granted that sacred Scriptures being divinely inspired are in the most literal sense the very words of God. This concept of inspiration flowed in upon the church from both the Judaistic tradition, which seems early to have had considerable strength in Rome, and from Greek culture on every side, and it is hardly surprising that the uniquely prophetic conception was forced into the background and ceased to be understood in its distinctiveness. But as long as the Scriptures continued to be read, it continued to exert an influence unobstrusively and found its way into men's minds without their quite realizing what was happening. Had it not done so, the revelation of God in the Scriptures would have been wholly hidden from the church and the very life of the church would have been destroyed, for, as Paul knew so well, only when men read the Scriptures in the freedom of the Spirit, which is the Spirit of the Lord and the Spirit that indwelt all the authors of Scripture, do they have eyes given them to understand what is written. There must be an inspiration not only of the Scriptures but also of the reader and interpreter of the Scriptures if they are to be heard and received as the word of life.

THE SCOPE OF INSPIRATION

It is impossible to deal with inspiration without introducing the subject of the canon of Scripture, because the canon is the church's way of pointing to the sacred writings in which it has heard the voice of God and marking them off from all other writings, religious and secular alike, as the ones that are uniquely the means of God's self-revelation. The canon has sometimes been considered no more than an official act of religious authorities setting their imprimatur upon certain writings and refusing it to others, and attempts have been made to determine the principles according to which they operated; why, for instance, the Jewish authorities included Ecclesiastes with its biting skepticism and excluded Ecclesiasticus, which seems to have a much richer religious content. The theory has been put forward in regard to the New Testament that it was apostolic authorship, or again that it was chronological closeness to the original events, which gained writings admission to the canon. To all such approaches the canon remains an insoluble enigma, and the impression is given that the determination of what books should be included in Scripture was entirely in the hands of men with their "reasons" which may or may not be satisfactory to us today. The explanation is more tenable that the official recognition had behind it a much broader and longstanding recognition of the writings in the life of the worshiping congregation and that canonicity was identical with authorization to be read in the worship of God. A writing, therefore, would have to establish its own essential canonicity by the nature of its content, and its recognition by the congregation was an act of witness in which it embraced the writing as necessary to its life as the people of God. It was the word of God to which the writings bore witness that called the people of God into being originally, that sustained them in being, and that remained ever at the center of their life as a word of promise and of judgment. The character of the sacred writings determined the character of this people. A different canon would have meant a different existence both for Israel in the Old Testament and for the church in the New. Canonization, therefore, did not imply that the church expected to find some divine truth in every word or phrase of every canonical writing but only that every canonical writing was an essential part of the sacred Scriptures through which God ever afresh revealed himself and his purposes to his people.

It is at this point that some Christians have their greatest difficulty, for there are some books of Scripture in which they find no divine self-revelation and which seem to them to be not only unnecessary but even misleading to the church. Luther found the law but not the gospel in The Letter of James,[14] and in his 1522 edition of the New Testament he left James and two other books unnumbered and marked off from the remainder of the New Testament in the index with a line. Calvin valued the book of Revelation much less highly than other books. Many scholars in modern times have expressed strongly their conviction that Esther and Ecclesiastes should never have been included in the Old Testament. But it is important always to ask on what basis these judgments are being made. Harnack and others have been prepared to decanonize the whole of the Old Testament, but when one examines the conception of the gospel on the basis of which this decision was reached, it is clear that soon much of the New Testament would have had to go too. The

---

[14] Robert C. Johnson, *Authority in Protestant Theology,* pp. 37 f., makes clear that while Luther failed to hear the gospel in The Letter of James, he did hear law in it and considered it an essential expression of the Word of God, which is both gospel and law.

decision for a new canon is certain to be a decision for a new faith and a new kind of church.[15]

The antipathy to Ecclesiastes is usually based upon his pessimistic outlook upon life, his denial of a future life, and the absence of that confident faith in God's activity in history which is so prominent in the prophets and psalmists. But is it not possible that the idealistic and unbiblically optimistic theology of the interpreters may be offended by Ecclesiastes' denial that a rational unity can be found in the phenomena of existence? Nineteenth-century natural theology was not open to a doctrine of God's hiddenness in his creation. No accusation can be made against Ecclesiastes of skepticism concerning God or concerning the order that God has established in his creation. His reverence before the reality of God as creator of all things is impressive. His skepticism is turned against the pretensions of man, such as were familiar in his time in popular Greek philosophy, the claim of human wisdom to penetrate the meaning of life or to fit all events into an orderly synthesis. He says in a more offensive way what Paul repeats when he tells the Corinthians that man by wisdom cannot find his way through to that knowledge of God and of himself which is his salvation (I Cor. 1:21). Thus, the recognition of Ecclesiastes as canonical and inspired does not mean that one should be able to find all the essential elements of an Old Testament theology in it but only that it reveals something of God's relationship with the world and of the meaning of a true faith in him that is necessary to the total witness of Israel to God. We meet the same problem in the books of Samuel and Kings, where much of the history seems purely secular and of a character that would be ridiculous to call inspired. The modern reader asks why he should give any heed to the petty struggles and intrigues of the princes of a tiny ancient Near Eastern nation that seem to have no spiritual significance and no importance of any kind for the modern world. Calling the text of the narrative inspired leads the reader to expect a message from God in every sentence. But this is only because the reader's mind is dominated by the Greek oracular conception of inspiration. Let him begin by asking why the total history of which those struggles and intrigues are a part is in the Bible, history that is indeed what we commonly call secular, and he

---

[15] See Karl Barth, *Dogmatik* I, pp. 523–548, on this whole section.

Barth used
extensively

comes upon the central Biblical truth that the God of Israel and of the Christian church is not concerned merely with religious happenings but with all happenings, not just with what happens in the secret places of the soul but also with what happens in the political, the economic, and the social situations where men live and act. Israel's covenant life with God compassed the totality of its existence. Understood in this light, even the most "secular" parts of Israel's history have something to say to us.

Perhaps now we are less likely to misunderstand the word "all" in II Tim. 3:16: "All scripture is inspired by God and profitable for teaching, for reproof, for correction." This may also be translated, "All scripture inspired by God is profitable. . . ." In the passage where this occurs, Paul is much more concerned with the equipment of the man of God for his task, that he may be armed with the word of God, which is "the sword of the spirit" (Eph. 6:17), than with establishing a doctrine of inspiration. Certainly he had no intention that Timothy should bow to the authority of the ritual laws of the Old Testament. But he *did* intend that Timothy should make full use of the Old Testament as one of the chief means whereby he might grow continually in his knowledge of God. Even with his repudiation of the law as a means of salvation, Paul retained a great respect for the law as a revelation of God's will for man through which came knowledge of sin and guidance in the way of obedience. Like Luther, he made no proposal for a revision of the canon. He only insisted upon a *Christian* reading of the Old Testament, that the Christian should find his key to the meaning of the Old Testament in the Spirit of God, which was poured into his heart through Jesus Christ and which he recognized as the same Spirit that had possessed the prophets, psalmists, and historians of the Old Testament.

Karl Barth has pointed out how in Protestant scholasticism and in most forms of literalism today the Bible is regarded as an inspired book completely apart from the inspiration of the interpreting individual or church. This inspired quality residing in the text is thought of as objective in a fashion that can be proved to be present by rational arguments. Barth holds that this development dissolved the mystery of the relation of God's Spirit to Scripture and so prepared the way for liberalism's identification of the divine element in

Scripture with religious and moral qualities that can be discerned in the central persons of the history. The inspiration of Scripture is not a divine quality in the text, or in the persons who are known through the text, but rather defines the relation of Scripture to God. It points to the source of Scripture in God: not in a God who dwells at a distance and has to intrude his word upon his people mechanically from without, but in a God who because of his love for his people dwells in their midst and holds communion with them through the Spirit. Therefore, the sincere outcry of this covenant people in prayer is witness to God in which God reveals himself. It is the prophet's fulfillment of the covenant relation in himself that makes him the man of God's counsel who can speak for God to the nation. The historical books are witness to what God has been to Israel, and Israel to God, within this covenant relation and so are a revelation for all time of what it means to live in covenant with God. But all of this means nothing to a person who does not yet know that all things in life depend upon God's relation to us and ours to him; in short, that unless God comes to us in the fullness of his Spirit to indwell our existence, we are lost. Therefore, that which opens the doors not only of the Old Testament but of all Scripture is the coming to us in Jesus Christ of Him who is the source and hidden content of all Scripture, the living Lord, who establishes his present sovereignty over us through his indwelling Spirit and so makes us to be one with all, in past and present, who have known the fulfillment or the hope of the fulfillment of life under his rule. We gain our understanding of the authors of Scripture through being possessed by the same Spirit who possessed them.

Verbal Inspiration

An element in Luther and Calvin, and also in Karl Barth, that has puzzled and confused many who have written concerning inspiration [16] is their insistence upon verbal inspiration — that the very words of Scripture are inspired by God. During the past century "verbal inspiration" in the English-speaking world has come to mean, wrongly, that each and every word of Scripture is infused with divine meaning, and must, at least in the original text, be free

---

[16] See J. K. S. Reid, *The Authority of Scripture*, p. 62. Reid is baffled by what seem to him contradictory assertions on verbal inspiration by the Reformers.

from all error of any kind. Inerrancy and verbal inspiration have been welded into one. It is at once significant that for Luther and Calvin verbal inspiration did not involve inerrancy. Both were aware of problems in the text of Scripture that had their source in its human genesis and transmission, and, much more than any Biblical interpreters for centuries before them, they were conscious of the importance of the human element in Scripture. And yet they spoke of the words of prophets and apostles as being the very words of God himself, and Calvin could even use the term " dictated by the Holy Spirit." This language is not rightly understood until we discover that both Calvin and Luther could speak of the words of the Christian preacher in the sixteenth century in the same terms. Here there can be no question of inerrancy, for they were well aware of the human weaknesses even of the ablest Protestant preachers. And yet they held that the Spirit of God must make the human words of the preacher the very words of God himself to men, or the gospel has not been rightly preached.[17] Not just the preacher as a person but the specific words of the preacher must be inspired by God.

Since the rise of historical criticism there has been a reaction against attributing inspiration to the specific words of Scripture. The inspiration is posited of the authors so that the Bible becomes a book through which we become acquainted with inspired men whose profound spirituality we must respect, even though we regard much of what they wrote as representing largely an outmoded religious viewpoint. It is against this separation of the man from his words that Karl Barth protests, asserting not that the words possess an inspiration apart from the inspiration of the prophet or apostle, but simply that we know nothing of the prophet or the apostle except through his words, and that each word they speak must be taken with the utmost seriousness, in the context of all their words and in the context of Scripture as a whole. Instead of escaping from the difficulties of the text to take refuge in an inspiring personality whom we envisage behind the text, we must remain with the text until in it we hear the very accents of the prophet or apostle. The revelation is *in the text itself,* in the words that confront us there in all their

[17] T. H. L. Parker, *The Oracles of God: An Introduction to the Preaching of John Calvin.*

strangeness, and not in a history or a personal biography or an event that we reconstruct by means of the text. The event of revelation is available to us only through the text of Scripture interpreted in the context of the church. It is through these words and no others that God intends to speak to us, and, when he does, we know that there is no other kind of inspiration than verbal inspiration. Far from implying any divinizing of the words of Scripture, verbal inspiration understood in its Biblical sense takes the words of the text with full seriousness as the words of real men, spoken or written in a concrete human situation, and yet at the same time words in which God ever afresh reveals himself to me. As in Jesus Christ, the divinity, far from contradicting the humanity, is its confirmation and fulfillment. It is just because the prophets and apostles are so indwelt by the Spirit of God that they are so robustly, freely, independently, and concretely human. The incoming of God's Spirit does not eliminate their human qualities so that they become mere puppets of God, but in the fullest sense it makes them *men* of God. It must be recognized, however, that, in the English-speaking world at least, the term "verbal inspiration" has become so widely a synonym for literal infallibility that it is difficult to use it without creating serious misunderstanding.

⌜ VII ⌝

THE AUTHORITY OF SCRIPTURE

As WITH inspiration, so also with authority, the full definition of its character should be drawn from within Scripture itself if it is to be a truly Scriptural authority and not an alien one attached to Scripture from without. And within Scripture the criterion of authority should be that which belongs to Jesus Christ, not just to Jesus in his earthly life but also to him as the risen Lord, the King and Head of the church. Many of the difficulties that have arisen in the past concerning the authority of Scripture have been the result of attributing to Scripture an authority that it does not claim for itself and that the New Testament church did not claim for Jesus Christ either in his earthly life or as the risen Lord.

THE AUTHORITY OF JESUS CHRIST

We are soon made aware in every part of the New Testament that the authority of Jesus Christ was *real* authority and of an overwhelming nature so far as those who came under it were concerned. Because he renounced every external form of compulsion, not only at the time of his temptations and throughout his life but also in his relationship to his church following his death and resurrection, and because he made himself so completely the servant of men, some interpreters have been inclined to speak only of his persuasiveness or the influence of his character and teaching and to suggest that the exercise of authority was alien to the nature of Jesus. This goes directly contrary to the witness of the Gospels. They report, first of all, the impact of his authority upon people in general and particularly upon those who disagreed with him. The impression that hearers carried away after listening to him preach or teach was that he taught with an authority that was novel to them. In part this points to the directness with which he proclaimed his gospel, a directness similar to the prophet's "Thus saith the Lord," without quotations of Scripture to validate the truth of what he was saying. But it may be more than this. The people were "astonished" or "awe-struck" by his teaching, which may indicate the awe engendered in them by preaching and teaching which proceeded from Jesus' consciousness both of his oneness with God and of the immediacy of God's Kingdom in his own existence. The confidence with which Jesus proclaimed the nearness of the Kingdom and its openness to men was based upon his knowledge of it as the reality of his own being. God's Kingdom of love and mercy and righteousness is God's rule in love and mercy and righteousness. Can there be any question that that rule was not just a future possibility but was a present actuality in Jesus' person? His ministry was a joyful obedience to God's gracious sovereignty, and in the concreteness of his obedience God's Kingdom came on earth in his flesh. It is not strange that words spoken out of that inner consciousness of God's present sovereignty should be felt even by casual listeners to have a peculiar authoritativeness.[1]

The religious leaders who found their established order challenged by Jesus' teachings and attitudes were conscious that he claimed for himself and his words an authority that transcended all their authorities. The law of Moses in its written and oral forms was the supreme authority for them, and they were confident that their beliefs and practices were soundly based upon it. Therefore, his critique, and at some points repudiation, of the established order seemed to them a repudiation of the authority both of Scripture and of tradition, an attempt to destroy the very foundations of religion. If Jesus had been content merely to present his teachings as a new interpretation of Jewish religion, to be debated in the rabbinical schools in a proper fashion, and so to make its contribution eventually as a new and valuable element in the heritage of Judaism, his fate might well have been very different. It was because he proclaimed his gospel to be the fulfillment for which the whole of the

---

[1] The Servant in Isa., chs. 40 to 66, who is destined to establish God's *rule* among men is the bearer of God's word (ch. 49:2). So also in Ps. 8 the man who *rules* for God is one from whose mouth comes a word that conquers God's enemies.

Old Testament was preparation, and his Kingdom to be the beginning of a new era in the life of Israel and of the world that required radical changes in the whole existing order, that his opponents were reduced to fury at finding themselves classified as representatives of a defunct religious order.

Jesus' consciousness of authority is evident also in his relation to John the Baptist. John had a widespread influence among the Jews of Palestine and also beyond Palestine. Those who recognized in him a true prophet of God and heeded his call to repentance would naturally regard his teachings and practices as possessing a divine authority. It disturbed them that Jesus diverged at many points from the teachings and practices of John, one of the most obvious of them being John's ascetic observance of periods of fasting and his great restraint at all times in regard to food and drink. Jesus and his disciples rarely fasted and quite unashamedly enjoyed dining in the houses of their friends (Matt. 9:14 ff.). When criticized for this, Jesus replied that " wisdom is justified by all her children " (Luke 7:35). He acknowledged himself a child of the same wisdom or word of God to which John was faithful, but he asserted his freedom to be a child of wisdom in his own way and not in slavish imitation of patterns set by John. He acknowledged that the word of God which he served and which was his life was the same word to which John and all who came before him were witnesses, so that the word not only of Scripture but also of John had absolute authority for him, but not in any slavish way. His baptism by John was an act of obedience to its authority. But because it was God himself to whom he gave obedience and not just certain words and practices reported in Scripture, it was no repudiation of the authority of God in Scripture or in the ministry of John for Jesus to speak and act differently from John, or from any of the earlier prophets, in his own obedience to the word of God.

Jesus' opponents challenged his authority on one occasion at least (Luke 20:1 ff.), and most likely also on others of which this one is representative. They asked him to tell them by what authority he spoke and acted as he did. What they undoubtedly desired to demonstrate was that he was pitting his human word and will against the whole divine order validated by Scripture. They had Scripture on their side and he did not. Jesus did not enter into a discussion with them to prove that Scripture was actually on his side and the bulwark of his authority. He did not attempt in any way to support his authority with an external structure of proof: he merely exposed their complete inability to understand *his* kind of authority because of their lack of openness to the authority of God in any of its manifestations. He used John the Baptist as a test. Was John from God, or did he speak only on his own authority? There was no room, however, even for John the Baptist in their closed system of revelation and authority. They had not taken John seriously as a messenger of God because they were satisfied that they had the totality of God's truth in Scripture and tradition. Yet they did not dare speak against John because of the widespread recognition of him as a true prophet of God. It could not have been clearer that their assertion of the authority of Scripture was only a concealed form of the assertion of their own authority and the authority of their religious system. They actually cared little or nothing about the authority *of God* and were so ill-acquainted with it, in spite of their familiarity with Scripture, that they would not have recognized it had it been directly before their eyes. The Gospel of John makes the same point when it states that there is an identity in nature between the authority of Moses and the authority of Jesus, so that awareness of the one must inevitably be followed by awareness of the other (John 5:46). He who was open and responsive to the voice of God in the word of Moses would be open and responsive to the same word in its new proclamation in Jesus Christ.

It is evident from this incident in which Jesus was challenged to declare himself that Jesus' authority is hidden, and, though it can be felt, it cannot be understood except where there is a willingness and humility to bow before it as the authority of God himself. If Jesus was not actually claiming this transcendent authority for his own gospel and person, then he was merely parrying words with his opponents when he refused to discuss with them the nature of his authority.

Most important of all, however, was the recognition of Jesus' authority by his disciples and by the whole early church. The response of the first disciples to his call was in itself a recognition of his authority. The Gospel of John represents them as understanding it from the beginning as the authority of God's Messiah, but the

Synoptics portray their apprehension of it as much less securely grounded during the first part of the ministry, becoming clearer at Caesarea Philippi, but not firmly established until the resurrection. What was to them a genuinely prophetic authority became a Messianic authority and finally the authority of One who was the manifestation of God himself. In John's Gospel there is a foreshortening of perspective, as in some medieval paintings, the end being seen from the beginning and Jesus being portrayed throughout as known by the disciples in his oneness with God. But even in John's Gospel the divine authority of Jesus is hidden from the world, and in some measure from the disciples, and revealed only to faith. It is only to those who are willing to receive him that he is the power of God, which establishes God's rule and authority in their lives and so makes them children of God. The world is blind to him.

In both John and the Synoptics his authority is absolute and unconditional. This was what made it seem so unreasonable to reasonable men. Jesus confronted men with an Either-Or. Either they were unconditionally under the rule of God and so new creatures in the life of the Kingdom, or they were, no matter how religious and moral they might be, rebels against the rule of God in the pride of their own self-rule. A man's old self had to die in order that he might come to his own true self as a subject or child of God. It should not be forgotten that in Hebrew usage to be a child of the Father was among other things to be under the authority of the father. Both " father " and " shepherd " were terms that expressed strongly a relation of authority. This absoluteness of Jesus' authority for believers determined the earliest Christian creed, " Jesus is Lord." His resurrection was both the revelation and the vindication of his Lordship, making clear once and for all that the authority of his word and person was not just that of a prophet but was indistinguishable from that of God himself.

It was, then, the revelation of divine sovereignty in Jesus that was central to his authority, and nowhere was the contrast between his authority and all that the world understood as authority and sovereignty so clearly demonstrated as in the cross. There Jesus seemed to be trampled upon by a variety of human authorities and to be helpless before them. His own royal authority seemed completely obscured. But the confession of the church, not only of Paul, for whom Christ crucified was the *power* of God, but of the whole church in its exaltation of the cross, was that the obedience of Jesus unto the death was the point in history where God's sovereignty over all powers and dominions was established once and for all. The cross was not a revelation of authoritative information concerning God as though one could extract from it a series of truths that would then be open to rational confirmation. It was the place where God revealed the true nature of his sovereignty in the midst of human history. It was the source of the Christian's knowledge of God (for Paul, Christ crucified was not only the power of God but also the *wisdom* of God), which was, however, a personal knowledge, the kind of knowledge that a subject has of his sovereign or that a child has of his father, and not a series of intellectual propositions that might later have an influence upon conduct. Nor was this revelation an infallible guide in the ethical decisions which Christians were to face so that they could appeal on each occasion to some word or act of Jesus or some aspect of the cross and resurrection as a ready-made answer to their problem. The earliest Christians, who all alike acknowledged the absolute authority of Jesus Christ, had very serious differences concerning what a Christian must do. When Paul and the Judaizers disagreed, there was no code to which they could appeal for unerring guidance except the truth of the gospel (Gal. 2:14). Faithfulness to the God revealed in Jesus Christ was the test both of conduct and of doctrine.

In questions concerning the form of church government Jesus had left behind no instructions that could be erected into a set of immutable laws. The Gospel of John represents Jesus as being perfectly aware that on many questions his followers would have no specific guidance in his words or example but would have to be led by the Spirit, which is his Spirit, into the needful truth. The authority of Jesus Christ in his church, then, while it asserts itself through the remembrance of his words, his actions, his death and resurrection, is extended to cover new situations by the fact that he himself continues to be present, to teach and to guide his church by means of the Spirit. And the genuineness of the Spirit, by which it is to be distinguished from false spirits, is the continuity of its ministry with that of Jesus Christ himself. Not everything that Christians claimed to know through being possessed and inspired by the Spirit was valid. It had to be tested by its conformity with the gospel.

To a later church the whole order that is reflected in the New Testament seemed to leave the church dangerously open to error both in doctrine and in practice. The faith was too precious to remain so poorly guarded and established! Therefore, an infallible Scripture and an infallible teaching authority in the church were instituted so that on no question could the church fail to have available an unerring and absolutely authoritative answer. A security was thus provided for the church that strangely, very strangely, had been omitted in its original founding. But the demand for this security was actually a distrust of the Word that is hidden until the Spirit reveals it and of the Spirit that is given through the Word.

THE AUTHORITY OF SCRIPTURE AS A WHOLE

It is not difficult to see that the authority originally claimed for the whole New Testament was simply a reflection of the authority of Jesus Christ himself. We see this particularly in the character of apostolic authority in the church. That the power and prestige of the apostles in the church was very great is unquestionable. They were ambassadors, plenipotentiaries, of Jesus, even in his lifetime, and their word shared with his word the power to open and close the door of the Kingdom, to forgive men their sins, to expel demons, and to heal the sick. To hear them was to hear him, and to receive them was to receive him. John's Gospel brings out strongly the authority of apostles as those who are " sent of Jesus Christ " in direct sequence to his own being " sent of God." Their oneness with him is in its nature like his own oneness with God. As *his* words and works correspond to those of God, so do *their* words and works correspond to his. Above all, an apostle was one who had known Jesus in his risen power. We can understand why it was so important to Paul to vindicate his own apostleship when its validity was questioned, and he vindicated it by his witness that he too was " sent of Jesus Christ," that he too was a witness of the resurrection, and that he too lived in constant oneness with Jesus Christ. Yet, great as was the authority of the apostles in the church, it was entirely a *derived* authority and not one that resided in them of themselves or because of their office. Just as Jesus' authority was wholly that of the sovereign God in him, so their authority was wholly that of the sovereign Christ in them. Apart from their relation with Jesus Christ and his with them, they had no authority at all. When Peter at Antioch seemed to Paul to be acting contrary to the truth of the gospel (Gal., ch. 2), it was Paul's duty to resist him. The decisions of an apostolic council of Jerusalem were not laws laid upon the church (Acts, ch. 15) but were issued rather in the form of an appeal that would be accepted as authoritative only in so far as it was recognized in the church as serving to bring men into obedience to Jesus Christ.

In the early church there must have been many diverse apostolic traditions, many of them now almost completely lost. We have only to think of how fragmentary in the New Testament are the evidences of the powerful Judaistic movement that opposed Paul and that undoubtedly had apostolic support. Why did some traditions perish while others remained to become an authoritative canon of Scripture in the church? It must have been because in some apostolic traditions the church recognized the voice of its Lord in a way that it did not in others. The authority of an apostle was not sufficient to keep a tradition alive, and writings of others than apostles could take precedence if the church heard in them the voice for which it listened.

New Testament Scripture, then, had in its very nature no authority except as witness to Jesus Christ. Its authority was hidden in the human documents — Gospels, letters, history — and could be recognized only by faith. The Prologue to John's Gospel makes this distinction very sharply when it insists that the prophets, symbolized by John the Baptist, were not themselves the Word of God but only witnesses to the Word. The error of Judaism was that it confused the witness with the Word (John 5:39), thinking to find eternal life in the words themselves when life was to be found only in the Word to which they pointed beyond themselves. The rabbis were not the last to fall into this error. There has been an ever-recurring temptation in the church to attempt to make the authority of the Word more concrete by identifying it directly and unambiguously with the words of Scripture. A hidden Word and a hidden authority seem too elusive and too indefinite for practical purposes. Where issues of doctrine and practice have to be decided and one needs to be certain where the line runs between truth and error, man in his impatience demands an external criterion that he can apply with readiness and confidence. He wants an authority with which he can prove that he is right and his opponent wrong. Therefore, he dismisses the hiddenness of God's authority in Scripture and externalizes it by making it inhere in every word of every document. Then, in his folly, but because of an uncertainty that plagues him, he undertakes usually to prove, by arguments that are supposed to be convincing even to an unbeliever, that the Bible is the word of God. Actually, he has done two things: he has made it impossible to be honest about the literary and historical problems with which the text of Scripture confronts us, since he has made the text an infallible revelation, and by binding Christ the Word to all the diverse words of Scripture he has silenced the word of really divine authority, which only Jesus Christ can speak. Jesus Christ no longer has the freedom that he had when he was here upon earth — to speak his own word even, if necessary, in contradiction to Scripture. He refused to be bound to every word of the Pentateuch or to the words and practices of John the Baptist. He claimed freedom in the Spirit to speak his own word in his own way. But once he is bound to an infallible Scripture, his freedom is gone and with it his authority. Roman Catholicism imprisons Jesus Christ within an infallible church; literal infallibilism imprisons him within an infallible Scripture. The New Testament sought to guard against this by insisting that both church and Scripture are earthen vessels for the treasure of the gospel, that the power and glory may belong wholly to God and not to men (II Cor. 4:7).

The Scriptures are so diverse in their witness that it is as though their authors (or Author) had tried to make it as difficult as possible to extract from them a code of doctrines and practices that would be fixed and final. The differences in the Synoptic Gospels, or between the Synoptics and John, or between The Acts and the Letters, serve as a safeguard against literalism and as a warning that these are witnesses to the truth and not the final truth of God itself. The authority of Jesus Christ who alone is truth, while it cannot be known except through the words of Scripture, is protected by the fallibility of the witnesses who claimed nothing for themselves but everything for the gospel that had been entrusted to them.

The Authority of the Old Testament

What, then, of the authority of the Old Testament? We have seen already that the Christian church embraced the Old Testament because it saw in Jesus Christ and in the church the continuation and true completion of the history of God's dealings with Israel, the fulfillment of that which had been promised in the Old Testament. The Old Testament, therefore, as the promise, was already in part the revelation of that which was to come. The early church preached its gospel, proclaimed Jesus Christ, and found guidance in the affairs of its life from the text of the Old Testament. Paul warned the Christians at Corinth against thinking that they could follow the letter of the Old Testament. That would lead them, like the Judaizers, into living as though they were Jews rather than Christians. The Old Testament had to be read under the guidance of the Spirit of the Lord. In this way the Old Testament writings as well as the apostolic traditions were made dependent for their authority upon Jesus Christ. The authoritativeness of the Old Testament lay not in itself but in its witness to the truth of the gospel.

The question remains, What kind of authority did the Old Testament authors claim for themselves, and is it alien to the authority claimed for it by the church? Part of the answer has already been given in our discussion of inspiration. Old Testament authors claimed a very great authority because they claimed to have had revealed to them no less than the mind of God concerning man. The prophet, in addressing the nation as though it were not he but God himself who was speaking in person, assumed for his words an authority that transcended all human authorities. Even the king, the anointed of God, was expected to bow in humility before the word of the prophet. " God has spoken; let all men obey." This authority of the spoken word of the prophet was transferred to the written word and was specially reinforced when the disasters of which the prophets gave warning became actuality. But as long as there were prophets speaking ever afresh with this kind of direct authority and in each instance saying something rather different, in spite of all similarities, from what had been said by earlier prophets, there was not likely to be any confusion as to where the center of authority lay — not in the prophet himself or in certain words received through him, but in the ever-living God, who maintained his authority over the whole life of Israel through the words of the prophets.

The author of Samuel-Kings was not concerned to preserve a verbally exact account of the history of his nation, a history that through divine inspiration would have in it no errors; on the contrary, his concern was to proclaim God's sovereignty in Israel's history and the subordination of all human authorities to God. The kings and people of Israel, in refusing to acknowledge and obey God's authority, had brought upon themselves the ruin of the nation. These writings are therefore, in spite of the inestimable value of the history contained in them, not infallible history, but rather a validation of the truth that God alone is king in Israel. The response that they seek is not the unconditional acceptance of their narrative as an inerrant account of historical events but rather the repentance of the hearers, humbling themselves before God, confessing the sins of the nation in the past, and yielding themselves in unconditional obedience to God in present and future. An examination of the documents of Genesis leads to the same conclusion. The priestly writer had no intention of writing authoritative geography, astronomy, or cosmology, fixing for all time how one should think of the world and the universe; what was essential to him was that Israelites should know that the God of Israel was the Creator of the heavens and the earth, and that it was by the same Word whose power for creation and destruction was known in all the history of Israel that he had in the beginning overcome chaos and brought an orderly creation into being. Thus, to locate the authority of Scripture elsewhere than where it belongs has the effect of preventing it from saying what it was intended to say. The authors are concerned that man should recognize the true order of his existence and should come under the personal authority of God. A recognition of their writings as authoritative, separated from the more costly acknowledgment and acceptance of God's absolute authority in the whole of life, would have been to them an empty and deceptive religious formality similar to the hypocrisy of those who were willing to give Jesus the title " Lord " but were unwilling to bend their wills to the will of the sovereign God, whose Word was Jesus' life.

Again we find the same kind of authority that we recognized

earlier in Jesus Christ. It resides primarily not in the authors or their writings but in Him to whom they bear witness, and in the writings in a wholly derivative fashion. There can be no recognition of the authority of the writings that is purely intellectual, for the sovereignty of God remains only a concept until in the response of faith man discovers his true freedom in unconditional surrender to the rule of God. To the human intellect this is likely to seem a form of spiritual tyranny, an unreasonable claim upon man. The force of the claim can be felt and resented, as the prophets and Jesus well knew, but in its true nature it can be understood only from within the circle where man in fellowship with God is willing to yield all authority to God and to be himself a servant.

The authority of Scripture, then, cannot be conceived as a static thing, a divine " quality " or " character " of Scripture, since it is the living God himself exerting *his* authority over man through his Word and Spirit. Word and spirit are inseparable, because Spirit is God's immediate presence, God acting in relation to man.[2] Apart from the activity of the Spirit, the words of Scripture are the residue of a past revelation but not the means of a present revelation. But God's word is by its nature always a word spoken by him to someone, to a *people,* and the first evidence of its authority is that it calls and claims this people to live in a unique relationship to God as *his* people. The concrete evidence that God has spoken with authority is that a people responds — or rebels. It is in this people and not in Scripture (or the oral predecessor of Scripture) alone that the sovereign authority of God receives visibility. The witness of Scripture is not an end in itself but exists for the sake of a more fleshly witness, the living witness to the reality of God in the total life of both the Old and the New Israel. This is basic to the whole Old Testament, but it appears with the utmost clarity in Isa., chs. 40 to 66, where God's revelation of his power and glory to the whole world is through his servant Israel, which does not carry Scripture as a book in its hand but lives with God's word as the core of its existence and as the sword with which it wins his battles for him.

It is not sufficient for God's word to reside in documents; it has to

---

[2] Robert C. Johnson, *op. cit.,* in a careful study of the whole problem of authority emphasizes the inseparableness of Word and Spirit if the authority is to be truly God's.

be a word that compasses the life of a people or it will not reach its goal, which is the establishment of God's rule in the life of humanity. Shut up merely in a book, it is robbed of its true authority no matter how obsequious the homage that is paid to it and the eulogies that are heaped upon it. Jesus, growing up in a Judaism that acknowledged the holiness of Scripture, that asserted the infallibility of its every word, and that yet failed to give God's word in Scripture freedom to rule within the present existence of the nation, must have been peculiarly conscious of this danger that the word of God should become imprisoned in the documents that were intended to bear witness to it. It was most likely for this reason that he set down nothing of his gospel in writing, but instead implanted it in the hearts and minds of a people. The establishment of God's sovereignty in human life could not be entrusted merely to a book; it had to be a word that captured men wholly for a new life in God so that their entire existence would be a witness to the reality of the life of the Kingdom. How else could men understand the paradoxical truths of the Kingdom, that absolute subjection to God was the secret of true freedom to live, or that dying unto self was not a grim sacrifice but rather one's birth into a life of incredible joy and richness with God? It was to his disciples as this witnessing people of God that Jesus gave himself and made them his body through which he would continue his ministry to the end of time. Thus, within Scripture itself, the authority of Scripture cannot at any point be separated from the authority of a witnessing people, which for us means the church.

This relation of the church to Scripture has frequently been misunderstood as though there were two authorities divinely established which somehow had to be reconciled with each other. Which is to have precedence, the Scriptures or the church? The church was established first, say some; to it was committed the truth of the gospel for all time to come and the task of interpreting its meaning to each new age; the church wrote the Scriptures; therefore, the authority of the church is superior to the authority of the Scriptures. Only the Scriptures are God's word, say others; therefore, any equation of the human traditions of the church with the divine word of God is blasphemy. But in the Scriptures themselves there is no such antithesis. The Scriptures came into being as the church's witness to the word of God through which alone a people of God was created and sustained and guided through the centuries. There is no church in Scripture that exists apart from the word of God or in other than obedience to it, and there is no revelation of God in the church apart from that revelation to which it bears witness in Scripture. Just as the apostles subordinated themselves to Jesus Christ, so the post-Apostolic church subordinated itself to the word of the gospel, which it could not hear in its full authenticity except through Scripture. It is only when it is forgotten that there can be no authority for Christians except the authority of the living God himself in his Word and Spirit that it becomes possible for Scripture and church to be set in rivalry with each other.

SOURCES OF CONFUSION

The misinterpretation of the Bible's inspiration, which we examined in Chapter VI, led inevitably to a misunderstanding of its authority. When the rabbis introduced the Greek conception of a text that, because it was divinely inspired, must contain divine truth in every detail, they became concerned with the authority of the words of Scripture rather than with the authority of the living God, whose word must be heard in the midst of the words. As we have seen, this led them, while intending to defend the authority of Scripture, actually to make use of Scripture in order to defend the authority of their established religious system. The word of God in Scripture was no longer free to set the established order of things radically in question. In Jesus Christ, the word of God recovered its freedom and asserted its unique authority in its own way — at a cost. But by the second century the revival of the Greek-rabbinic concept of inspiration was at least beginning to conceal the authority of Christ the Word behind a statically authoritative text of Scripture. This in turn brought in its train, as it had in Judaism, the development of an authoritative tradition of the church alongside Scripture in order to secure a revelation that would be revelant to the ever-changing problems of humanity. This in itself was an indication that Scripture had become the record of a past revelation from which inferences could be made rather than the medium of a present revelation. The canon now marked not the area in which God's voice could ever be heard afresh, but instead the point at which God had ceased to speak, so that his church had to take over the function of speaking for him. Jesus Christ was no longer present himself as the Head of the church in his Word and Spirit, so that the church must now have its own human head, fully accredited and empowered to speak for Jesus Christ. It should be emphasized that this outcome was the direct consequence of the church's ceasing to understand how God in each new age asserts his own authority over the life of the church and of humanity through Scripture. And it was only to be expected that the dynamic and mobile authority of the church would take precedence over the now static authority of Scripture.

In the Reformation there was an essential, though not complete, recovery of the Bible's own understanding of itself and of its relation to the church. Luther and Calvin were both aware that the gospel had become imprisoned within the church in such a way that the authority of the words of Scripture could be used to defend the established order of doctrines and practices against the critique of the prophetic and apostolic Word. What men were hearing in Scripture was largely an echo of their own voices rather than the totally other voice of God. The revolutionary power of the rediscovery of the Bible by the Reformers was that the Word within the words of the Bible had its authority and freedom restored to it. Yet in their writings they did not get completely free from the earlier ways of thinking of inspiration, revelation, and authority. The age out of which they came left its mark upon them. While insisting upon the hiddenness of the revelation in Scripture so that it is evident to faith alone through the present action of God's Spirit and bears within itself its own proof, they could not refrain from suggesting that there are certain external characteristics which should make even unregenerate men aware of its authority. And while insisting upon a Christological approach, Jesus Christ being the center from which the whole of Scripture must be understood, they fell back at times into the conception of a divinely inspired text, in every part of which it should be possible to find something concerning Jesus Christ.

In Protestant scholasticism the Greek-rabbinic-Roman conception of inspiration pressed back into the church through diverse channels. In order to read the Old Testament in the original Hebrew, Protestant scholars studied with Jewish rabbis and so came in contact both with their traditional awe before the sacred words of Scripture and with their use of allegorical interpretation for extracting the meaning. There was also the pressure of the Roman Church, which claimed to have an infallible doctrine and church order based upon an infallible Scripture and tradition. Could Protestants claim for the Scriptures on which they had to place their entire reliance a less definite and concrete authority than did the Roman Church? In the seventeenth century there were some scholars who alleged that not only the words but the very punctuation of Scripture was dictated by the Holy Spirit, and that to suggest there was error in any part was to impute error to the Holy Spirit of God, which was blasphemy. Because of this literalism, both in Protestantism and in Romanism, the Scriptures were regarded as authoritative in an external way. They contained an authoritative history of the world from the time of the Creation. All their statements were statements of fact.

Fortunately, there were inconsistencies in Protestant scholasticism. Contradictory principles existed alongside each other. There was a desperate earnestness to hear God's own guiding word in Scripture coupled with the conviction that every detail must in some way contain this word. The strength of Puritanism lay in its willingness to bow in unconditional obedience before the word of Scripture, but its most dangerous weakness lay in its inability to make any distinction between the divinely authoritative word and the human words. God's command to slay the Amalekites was equally authoritative with the command to love one's enemies. Also the erection of Scripture into an absolute authority in and of itself and apart from the witness of a responsible church left the way open for the intrusion of irresponsible authorities, each claiming to possess the only valid interpretation of Scripture on which the only true Christian church could be built.

"Scripture its own interpreter"[3] was a valid and important principle of the Reformation in so far as it meant that Scripture must be interpreted from within itself. This was something much more than a collation of texts so that the one might be used to illuminate the other. It meant that Biblical words must receive their definition from within the context of Scripture and not from some

[3] See ch. 2, p. 159.

outside source. It was based on the recognition that the Biblical writers have their own unique meaning for words. When they say " God " or " love " or " fear," they do not mean what other men mean by God and love and fear. The revelation of Scripture is to be interpreted not in the light of knowledge gained from some other source but in its own light. We must not take the claim made by the words of Scripture themselves that they are inspired and inject into the word " inspired " a meaning drawn from some source other than Scripture. " Scripture its own interpreter " was not intended to mean either that no interpreting church was needed any longer or that every man was his own interpreter. And yet both these meanings were placed upon it in post-Reformation centuries, much to the confusion of Protestantism and as one of its most prolific sources of sectarian division. The authority of Scripture that should by its nature be the most unifying of all forces, since it is the assertion by God of his sovereignty in the life of humanity, was transformed into the most divisive of all forces, enabling men to validate stubbornly those elements in the life of their own church which divided them sharply from their fellow Christians.

THE CONSEQUENCES OF HISTORICAL CRITICISM

The demonstration by historical criticism of the thoroughly human character of the Biblical documents is usually held responsible for their loss of authority in the modern world. And in so far as critics went beyond literary and historical analysis to pronounce the content of Scripture to be merely religious phenomena and to deny the reality of a revelation of God, they bear this responsibility. But the question must be asked why in so many minds the recognition of the humanity of Scripture was thought to entail the denial of its divinity. Both liberals and orthodox seemed to agree at this point. The one said, " Because it is wholly divine, the human authors must in their writing have been kept free from the errors and imperfections that are the usual mark of humanity." The other said, " Because it is wholly human, we can no longer speak of divine revelation." But both were operating with something less than Christian conceptions of humanity and divinity. The Christian of the New Testament is defined as a man in whose humanity God dwells as in a temple. But Paul and Peter did not cease to be sinful, erring humanity when the Spirit of their Lord possessed them and spoke and acted through them. Their inspiration did not set them beyond the possibility of error. Yet their fallibility was no obstacle to God in establishing the authority of his truth among men through them. It would be a sorry outlook for the church and for mankind if God could use no witnesses to his truth except infallible men. It belongs to the nature of his grace that he has always been able to accomplish his purpose through men who were far from perfect and to make his voice heard in spite of the inadequacies of his spokesmen. Who, then, has the right to demand that Biblical documents be infallible in order to be credible? Or to conclude that, because the documents bear upon them the marks of their time-bound humanity, they cannot be the medium of divine revelation? If we take our starting point with Jesus Christ and his apostles, then we have to say that no witness to revelation would be credible unless it were visibly the witness of fallible men, since, except in the person of Jesus himself, infallibility and humanity are contradictory terms. But we have also to say that the honest, undisguised humanity of the witnesses, far from being an obstacle to revelation, convinces us of their integrity as they tell us what they have seen and heard. There is no reason, then, why the establishment of the fully human character of Scripture by historical criticism should have destroyed confidence in Scripture as God's revelation except that so many persons had a false or superficial idea of revelation. If this is so, then one of the constructive achievements of historical criticism has been in clearing away such false conceptions to make room for a truer and more Biblical one.

The recent volume, *Revelation and the Bible* (1958), edited by C. F. H. Henry, marks an attempt by conservative scholars to take more account of the human phenomena of Scripture without abandoning the dogma of the infallible text. It is noteworthy how even among the most progressive conservatives this dogma still takes precedence over all others. The newly organized " Evangelical Theological Association " requires of its members only that they agree to the infallibility of Scripture. The essays in the volume edited by Henry reveal that behind this façade there exists a wide diversity of theologies, all of them ostensibly based on the infallible text. The most vital of them show clearly the influence of theologians of our day for whom there is no infallible text. It is no accident that the essayists most alive as theologians have the least to say concerning infallibility and those whose thinking is most wooden make most of it. By its very nature the dogma has a paralyzing effect upon the inquiring mind, for it warns the scholar that his standing as a Christian will be set in question if he discovers in the text of Scripture any clear evidence of human fallibility. An evangelical theologian should be sensitive to the denial of the doctrine of justification by faith alone through grace that is inherent in this attitude. To say that our salvation in any degree depends upon the views we hold concerning the authorship of books of Scripture or our estimate of the relation between Chronicles and Kings is to trust in something other than God's grace and truth in Jesus Christ. Faith is the response of our whole being to God's approach to us in the gospel, and by its nature it sets us free to read the Scriptures unafraid of what we may find there if we read with an honest and open mind. Only God himself can receive man's unconditional submission without robbing him of his freedom. Both an infallible Scripture and an infallible church are attempts to make God's hidden sovereignty visible, tangible, and even manageable, but they show themselves usurpers of the place that can be occupied by God alone by the fact that in receiving man's unconditional submission they are forced to take from him his freedom to inquire or at least to set a definite limit beyond which it cannot go.

We have now to ask why historical criticism, having opened the way for a recovery of a true understanding of Biblical authority, produced no adequate restatement of the doctrine of Scripture. Why was it left to conservatives who were unfriendly to free historical investigation of Scripture to defend its authority? Critical scholars seem to have been under the misapprehension that the doctrine of infallible authority which their researches had made untenable was intrinsic to the Scriptures themselves and indeed was the doctrine held by Jesus and Paul. Therefore, a reassertion of the authority of Scripture, it seemed to them, would have to be upon some totally different basis.

Attempts at Critical Reconstruction

C H Dodd

The volume on *The Authority of the Bible,* by C. H. Dodd, published in 1928, and again in 1938 with little change except a preface that exhibits a rather different point of view from the body of the book, is illuminating at this juncture. Dodd's aim is " to approach the Bible not as a collection of dogmatic texts, but as literature in the full humanist sense, in the belief that such an approach will most surely lead to the discovery of its unique qualities as religious literature " (p. 9). There are apparently in his mind only two alternatives, the literalistic view for which the texts are inerrant statements of dogmas, and the humanist view that the divine authority must reside in the unique qualities of the religious literature as human documents, qualities that should be demonstrable by the historian. All authorities, such as Bible and church, are erected by human decisions, so that the ultimate authority is man's observation and reason (pp. 14-15). The realities of the material world exert an authority upon the mind of the scientist, forcing him to think in a particular way and not just in any way he pleases. As he does so, he himself becomes an authority or expert. An authority is therefore a person whose mind is open to the realities, and we have no difficulty in accepting such authorities in the realms of science, art, education, and elsewhere. " The expert in religion is the saint or the prophet — the man of inspired character or the man of inspired vision." (P. 24.) The authority of the Bible is thus " the authority of experts in the knowledge of God, masters in the art of living, the authority of religious genius " (p. 25). " The dominant personalities of the Bible are of this order," i.e., religious genius, and in Jesus " religious genius reached its highest point " (pp. 27, 28). Geniuses are defined as " men who by reason of some innate spiritual faculty, and by reason of the faithfulness with which they have followed its impulse, have attained experience of divine things fuller, deeper, and more compelling than comes to the ordinary run of men " (p. 25). Three periods — the Mosaic, the eighth- to sixth-century prophetic, and the New Testament — " were flowering times of the spirit, when genius in the sphere of religion asserted itself after its own incalculable fashion " (p. 28; note the small " s " signifying that the spirit which flowers is the human spirit). The genius of the prophets was identical with their inspiration, and the authors of the Pentateuch, being lesser geniuses, are held to be less inspired. This religious genius, or mastery in the religious life with which it is equated, is as readily recognizable as the genius of the Greek architect displayed in the Pantheon, or the genius of Shakespeare evident in *King Lear*. It has about it nothing of mystery (contrary to what one might have been led to deduce from the prophets' own statements about it). It is not divine revelation but intrinsic human genius that lends to the words of the prophets their authority.

The whole approach is naturalistic.[4] It is said of primitive nābī'ism that it "from time to time threw up men of real religious genius" (p. 54). The claim to be inspired by God's Spirit belonged only to the cruder prophets who had hardly emerged from paganism: "Prophets of the eighth- and seventh-centuries have little to say of the ruach or 'spirit'" (p. 58). Significantly Dodd makes no mention of Ezekiel or Second Isaiah, for whom the Spirit of God was of the greatest importance. Prophetic visions are explained as produced entirely from within "by the projection of ideas in a symbolic form." God enters the picture as "a numinous emotion" suffusing the ideas of the prophet. One wonders how the prophets would have reacted to Dodd's description of them: "In the prophetic experience we have an elevated idea, suffused with intense emotion, entering consciousness in dramatic forms created by imagination and uttering itself in poetical language" (p. 81). The language re-creates the same experience in the hearer, so that revelation is essentially a direct communication of ideas and experience. The great achievement of the eighth-century prophets was in ethicizing God's character, having discerned that "God must himself be at least as good as they saw he expected men to be" (p. 98). Amos made God

---

[4] In Dodd's later book, *The Bible Today*, one seems to be confronted with a quite different point of view. Here he denies specifically that "the church of God's elect consists of people with a natural genius for religion" (p. 106). The Bible is "a unity of diverse writings which together are set forth by the church as a revelation of God in history." The Old Testament is intelligible only as containing the promise that is fulfilled in the New, so that each has to be understood in the light of the other. Both are recognized by the church as authoritative in revealing God. The Bible is the record of God's agelong search for man that he might reveal himself to him and win man's obedience. But it is the earlier book rather than the later one that still circulates most widely — now in a paperback edition.

just and Hosea made him gracious. Of course, the ideas of the prophets are recognized by us as most imperfect, but there was in them " a creative power " that makes it permissible to regard them " as a revelation of truth itself to the seeking mind of man."

This same category of religious genius is used by Dodd in his consideration of the New Testament, especially in interpreting the experience of the apostles. He finds it a complicating factor that the New Testament writers were so much under the influence of Jesus (p. 36). Only in regard to Jesus himself is it necessary to speak of an authority greater than that of genius. Jesus is for him a religious genius, but more than a genius. " At the risk of raising philosophical problems which we are not in a position to solve, may we not say in general terms that for Christians, even for Christians who would hesitate to assent to any traditional creed, Christ is in some way identical with ' that of God in us,' the inner light, the indwelling Spirit, whatever it is that we live by at our best. His authority, therefore, is the one and only authority we have declared to be absolute, the authority of truth, the authority of God. There can be no discussion of it." Here Dodd shows his awareness of a mysterious claim of absolute authority that resides in Jesus Christ, but he sharply differentiates it from prophetic and apostolic authority, which is only the relative human authority of religious genius. But does he not also suggest that this unique absolute authority is not really unique when he makes Christ identical with " that of God in us " ? Does " that of God in us " share this absolute authority with the Jesus Christ of the Gospels? Or is " that of God in us " in the last resort only another symbolic name for religious genius that has already been equated with inspiration? Dodd distinguishes three stages in revelation and so three degrees of authority: the first, " the inspiration of individual genius, conferring not inerrancy but a certain cogent persuasiveness "; the second, " the appropriation of ' inspired ' ideas by a whole community, whose experience through many generations tests, confirms, and revises them "; and the third, " the life of One in whom his followers found so decisive an answer to their needs that they hailed him as the Wisdom of God incarnate " (p. 284). Why the claim of the apostles for Jesus as the Wisdom of God should be more credible than the claim of the prophets to have heard the word of God is never at any point explained and remains an arbitrary judgment.

It is obvious that "religious genius" is not a Biblical category but one drawn from the general observation of human life to explain unusual human achievements. It points to innate qualities of the human person that make the unusual insight, ideas, or creative works possible. Its inappropriateness when used in relation to prophets, apostles, or Jesus himself is evident in their insistence that all that they know or speak or do comes from a source beyond themselves. The man is lost in the message. What constitutes Paul an apostle is not the genius that resides in him but the fact that Jesus Christ calls him, commissions him, and abides in him in the power of his Word and Spirit, so that men through him know Jesus Christ. Sören Kierkegaard, in his essay "Genius and Apostle," furnishes a valuable analysis of the difference between the two categories: a genius is born one; an apostle is called to be one. A genius brings something new that is, however, assimilated by the race; an apostle brings something new whose newness remains through all time. A genius is what he is through that which he possesses in himself; an apostle is what he is by divine revelation and authority. But if one has dismissed "inspiration by the Holy Spirit" as an idea that belongs to a crude and superstitious stage of religion and can see in the Scriptures as a whole only the documents of human religion, the distinction between genius and apostle disappears and one is forced to locate the authority of Scripture in some superior quality or power residing in the authors of Scripture, or in the religion of Israel in combination with the religion of the New Testament.

It is partly in reaction to the subjectivism of this viewpoint that H. H. Rowley [5] attempts to establish objectively the divine authority of Scripture. His criticism of Millar Burrows' identification of "our own best judgment" with "the Holy Spirit" would apply equally to Dodd's identification of man's genius with inspiration. A highly competent historian such as Rowley is well aware of the fallible character of all human documents, even Scripture. "None of the media of revelation is infallible, and hence the authority of the media

[5] H. H. Rowley, "The Authority of the Bible: An Apologetic Appealing to Objective Evidence," *Encounter* (Winter, 1957).

is never absolute." What he wants, however, is to establish in some objective way, demonstrable to human reason and not requiring faith for its recognition, the intimate relation between God and the Scriptures. The whole of the Bible he holds to be inspired but some parts in a higher degree than others. There are various levels of inspiration. " Viewing the Bible as a whole I find a surprising measure of inspiration and therefore of authority marking it." But by what criterion he measures the inspiration and exactly what he means by inspiration he does not say clearly. It is plain, however, that he considers this evidence which the Bible gives of its own inspiration and authority to be entirely too subjective. " Two things are now required of him who would maintain the authority of the Bible. He must first establish some test whereby these levels may be judged; and he must produce evidence that can approve itself to reason that the Bible is the Word of God, even if not all in the same degree. He must point to some evidence of the hand of God in the Bible that can be objectively tested by reason. If he can produce such evidence, he may hope that men who accept the arbitrament of reason will recognize the hand of God and will therefore approach the Bible with humility and reverence to receive the word of God. Their spirit will be susceptible to the influence of the divine Spirit."

This seems to be a curious reversion to the tradition of rational orthodoxy that began, as Rowley does, with a revelation of God in nature, history, and experience, received by man through his reason, and preliminary to a supernatural revelation confined to Scripture that can be known only to faith. The fact that the revelation of Scripture can be perceived only by faith evidently poses a problem, since it seems to exclude from access to it the very people who need it most, those who have intelligence but no faith. The problem, then, is how the intelligent man may be induced to take Scripture seriously. The rational orthodox theologian was confident that by certain evidences, such as the correspondence of prophecies with later events and the presence of power to work miracles, he could prove convincingly that the Bible is the word of God. Rowley presents this old argument in a new form. The remarkable correspondences in various parts of Scripture — between the description of the Suffering Servant in Isa., ch. 53, and the actual events of Jesus' death; between God's deliverance of Israel in the exodus and of the new Israel in the redemptive work of Christ — are to him a " signature of God " upon the external events of history that any reasonable person should be able to see. The spread of Christianity through the world validates a revelation that promised a world mission. It may be freely admitted that events such as the birth of Israel in the exodus and the birth of the church as a consequence of the death and resurrection of Jesus present a baffling aspect to the historian who wants to explain all that happens in terms of cause and effect, and they point him at least to the possibility of a power's being at work from beyond history. But this can hardly claim to be " rational proof of the activity of God," and to rest the authority of Scripture on any such dubious basis could have the opposite effect to that which is desired. The deeper theological question must be asked, whether the word of God can be based upon reason or submitted to a criterion of reason without making man rather than God the ultimate authority, and, moreover, whether this procedure does not betray a serious misunderstanding of the nature of the authority claimed by Scripture. It is inconceivable that Jesus should have felt it necessary to provide any such external signs visible to reason in order to prepare men for the recognition of his authority and as a kind of steppingstone from reason to faith. The revelation of God in him creates by its own power the faith that is necessary to receive it; in its light men have their blindness taken away and see light. Faith is not a precondition of hearing God's word but rather is the response of the whole man (the man who is always in some measure an unbeliever) to God's call in his Word. That a historical scholar such as Rowley should fail to recognize this and should resort to a device of this nature in order to reinforce the authority of Scripture indicates once more the vacuum that was left when historical criticism had done its work most thoroughly.

If further evidence of the same dilemma is needed, it may be found in the symposium published under the auspices of the World Council of Churches, *Biblical Authority for Today*.[6] Scholars from the continent of Europe, from Asia, from Great Britain, and the United States, representing many different churches, contribute to

[6] A. Richardson and W. Schweitzer, eds., *Biblical Authority for Today,* a World Council of Churches Symposium on " The Biblical Authority for the Churches' Social and Political Message Today."

the volume. Their primary intention is to clarify the nature of the Bible's authority in relation to the social and political questions of our time, but in order to do this they are compelled to deal with the prior question of how rightly to interpret Scripture. A number of the essays, in particular those of Professors Nagy, Muilenburg, and Eichrodt, make extremely valuable contributions, and the statement of guiding principles for the interpretation of the Bible, accepted by the group, is admirable as far as it goes, but a number of the essays leave the impression upon the mind that the Bible can no longer be expected to be our source of guidance in the perplexing ethical problems of the modern world.

The viewpoint of some of the essayists may be summarized in the words of one without too great injustice.[7] The Bible is the authoritative witness to " the redemptive activity of God culminating in Jesus Christ," and apart from it " there is no way that reason by itself could come to the conclusion that ' God was in Christ reconciling the world to himself.' " The God who forgives and reconciles makes ethical demands upon those who are forgiven and reconciled, so that the receiving of his grace must issue in a new kind of life not just in individuals but socially and politically. But the social and political responses of the Israelites or of the early Christians as described in the Bible cannot be taken as authoritative patterns established for all times. In the past Christians have done this to their hurt, using the Bible " to defend ethical standards advantageous to powerful, dominant groups," finding a sanction not only for slavery but also for other tyrannous practices in texts of Scripture, and validating the extermination of their enemies as the enemies of God. Not even the words of Jesus can be taken as adequate ethical instructions for our time, since they were in many instances directed to situations peculiar to the life of Jews in the first century A.D. and were given in expectation of the imminent end of the age. We can find guidance in his words and in many parts of the Bible, but always we ourselves have to distinguish between what is valid and what is obsolete. Where, then, lies the authority? The

---

[7] Quotations in this paragraph are taken from the essay by Clarence T. Craig because of the clarity with which he states the difficulties in applying the Bible ethically and because his assumption concerning " other sources of guidance " is representative of the standpoint of a number of the essayists.

ultimate ethical authority resides in " the Christian consciousness," or, perhaps more truly, in the will of God as apprehended by the Christian consciousness through a variety of channels of which the Bible is only one. God's will is known to Christians also through natural law, which is the rational man's perception of a divine order in human life, through the traditions of the church, and through the internal witness of the Spirit quite apart from Scripture. The Bible may have a primary authority, but it cannot be permitted to have sole authority. The best that can be said is that " if the Bible is used by a Spirit-filled inquirer, in the light of the best traditions of the church, the moral experience of the race, and an accurate knowledge of the contemporary situation, it will prove an invaluable source of guidance in dealing with our social and political problems."

A number of the contributions follow this general pattern, while showing individual variations. The recognition that the Bible can no longer be used as a code-book of ethics, which is a valid and valuable outcome of modern historical investigation, becomes the basis for asserting the inadequacy of the Bible, however interpreted, to serve as an absolute and unique source of authority in ethical questions. While the " saving " revelation of God is in Jesus Christ alone and is known only through Scripture, the " guiding " revelation of God from which the Christian learns what he must do in obedience to God is given through a variety of channels of which the Bible is only one. Reason, conscience, general human experience, and the traditions of the church must all be taken into account.

It may readily be granted that these are factors in all our thinking, but the question remains, Where, then, does the ultimate authority reside? Who is to weigh these various authorities or revelations and determine which is primary and which may be ignored in a given situation? Surely no one could be so naïve as to expect all of them to fall automatically into a God-given harmony. If the ethical patterns of Scripture are time-bound and relative to the society in which they originated, so also are the dicta of reason, conscience, and natural law time-bound and frequently a mere reflection of the general culture of the time and place. The effect, then, of the generalizing of the ethical revelation is to place the ultimate authority squarely in the hands of man himself, and there is nothing to prevent him from absolutizing it by identifying his judgment with the will of God. It is man who holds the balance between the authority of Scripture and the authority of the values of his culture (which is the actual content of what he calls natural law). This is an excellent safeguard against the values of our culture being set radically in question by the word of Scripture, and has in history been man's surest defense against the cutting edge of the word of God.

Muilenburg

Only in two of the essays is the authority of Scripture for the whole life of man recognized in its true character as the establishment of God's sovereignty in and through his Word and as a sovereignty that is safeguarded by Scripture itself against the confusion with various forms of human sovereignty that inevitably follows when other revelations are validated alongside the revelation of Scripture. Muilenburg's essay, like the others that have been mentioned, agrees that " the nature of the Bible forbids us to find within it any external ethical system. . . . The Bible is a *sacred history,* and a distilling of permanent laws and principles from it is not in keeping with its fundamental meaning and character." But he goes on from this directly to show how " the Bible does offer us all kinds of guidance and direction in the discernment of our duty and obligation." There is for him no lumping together of Bible, tradition, natural law, and human reason as mutually supplementary revelations of the will of God for man. Rather, he maintains the uniqueness of the Biblical revelation. Man's responsibility " under a judgment higher than his own " and "under a sovereignty higher than the sovereignty of nations " is " grasped within the unique community of the covenant people." There and there alone does man know what kind of person he is, and it is there that he understands the nature of the obligation under which he lives. The urgency of the Biblical demand for justice is rooted in the covenant relation in which Israel is called to respond to God with a love and justice and faithfulness that are a reflection of the nature of God himself. Ethics is the outcome of theology, and the distinctiveness of Israel's relation with God results in a distinctive ethic. The prophets spell out the implications of this ethic with a concreteness that we cannot brush aside as applicable only to ancient Israel. The poor are the responsibility of all Israel. Justice must be done to every man. Every person is of infinite worth to God. Man's body is sacred.

These and many other implications of the covenant relation are made very plain. But it is within the church that the implications of God's absolute sovereignty must be spelled out, not by the church apart from Scripture but by the church as the custodian and interpreter of the revelation of Scripture. All nations are claimed by God as his own and they cannot attain their true life until they come under his sovereignty, but the meditation of his authority to them is through the Scriptures and the church.

Nagy's essay presents a similar interpretation. He too agrees that the Bible has "no mechanical authority for the right ordering of social and political life, set out in paragraphs like a legal code, but a spiritual and religious authority." "The authority of the Bible is the living, concrete authority of Jesus Christ, who speaks by means of it as the Lord and King appointed by God." In him the Bible has a unity of meaning so that, wherever its message is truly heard in repentance and faith, his Kingdom is established, a Kingdom that "cannot be indifferent to any human concerns, which include social and political affairs." "The unique and basic importance of the Bible, for social and political problems as for others, is that, being the Word of God, it relates all problems to this one center, the Kingdom of God realized and to be realized through Jesus Christ." "When the sovereignty of God's Word has been accepted for all our thinking and living, then in the free and responsible Christian conscience the right solutions will be found." Like Muilenberg, he points to the fact that only in the Biblical revelation of God is man revealed truly to himself, and that basic to all social and political problems is man's understanding of himself. "Behind every political system and every social ideology there is a definite anthropology, i.e., a definite idea of what man is and ought to be, of what can be made with him and out of him." Also, the Scriptures reveal to us God's ordering of human life in marriage, family, nationality, work, economic activity, law, the state, etc. The divine purpose of each of them within the totality of God's purposes is made clear, and limits are set upon each of them in relation to God and to each other. We are not given ready-made solutions to all the problems of life that would make it unnecessary for us to use our own powers, but only "decisive directives." "God's Word to us on social and political problems must be worked out afresh for each generation in relation to the whole Biblical witness." Natural law and all secondary sources of revelation he rejects as leading eventually to an undermining of the authority of Jesus Christ over his own people. Doctrines of natural law " always depend on a non-Biblical conception of human nature," and appeal to us because they provide a basis on which to assert our own human judgment in opposition to the will of God revealed in Jesus Christ. Events of the past thirty years in mid-Europe seem to him to accentuate the importance of this issue.

THE UNIQUENESS OF THE BIBLICAL AUTHORITY

In the preceding discussion it has become apparent that the most important difference between the various scholars under consideration has to do with their concept of revelation. Both Dodd and Rowley assume a general revelation of God in the life of humanity. For Dodd, revelation is present in all history. Because of sin the divine meaning is obscured in " long stretches of human history," but nevertheless " there is some disclosure of a divine meaning in history as such." For Rowley, " revelation is God's unfolding of his own nature and will, and it has many channels outside the Bible " — nature, history, experience, personality, etc. The majority of the essayists in *Biblical Authority for Today* seem to make a distinction at this point, finding in Scripture a unique revelation of the gospel, but broadening the media of revelation to take in tradition, natural law, and human reason where the law of God or the ethical criterion is concerned. This broader viewpoint reflects the theological climate of our time in which any insistence upon an exclusively Biblical revelation has seemed unintelligently narrow and harsh, and it has been taken for granted very widely that God reveals himself to man through a multiplicity of channels — through nature, history, the individual conscience, the riches of culture in literature and music, and a hundred other ways. Theologians were for a time accustomed to talk quite loosely about " God's revelation in history," until in 1933 a nation with a mystic faith in what God had revealed to them in the rebirth of their nation in that year set out to claim the destiny that seemed to be indicated by the revelation. In its popular form this broad view of revelation makes no distinction between " saving " and " guiding," and perhaps no distinction *can* be made that is ultimately real. If God has revealed himself in all these ways, then God can be known through them, and this knowledge of God is salvation. Any attempt to maintain the distinction that it is only a " guiding " revelation, with value for ethics, that one finds through these diverse channels, and not a " saving " revelation, is likely to fail. It seems to have more the character of a formal theological concession while the doctrine that remains in force practically is evident in the definition of the sources of ethical criteria.

The question of the validity of a natural revelation alongside the Biblical one lies at the very center of the theological debate of our time and is of a dimension that forbids any extensive discussion of it here. Elsewhere [8] I have tried to show that it is the crucial issue in determining the character of the church and its ministry. When revelation ceases to be understood as Biblical in an exclusive sense and is widened to take in all that seems to be of value in human life, the ministry becomes the " ministry of truth in general " and no longer the ministry of Jesus Christ, with its nature determined entirely by him. Preaching becomes the communication of moral and spiritual truths that seem to have proved their value in human life rather than the ministry of the word in which the preacher puts himself unconditionally at the service of that strange and troubling word of Scripture which has sometimes seemed almost to destroy men and their constructions (and even the preacher and his cherished values) before it is able to redeem them. But most important of all is what happens to the Christian congregation when it thinks it has a " revelation of God " through nature, tradition, conscience, and common sense on which it can rely in addition to the venerated but rather difficult revelation of the Scriptures. Why should a Christian wrestle with the intricacies of nearly a million words of ancient religious documents if he has much simpler ways of knowing God's will? Inevitably the Scriptures recede, and with them recedes the Biblical understanding of a God who as the Father Almighty lays claim to the entire life of his people in the world. The Christ, who discourages followers who are not willing to put themselves unconditionally at the service of his mission but offers those who are truly open to him the joy and strength of a life in God, ceases to be known. And the Spirit of God, which is God no longer worshiped

[8] James D. Smart, *The Rebirth of Ministry: A Study of the Biblical Character of the Church's Ministry.*

at a distance but taking possession of one's very being, becomes a
stranger in the church. In short, as the Scriptures recede, the unique
nature and reality of God as Father, Son, and Holy Spirit, is forgotten and is replaced by some other conception of God that is
only vaguely Christian. One has only to consider how little
understanding there is of a Trinitarian faith in wide sections of the
church to realize how true this is. The uniquely Christian faith in
God can be sustained only by an openness of the church to the
unique revelation of the Scriptures.

But it is more than the doctrine of the Trinity that is at stake. That
doctrine is not a statement of abstract truths concerning God but
rather a description of God's action in his coming to man. God the
Father Almighty, Creator of heaven and earth, came into the life of
our humanity in Jesus Christ in order to establish his kingdom in
the midst of time. In the perfect obedience of Jesus in our flesh, in
word and action, in death and resurrection, God's sovereignty was
revealed as man's only hope of true freedom and blessedness. But
if that hope were to be known to all men, there had to be men and
women who in oneness with Jesus Christ would be witnesses before
the world of what life becomes when lived under God's sovereignty.
The oneness with him that the disciples knew in Jesus' lifetime was
not sufficient; their inner resistance to him had to be broken by the
cross, that his Spirit might take possession of them unconditionally
for his ministry. The church was therefore not just a new religious
organization with a superior conception of God and a superior way
of life; it was a human fellowship whose members were bound to
one another not by natural liking but by their sharing of a common
life in God and who were unconditionally at God's disposal that he
might use them to bring the whole of human life under his sovereignty. Each member knew himself committed by his faith to this
ministry. It is *this* understanding of what it means to be the church
which fades and disappears when the authority of God's word in
Scripture is weakened and drained away by the legitimation of
another less demanding revelation of nature and tradition.

Has Scripture itself anything to say on this issue? Proponents of
natural revelation usually quote the Nineteenth Psalm in support of
their position: "The heavens declare the glory of God; and the
firmament showeth his handiwork," or the third chapter of Ro-

mans, where Paul speaks of a knowledge of God's will possessed by all men that makes them to be without excuse in their sin and disobedience. Both are weak supports. It is basic to both Testaments that God is creator of the world and of all mankind. As creator he has left the signs of his handiwork upon all that he has made, and as the sustainer of his creation he has set restraints upon all men to prevent them from destroying themselves utterly. But it is the psalmist who knows God from within the covenant life of Israel who is able to recognize God's handiwork in the starry skies. There is no suggestion anywhere in the Old Testament that, apart from God's revelation of himself in Israel, men are able to know and praise him through the contemplation of his works. On the contrary, it is everywhere assumed that the nations beyond Israel can know God truly only through the witness of Israel. So also with Paul in Romans, the knowledge that the Gentiles have had of God's will does not constitute for Christian Gentiles a second revelation apart from and supplementary to a primary revelation of God in his word, but is like the law in Israel, a knowledge of God so corrupted by human sin that no dependence may be placed upon it at all. Now that God has declared his will for man in Jesus Christ, both Jew and Gentile must draw their knowledge of him wholly from the gospel, and, in so far as the Old Testament law continues to be a source of guidance for the Christian, it must be within the context of the gospel and not as an independent supplementary revelation of God's will. It was on this issue that Paul was so sharply at odds with the Judaizers who made the Old Testament law a secondary revelation that justified them in maintaining much of their Jewish nationalism and many of their Jewish traditional practices. Such secondary revelations have a long history in which they have frequently provided Christians with a validation of institutions and practices that were dear to their hearts.

The exclusiveness of the New Testament concept of revelation is inherent in the canon but comes clearly to expression at a number of points. In Luke 10:21-22, where Jesus speaks of the unique power and knowledge that his disciples now possess in the gospel, he contrasts this with the blindness of the "wise and understanding," a reference undoubtedly to the religious leaders of Judaism. Such knowledge and power have been delivered to him by his Father and are inseparable from his intimate relation with his Father, which he has been able at least in some measure to share with his disciples. So also in John's Gospel the revelation to Jesus of what God is saying and doing is communicated by him in turn to his disciples, and the responsibility rests upon them that this revelation of grace and truth should reach a world that without it remains in darkness.

It is a misreading of the Prologue to John's Gospel that fails to identify the eternal Word with Jesus Christ and so makes of the Light in ch. 1:9 a divine light that quite apart from Jesus Christ lightens every man who comes into the world. Throughout the Gospel of John, Jesus, in whom the eternal Word becomes flesh, is the light that shines for every man. It is said emphatically that both before his incarnation when he was known in the witness of the prophets, and in his earthly life, the world of men rejects his light and clings to its darkness. The world is portrayed as being in darkness until God sends his light. The Word descends into man's darkness to bring him light and life. Apart from the Word, God cannot be rightly known: " No man comes to the Father, but by me " (John 14:6). Whether these passages reflect the mind of Jesus or only the mind of the early church is impossible to determine, but they are conclusive evidence of how the church of the first century understood the revelation from which it had its life. It is impressive that Paul states the same exclusive concept in I Cor., ch. 1, when he distinguishes sharply between the wisdom of men by which they thought to know God and failed and the wisdom of God that cannot be known except where man lets his whole existence be set in question by the cross. Christian knowledge is " a secret and hidden wisdom of God, which God decreed before the ages for our glorification " (I Cor. 2:7), hidden from the wise but revealed to those who die with Christ in his death and rise with him in his resurrection into the life of the Spirit (I Cor. 2:10).

Why is this New Testament assertion of the absolute uniqueness of the Christian revelation so little understood or regarded either in the church at large or among theologians? Why is it so lightly dismissed as an impossible narrowness? Here conservative theologians such as B. B. Warfield and a host of others bear a heavy responsibility for confusing the issue. Instead of defending the absolute uniqueness of God's self-revelation in Jesus Christ and in the witness of Scripture to him, they set out to defend the text of Scripture, the accuracy of historical narratives in Scripture, the inerrancy of every word of Scripture, and the absolute authority of a body of doctrines traditionally derived from Scripture. In the essays of Warfield on the inspiration and authority of Scripture, it is striking how little there is about Jesus Christ. He becomes little more than one of the chief supports for the all-important doctrine of the infallible Scripture. An impersonal authority of sacred documents is substituted for the personal authority of the living God, asserted by him through his Word and Spirit. Thus, while the conservative defenders of Scripture reminded the church that in Scripture there resided an authority that was sovereign, they confused the mind of the church concerning the nature of this authority and engendered a passionate and widespread reaction against what seemed to be a " paper pope." Their example is a warning to us in a time when the Scriptures are recovering their authority as a unique and indispensable witness to the revelation of God. Zeal without discernment may lead again to an undiscriminating attribution of authority to Scripture. The surest safeguard is that all authority in Scripture and in the church should be brought to the test whether or not it is the kind of authority that is validated in the person of Jesus Christ. We dare not recognize any authority that stands in contradiction to the sovereignty of God in him.

[VIII]

THE DEATH AND REBIRTH
OF BIBLICAL THEOLOGY — I

Neglect of
the history
of
interpretation.

T HE DISCUSSION in church and theology of the basic questions with which the preceding chapters have dealt is greatly impeded by the widespread neglect of the history of interpretation. There are few seminaries in which it is taught; the literature on the subject (especially in English) is scanty and much of it deficient in its grasp of the nature of the problems; and yet no student of the Bible can hope to understand the widely divergent and even mutually contradictory approaches of competent contemporary Biblical scholars unless he knows something of the successive stages through which Biblical research has moved during the past two hundred years. The problems that confront us in our understanding of the Bible are most of them the product not of our generation but of developments that began two centuries or more ago, and they have come through various phases on their way to us. The slowness with which the church's ablest scholars have worked their way toward solutions, rarely in a direct line but more often by tacking boldly to and fro, should warn us of the magnitude of the problems and should make us distrustful of all facile answers. We need also to learn to appreciate the importance of achievements in the past by scholars with whose point of view we find ourselves in radical disagreement. The direction and character of their thinking may seem to us perversely awry (as, for instance, D. F. Strauss) and yet may provide an important and valuable contribution to the total process and may point to realities in the Biblical phenomena that we neglect at our peril.

History is particularly valuable in combating naïve false assumptions. The theological student who is introduced to historical criticism in college or seminary comes frequently from a church where the use of Scripture has been completely uncritical, so that to him the approach is new and modern. He thinks of it simply as the intelligent approach in contrast to the unintelligent one. Therefore, he may develop a somewhat arrogant pride in what is no more than a smattering of superficial historical information that leaves him without any real grasp of the meaning of Scripture as a revelation of God to man today, and he may scorn the "ignorant literalist" who unknown to him has been more open in his Bible reading to a word of judgment and promise from God than he himself. An introduction to the positive and negative achievements of historical criticism would dissipate his pride and make him aware of the sobering complexity of the problem in which he and his church are involved.

Again, one hears it said that the present theological emphasis in Biblical studies is only a passing phase, perhaps even a passing craze, engendered by the theology of crisis, one of those extreme reactions from which we shall presently recover and return to a sober, balanced, and less dramatic historical science of the Bible. But when we discover that historical-critical scholarship in the first century of its life was consciously and deliberately a theological discipline, that it lost its theological character (or, more truly, its sense of theological responsibility, since it merely took on a less formal and less recognizable theological character) only in the later years of the nineteenth century, that its loss of theological interest soon began to result in a loss of relevance for the life of the church, and that the recovery of theological interest and concern has already given it new significance for Christians, it begins to seem as though the purely historical phase may prove to have been the passing phase.

Or again, it may be the project of demythologizing that seems to be most modern and relevant. We must clear away the myths of Scripture, we are told, distilling from them their intrinsic significance, or modern man will be offended by these transitory ancient elements in Scripture which have meaning only for the ancient world, and he will never come face to face with the true and decisive offense of the gospel. But this is no new problem. It needs to be faced more courageously by the church in the present, but we should be warned by the history of rationalist interpretation in the eighteenth and nineteenth centuries that scholars have always been inclined to dismiss as mythological anything in Scripture that does not fit into their world view. Demythologizing usually begins with something obvious and indefensible, such as the primitive concept of a three-story cosmos, and gradually works its way to a point where belief in an incarnation of God can be included in the same category.

The Theological Context of Biblical Scholarship

Biblical scholarship always exists in some theological context, since no scholar who is devoid of religious convictions (were such a thing possible) would be likely to busy himself with the Biblical documents. Since the forces of life refuse to be sealed off in separate compartments of the mind, one's theological convictions are certain to exert an influence, even though unconsciously, upon the evaluation of Biblical phenomena. A generation ago it was taken for granted in most quarters in America that a man who held critical views rather than traditional ones on problems of Scripture was a "liberal" or "modernist" in theology. J. Gresham Machen so identified the two in his writings that, after a long and damning analysis of modern immanentalist theology in which he demonstrated convincingly its unbiblical character, he would announce in conclusion that he had now demolished higher criticism, even though the latter had received practically no consideration. But at the opposite extreme many eminent critical scholars made the same assumption: that critical scholarship was possible only upon the basis of a liberal theology of some kind and that defection from liberal theology was likely to injure a man's competence for honest scientific work in the Biblical field.

The absurdity of this assumption becomes evident upon even the slightest acquaintance with the history of interpretation. Scholars of widely varying theologies have made their contributions to the progress of the science, and a resumé of the theologies of active scholars today would show variations all the way from the most liberal to the most conservative. Even those who find it necessary to tie themselves tightly to the dogma of inerrant original texts of Scripture show signs of wanting to take account, so far as it is possible for them, of the results of historical research.[1] Yet, we fail to understand the theological antipathies that are deep-rooted not only in the tradition of orthodoxy but also in the tradition of critical scholarship, and that continue to create complicating tensions in the life of the church, unless we know something of the earlier history of the relationship between the two.

A historical approach to the Biblical records may have had its seeds in Luther's concentration upon the simple literal meaning of the text and Calvin's willingness to recognize a historical process in the formation of Scripture. But the seeds had little opportunity to grow and ripen in their appropriate seed plot, that is, within the exposition of Scripture as practiced by the successors of the Reformers. Protestant scholasticism in its exaltation of the text of Scripture venerated the words themselves as divine, the very words of the Holy Spirit. The freedom of a Luther in the interpretation of Scripture became a thing of the past. Isaac de la Peyrère, of the French Reformed Church, published a book anonymously in 1655 in which he distinguished different elements in the Pentateuch and raised questions about the human story that lay behind the documents. He expressed the view that there must have been men on earth before Adam, since otherwise there was no explanation of how Cain found a wife. His authorship was discovered, and for the temerity of his views he was thrown into prison in Brussels and released only when he disowned his printed statements. In such an atmosphere the historical investigation of Scripture could make little progress. In both Protestant and Roman churches the first tentative essays in critical research were violently suppressed because they seemed to shake the security of the traditional order. Richard Simon, an Oratorian monk, was excluded from his order when he produced a critical history of the Old Testament in 1678, and most of the thirteen hundred copies of his book were burned. It was not until 1776 that one copy that had survived was found and was translated into German by J. S. Semler.

Because there was no room for it in the church where it belonged, the historical investigation of Scripture was forced to find its home

[1] Warren C. Young, "Whither Evangelicalism?" *Bulletin of the Evangelical Theological Society* (Winter, 1959).

elsewhere. Orthodox churchmen might frown on it, but humanist scholars gave it encouragement. They were interested to learn the human story behind all ancient documents and saw no reason why Biblical documents should be excepted. Thus Hugo Grotius' *Annotations to the Old Testament* in 1644 combined philology and text criticism in order to disclose the history behind the Bible, refusing to permit meanings to be read into the text from the New Testament or from dogmatic theology, and insisting that the Old Testament be allowed to tell its own story. Because of his own theological viewpoint he dismissed the idea that the Old Testament text was the medium of a present revelation, and was willing only that moral values should be found in it. In England, a friend of Grotius, Lord Herbert of Cherbury, advanced a similar viewpoint, making the test of a genuine revelation in Scripture whether or not it corresponded to the teaching of man's innate reason. John Spencer, toward the end of the century, deduced a pagan origin for the Hebrew laws of sacrifice and set the Old Testament in the broader context of all human religion. And Thomas Hobbes, in his *Leviathan,* tried to let the Pentateuch itself furnish evidence concerning its origin. The philosopher, Baruch de Spinoza, in his *Tractatus Theologico-Politicus* in 1670, established sound rules of exegesis, repudiating the contemporary practices that extorted false meanings from the text, and taking it as basic that each text should be read in its historical context. He saw the necessity of a history of Biblical literature in order to provide the proper background for exegesis. For his views Spinoza suffered severely at the hands of both orthodox Jews and orthodox Christians.

By 1700 the iron grip of uncompromising orthodoxies had begun to relax at least in some regions of the church. They were discredited in the minds of many by the devastating wars of religion that they had provoked and by the cruelty with which they had tried to beat down opposition. An increasing number of men wanted a less enthusiastic, more reasonable, and more humane religion. This led to some curious combinations. A theologian such as Samuel Werenfels in Basel, who had his like in many other places, combined the humanist tradition of Erasmus, with its emphasis upon reason, with the orthodox Calvinist tradition, with its emphasis upon correct doctrine, and warmed the mixture with an infusion of Moravian pietism. John Wesley's father in England found a similar standpoint sufficiently attractive that as a youth in school he broke with the stricter Puritan tradition for which both his paternal and his maternal ancestors had been willing to sacrifice life and fortune and returned to the Anglican church. But many were willing to dispense with the Calvinism and pietism and to profess a Christianity that was a religion of reason from which all supernatural elements and unreasonable doctrines had been stripped away. It was in this new atmosphere of the eighteenth-century church that the historical investigation of Scripture at last was given its opportunity, and it is not surprising that it found its friends among the more rationalist churchmen and its bitter enemies among the orthodox. But the situation was a new one, because it was now possible in Europe for a professor of theology to engage in critical scholarship without being banished from his office. He might be attacked and in some instances humiliated, but at least he now had legitimate standing ground within the church.

It could be predicted that with such an origin Biblical scholarship in the critical tradition would be more likely to draw its theology from the Renaissance than from the Reformation, and that it would have a strong bent toward rationalist humanism. J. S. Semler, in the latter half of the eighteenth century, symbolizes this development. In him the whole tradition of scientific method developed by the Enlightenment gave new shape to theological method, emancipating theology from its outworn scholastic garments and introducing a totally new freedom of thought. He believed that he was strengthening the church in freeing men from a tyrannical doctrinal system to think for themselves. In regard to the Bible he distinguished between the divine content of truth and the human receptacle and called for the application of the same critical scrutiny that was devoted to other ancient literature. Judging the truth of Scripture by the criteria of rational theology, he found universal and eternal truths in the New Testament but pronounced the Old Testament narrow, national, Jewish, and time-bound. Revelation for him consisted of eternal religious and moral truths. But when the writings of Semler and others like him are examined, it becomes evident that their rationalist spectacles determined in a large measure what they saw in both Testaments. They wrote lives of Jesus in which they cleared away such antique features as his dealings with demons, explained his miracles in a naturalistic fashion, and produced a portrait of a superb eighteenth-century rationalist religious teacher. In the Old Testament everything that was peculiarly Jewish was brushed aside to leave only those elements of religion and morality which would be acceptable to sensible men.

Here we recognize a tradition that was to persist through two centuries, experiencing many changes in detail but retaining its basic orientation. A discipline that was nurtured in the womb of Renaissance thought would retain the marks of its origin through all variations and would have in its blood stream a gratitude and loyalty toward the humanist tradition and a distrust and hostility toward the orthodoxy that tried to strangle it from its very birth. It is ironic that in recent years spokesmen of orthodoxy complain sometimes that critical scholars dismiss them without a hearing. They forget that in the seventeenth and eighteenth centuries in Europe and in the nineteenth and early twentieth centuries in Britain and America, pioneers of critical scholarship had to pay a heavy cost for the right to be heard as long as orthodoxy had control in high places. Also, a careful reading of the history of interpretation would set some question marks against the theory of an inerrant text in the minds of orthodox theologians if they would contemplate the havoc that it has wrought. Defending it today is like trying to continue a battle that was lost, and well lost, two hundred years ago. It is only an unthinking traditionalism, blind to the new and more vital issues with which God confronts us, that continues unabated the orthodox hostility of that time toward all critical scholarship. But equally fallacious and unthinkingly traditional is a critical scholarship that holds to a humanist theology in conscious or unconscious antipathy to any theology that even remotely resembles orthodoxy. It is curious that today both the orthodox and the liberal or humanist scholar, when they protest against new developments, do so as doughty conservatives who are defending the heritage of the past against the threat of the new.

THE BIBLICAL SCHOLAR ORIGINALLY A THEOLOGIAN

For a full century after Semler began his work, there was no question in anyone's mind but that the Biblical scholar was a responsible theologian of the church. This fact is forgotten in the English-speaking world where critical studies of Scripture have had a much briefer history. From 1750 to 1850, which may be defined as the early theological period on the Continent, only the slightest essays in critical research were attempted in Britain or America. Coleridge wrote his influential *Confessions of an Inquiring Spirit* early in the century. Connop Thirlwall published a translation of Schleiermacher's commentary on Luke's Gospel in 1825, in his preface criticizing the theory of verbal inspiration, and he was so brutally attacked because of it that he did nothing more of that kind. In 1846, F. D. Maurice, who was not noted for his timidity, advised Caroline Fox not to translate Schleiermacher's sermons because of the English hostility to German theological works.[2] E. B. Pusey visited Germany in 1825 and on his return wrote an essay on certain aspects of critical scholarship, but he was criticized by Keble and John Henry Newman so sharply for seeing any promise of good in it that he avoided all contact with it for the rest of his life and later persecuted bitterly the instigator of the 1860 publication of *Essays and Reviews,* which advocated a historical approach to Scripture.

The consequence of this general atmosphere which extended through the whole English-speaking world was that the battle for the establishment of critical scholarship in the churches of Britain and America was a century or more late and developments were telescoped into one generation that on the Continent were worked out with thoroughness over a long period. As in Europe, so also in Britain and America the pioneers were theologians, men such as A. B. Davidson, W. Robertson Smith, and C. A. Briggs in Old Testament, and B. F. Westcott, F. J. Hort, and others of similar type in New Testament. But already in Germany a purely historical science had taken the place of one that was both historical and theological, and in America, where German influence was stronger than in Britain, this new development cut the theological era so short that it almost passed unnoticed. Gerald Birney Smith, in an article in the *Journal of Religion* in 1925, bore witness both to the shallowness of the theological rootage of American Biblical scholarship in the nineteenth century and the loss even of that slight rootage by the end of the first quarter of the twentieth century. " During the nineties ' Biblical theology' began to be emphasized in several theological seminaries. But by the beginning of the twentieth century the vogue of this new [*sic*] discipline was waning, and the subject itself gradually disappeared. . . . Biblical scholars came to be more and more interested in the task of recovering the details of an ancient culture and in reconstructing the history of that culture. The question of the relationship of Biblical scholarship to systematic theology eventually ceased to concern them." [3] Naturally an interest so slight and so brief failed to produce any significant fruit, so that in America it is hardly true to speak of a death and rebirth of Biblical theology.

The story in Europe was very different. A critical and historical approach to Scripture was substituted for an uncritical one, but the determination to understand the literature and history was coupled with the expectation that theology would be greatly enriched by the clarification of the meaning of Scripture. One of the sources of confusion in the preceding period had been the failure of theologians to discriminate between a dogmatic theology and a Biblical theology. In 1787 Johann Philip Gabler called for a clear distinction between the two, the Biblical theologian confining himself to the task of elucidating the theology intrinsic to the various Biblical documents and the dogmatic theologian dealing with the faith of the church that is built upon the Biblical basis. It was clear to him that Biblical theology required a historical approach, but he had no intention of divorcing the historical from the theological task. The crowning achievement of Biblical scholarship was to be the writing of a Biblical theology in which the Bible would speak for itself without being forced into the uncongenial forms of the dogmatic theologians. It was in line with this that in 1792 C. F. Ammon produced an *Outline of a Purely Biblical Theology,* and in 1796 appeared a *Theology of the Old Testament,* by G. L. Bauer.

That Biblical scholars counted themselves theologians is evident from the broad responsibilities they undertook in the faculty of theology. De Wette published works on Protestant theology and Christian ethics and edited the letters and papers of Luther. He also worked in both Testaments and published in 1831 a *Biblical Dog-*

[3] Gerald Birney Smith, " A Quarter-Century of Theological Thinking in America," JR, V (1925).

matics of the Old and New Testaments, or a Critical Portrayal of the Religious Teaching of Hebraism, Judaism, and Early Christianity. The historian and the theologian were united in one soul. Ewald, who wrote the first full-scale history of Israel as well as many other volumes on the Old Testament, published no less than seven books on the New Testament. The age of intensive specialization had not yet begun.

The work of each of these scholars bears plainly upon its face the marks of the particular theology that he found most convincing. This was eventually to be one of the main phenomena that provoked a reaction and inspired the attempt to establish a pure (i.e., untheological) science of Biblical research: diverse theologies and philosophies led to such diverse conclusions from the same evidence. Eichhorn was a rationalist theologian who saw Moses as the great rationalist educator and read the books of the Old Testament as " the record of the rational religion of antiquity in which we can follow the gradual ascent of human reason to the lofty doctrine of monotheism." [4] Gabler and others were quite confident that they could distinguish " what conceptions belong to the permanent structure of Christian teaching and so concern us directly and what ones are spoken only for the men of a particular age." [5] A line could be drawn between the mythical and the historical, between unworthy forms of religion and the truly reasonable and divine religion.

De Wette was strongly under the spell of the philosopher Fries and worked out a theology that, he hoped, would avoid the weaknesses of both rationalism and orthodoxy. As a consequence, he was regarded as a pietist by the rationalists and as a rationalist by the pietists, an almost sure sign that he was breaking through traditional attitudes with courage. Delitzsch had his orthodox Lutheranism to which he was devoted and went through severe spiritual struggles at each step of progress in his critical pilgrimage. Vatke, going from Hegel to the study of the Old Testament, carried his Hegelian philosophy of history with him and tried to explain the history of Israel as a progress of thesis, antithesis, and synthesis, a pattern into which the facts could not be forced but a principle of development

[4] H. J. Kraus, *Geschichte der historisch-kritischen Erforschung des Alten Testaments von der Reformation bis zur Gegenwart* (1956), p. 126.

[5] W. G. Kümmel, *Das Neue Testament. Geschichte der Erforschung seiner Probleme* (1958), p. 117.

Read this book

that helped break through the old static conception of Israel. In the New Testament F. C. Baur applied the same principle to the early history of the church, identifying Jewish Christianity as the thesis, Gentile Christianity as the antithesis, and Catholic Christianity as the synthesis, a schema that, while it ultimately was to prove inadequate, provoked scholars to think in terms of historical development.

In Britain, where critical scholarship was not introduced until about 1860, its character was greatly influenced by the soil in which it grew. The earliest German scholars in the mid-eighteenth century grew up in an atmosphere of rationalism or mingled rationalism and orthodoxy. The earliest British scholars grew up in the mid-nineteenth century in an atmosphere of evangelicalism. W. Robertson Smith, a brilliant Old Testament scholar, was a theologian of no mean ability, deeply loyal to an intelligent Reformed tradition in doctrine, whose service to the Christian church, however, was tragically cut short by a misguided but successful process against him. A. B. Davidson considered himself both historian and theologian, and his works show more emphasis on the theology than on the history. T. K. Cheyne could write in the preface to his *Founders of Old Testament Criticism* (1893): "We cannot be mere historical or literary critics; we feel that we must contribute, each in his degree, to the construction of an improved Christian apologetic for our own age."

A scholar of a very different character, whom we usually associate with Plato rather than with the Bible, is Benjamin Jowett, who suffered severe persecution from Evangelical and Anglo-Catholic leaders for his early and outspoken advocacy of a historical and critical study of Scripture. Having had a rigid evangelicalism forced upon him in his home, he reacted passionately against it and longed to see a more intelligent theology established in England. He was a liberal in his views, largely as a protest against the severities of evangelicalism, but one who so desired that the Bible be rightly heard that he would have spent his life as a theologian and exegete had he not been dissuaded from it by the ferocity of religious leaders in high places. He paid dearly for having an essay in the *Essays and Reviews* of 1860. Westcott, Lightfoot, and Hort were to fare better at the hands of the church and were to establish in England a tradition of capable critical scholarship of a conservative and evangelical quality. Perhaps it was because the distrust of German Biblical scholarship was so strong in England that the initial period in which theological interest was combined with the historical and critical concern lasted much longer and was much more productive than in America.[6] Yet here also, as in Europe and America, the theological responsibility of the Biblical scholar was to recede and vanish. Why it did so we shall have to examine with care, but first we must give attention to another significant, but at the time unappreciated, development in the early period in Germany.

Two Warning Voices

It was generally assumed that historical method, because it would uncover the truth about the past, would be certain to prove a handmaid to reasonable and intelligent faith. All one had to do was to be honest in reading the documents, whereupon the crude conceptions of deity, the superstitions, and the primitive religious practices that were an embarrassment in Scripture would fall away and leave only a pure religion and a faultless Jesus, the sum of all perfection. The first suggestion that a more rigorous historical method might produce other and less reassuring results came with Lessing's publication in 1774 of fragments of the writings of Hermann Samuel Reimarus on the life of Jesus. Reimarus had died in 1768. He was for years a professor of Oriental languages in Hamburg and an advocate of a religion of reason, which he much preferred to the faith of the church in any of its forms. He did not examine the Gospels as an impartial spectator but as an impassioned antagonist. Nevertheless, he was a thorough historian and submitted the documents to a searching criticism. "This was the first time that a really historical mind, thoroughly conversant with the sources, had undertaken the criticism of the tradition."[7] The Jesus whom he brought to light was not the figure with whom men had grown familiar and content. He was a Jew not only in his physical features but also in his thought-forms and in his religion. The Kingdom of God that he proclaimed was the new political era that all his countrymen were expecting to dawn soon. Jesus told men that it might come at

---

[6] This conservatism had also a wasteful aspect. In English Johannine studies between 1880 and 1920, able scholars expended their energies in defense of the apostolic authorship of the gospel almost as though the fate of Christianity depended upon the issue.

[7] Albert Schweitzer, *The Quest of the Historical Jesus,* p. 15.

any moment and lived in this tense expectation. He had no intention of founding a new church or of breaking with Judaism in any way. That he did no miraculous works is evident from the fact that he paid no heed to the demand of his contemporaries for a sign, that is, for a miracle to vindicate his divine power. He hoped to be acclaimed Messiah and to have the people rally behind him in a successful revolt against Rome, and when he was disappointed he died in despair. The story of the resurrection was invented by the disciples in order to provide a basis for continuing their movement.

The embarrassment of Reimarus' portrait was that he made Jesus' Jewish features, such as the eschatological tension and his conformity to religious practices of Judaism, essential to him where these had formerly been dismissed as unessential to the real Jesus. Also, the outcome of his application of the historical method to the sources suggested that perhaps the rationalist theologians of the church had arrived at their portrait of Jesus by disregarding whatever displeased them in the sources. But Reimarus was only one voice against many — and he was dead. He could be safely disregarded. He was disregarded completely until D. F. Strauss brought him again to the fore; then, late in the nineteenth century, he came to be recognized as a pioneer in having discerned the Jewish and eschatological character of Jesus' preaching. The warning of Reimarus, however, should have been that, while objective historical investigation is essential in letting the sources speak for themselves, there are realities behind the sources that historical method itself is not able to disclose. The historian must know the limitations of his method. Both Reimarus and his opponents failed in their attempts to draw the portrait of Jesus. By this the question could and should have been raised sharply: Why should there be such difficulty? and How, then, is this Jesus to be known?

D. F. Strauss   The second warning voice came sixty years later when D. F. Strauss published his *Life of Jesus* in 1835. The shock that he gave to Christians of all complexions, orthodox and rationalist alike, was in challenging the validity of the image of Jesus that they were drawing from the New Testament. Orthodox and rationalist might disagree with each other radically at many points, but they were united in regarding the Gospels as historical documents through which they could have direct access to Jesus as a historical person.

The orthodox accepted as historical some elements in the story that the rationalist dismissed as mythical, so that the Jesus of the one was a divine wonder-working Savior while the Jesus of the other was the supremely reasonable religious teacher. But both built their structures with complete reliance that a Jesus was historically available to them in the New Testament. There was no mystery about knowing Jesus, disagreement perhaps on details, but no reason for any mystery. Therefore, Strauss shattered both structures by setting this common assumption in question, and he could look for support in neither direction. First he evaluated the Gospels as historical sources and came to the conclusion that the form of the New Testament narration is not that of a historical report but that of a myth.[8] It describes primarily not the movements and words of a man among men but a divine being appearing for a time on earth, conquering unseen evil powers and ascending in triumph to heaven. Concerning such a story, the historian who approaches his sources without assumptions has to say that the events described are not what he recognizes as historical events and the person described is not the kind of human being that he finds everywhere else in history. The logical, psychological, and physiological laws that apply to human persons do not apply to this person.

That there was a real human person called Jesus round whom this mass of mythological narration had grown up in the first century A.D. was not questioned by Strauss, and occasionally he suggests that we may discern the figure of a Jewish teacher who lived in tense expectation of the Last Days and the coming of God's Kingdom on earth, but his constant insistence is that Jesus as a man is not available in the New Testament records, since their authors had no interest in portraying the man Jesus. Glimpses of his human life are only incidental, but are sufficient to suggest the invalidity of existing portrayals of the Jesus of history. Later, Strauss was to describe the real Jesus as a noble spiritual enthusiast whom we would never choose as a religious leader, but his more consistent standpoint was that Jesus was so deified in the records that too little was known of his personality for men to base their religious consciousness in any way upon him. We can well understand that the orthodox

---

[8] A. Schweitzer, *op. cit.*, pp. 68 ff. Karl Barth, *David Friedrich Strauss als Theologe, 1839–1939.*

churchmen found themselves more at home with the rationalist life of Jesus by Paulus than with Strauss, because Paulus at least left them a historical person on whom to pin their faith. Strauss himself had drawn from Hegel's philosophy a faith that in Jesus a God-manhood was realized that made him the supreme manifestation of Spirit, or truth, in history. Since no idea can ever be perfectly realized in the human sphere, it did not trouble him that there should be flaws in the manifestation. He felt himself free, therefore, to let the New Testament records be what they were and tell their story in their own way.

Both Reimarus and Strauss raised questions about the historical approach to Scripture that should have commanded the most thorough theological investigation. Their questions were brushed aside and even today in many quarters continue to be brushed aside. Does the Christian faith stand or fall by the validity of the picture of the man Jesus that is extracted from the Gospels, or is this a Jesusolatry unknown in the New Testament church and actually a device by which men are able to incarnate their own religious and ethical ideals in Jesus? The question also concerns the Old Testament. Is the historian able to portray objectively the religion of the prophets or of the psalmists so that merely by psychological penetration we can understand what God was to them, or does he merely bring us to the point where face to face with prophet or psalmist a dialogue is possible between them and us in which the God who was known to them may actually make himself known to us? To what extent can historical scholarship penetrate the meaning of Scripture, so that it reaches beyond the description of religious practices and ideas and experiences and discloses the actual content of God's revelation of himself to man?

Rationalist theology identified the revelation of God with eternal truths and principles that it was able to separate from their temporary excrescences and find ready to hand in an authoritative form in Scripture. Orthodox theology identified the revelation of God with the entire text of Scripture but specifically with the doctrines that it found immediately present in Scripture. But now Strauss, like the naïve child in the story of " The Emperor's Clothes," blurted out what he saw in Scripture with the clear eyes of the historian — not what all men had been taught to see and so thought they saw but rather what the text itself actually portrayed. To many Christians ' he had taken away their Jesus, and they knew not where he had laid him. Had they known their day, they would have thanked Strauss for his negative achievement and would have read their New Testament afresh, understanding as they had not before that flesh and blood, that is, historical and psychological penetration, cannot pierce the secret either of Jesus or of the meaning of Scripture as a whole.

Because Strauss was not understood, Biblical scholarship became dominated by an inordinate confidence in the power of historical interpretation to disclose the ultimate meaning of the text of Scripture. History was to be the instrument whereby man would at last get at the truth of things. The method was already fully developed in the secular sphere and in the hands of great historians had brought a totally new understanding of what had actually happened in certain periods of the past. It had disclosed a new and fascinating world behind the Scriptures. Everything depended upon the objectivity of the historian. He had to put aside as completely as possible all his own prejudices and preferences. He would then be able by a critical examination of the evidence to declare the facts with certainty. This offered an enticing prospect to the Biblical scholar. It was only too clear to him that the defect in Biblical science thus far had been that each scholar approached the text of Scripture with a fully defined theology or philosophy that he hoped would be vindicated by what he found there. Exegesis had been emancipated from the dominance of an orthodox theology that assumed that it was present everywhere in the text. The old tyranny was gone, but in its place was confusion, as each interpreter found his own private theology in the text. The vitiating factor was the theology of the interpreter. Therefore, the cure was for Biblical scientists to divest themselves of all theological presuppositions and approach the text of Scripture with a mind that was practically a *tabula rasa*. The logic of the argument was irresistible. The dominance in European culture of a positivist philosophy with its devotion to facts and scientific method provided an appropriate background. But the assumption on the basis of which this Biblical science was to proceed for three quarters of a century was the one that Strauss had already shattered in 1835 — the assumption that the Biblical documents are historical

the false assumption of historicism

records that may be expected to yield their full content readily to the competent and unprejudiced historical investigator.

THE TRIUMPH OF HISTORICISM

In the mid-nineteenth century Biblical scholarship, then, underwent a profound change. The demand that for the sake of historical objectivity the scholar should put aside his theological convictions in his approach to Scripture was recognized as so difficult to effect that he frequently decided to withhold himself entirely from theological interests and pursuits for the sake of his science. He should be content to be a descriptive historian. But this was only one factor in the change. Closely related to it was the substitution of the word " religion " for " revelation." Ewald, in his *History of the People of Israel,* aimed to write the story of the development of " the perfect true religion." Religion is a human phenomenon that can be observed and described in its practices and ideas and experiences. God enters the picture then only as the idea of a particular man in a particular time. Revelation in which God reveals not just something about himself but himself as a living, acting God, who can be known to man only in a personal relationship in which man responds to him in faith and love, is a reality of a kind with which historical science has not the equipment to deal. Therefore, it is in the nature of things that the historian who refuses to be a theologian can make the materials that confront him in the Bible manageable only by dismissing the Biblical reality of revelation and substituting for it an *idea* of revelation that is only one of the factors in man's religion.

The idea of development was in the air early in the nineteenth century and began to be applied as a principle of explanation to all manner of phenomena. Earlier scholars had had very little comprehension of the various stages of growth that can be recognized in the institutions, social life, and religious ideas of the Hebrew people. The Bible was interpreted on one level and in static terms without any clear distinctions between the different periods. J. G. Herder, at the end of the eighteenth century, had brought to his Biblical studies a more highly developed historical sense. The rationalist may have considered all primitive forms and expressions crude and low, but Herder's romantic mind appreciated the possible profundity both of the child and of the primitive man. Herder, however, was not much heeded until later. William Vatke and F. C. Baur as disciples of Hegel, while they tended to force phenomena into an artificial schema, nevertheless taught men to look for signs of development. The new principle was of great value in bringing order and meaning into the vast complex of Biblical phenomena. But, as so often happens with new discoveries, too much was expected of it. It was thought that each event, each document, each custom, each law, each idea, had only to be given its proper place in a process of development and it was thereby accounted for. A demonstration of historical origin was taken to be a demonstration of significance. When ideas of God in Israel had been ranged in ascending order from the most primitive to the most intellectually acceptable, it was taken for granted that we now understood how man came to believe in one God of truth and holiness. It was unnoticed that history, in order to explain the God of the Scriptures, had had to reduce him to a sequence of abstract ideas.

There was also in the air a belief in the inevitability of progress. S. R. Driver,[9] in his commentary on Genesis, could write: " Progress: gradual advance from lower to higher, from the less perfect to the more perfect, is the law which is stamped upon the entire range of organic nature, as well as upon the history of the civilization and education of the human race." Not yet had Spengler and Toynbee pricked the optimism of modern man with their graphs concerning the decline of civilizations, nor had twentieth-century catastrophies made man doubt the inevitability of his own progress. A schema was superimposed upon the Old Testament by which Israelites were depicted in their slow but sure growth from the lowest forms of religion to the highest. Everything in the earliest stage had to be primitive and low. Therefore, Israel in the desert was assumed to have been on a level comparable to modern nomads. Moses had to be denuded of all profound significance and represented as merely a noble pagan. All prophets before Amos had to be reduced in stature by assuming that later writers had removed at least some of their pagan characteristics and endowed them with virtues of the great prophets. The growth of a higher faith in Israel was portrayed as the result of the clash between the nomadic religion the Israelites

[9] S. R. Driver, *The Book of Genesis,* p. 56.

brought with them from the desert and the more developed Canaanite religion and culture of Palestine. No psalm that showed loftiness of conception could be attributed to the period before the eighth century, since it was Amos who first pointed Israel toward a higher level of religion. The supreme achievements of prophetic religion were explained not as the product of revelation but as the end result of a natural historical process.

Such a viewpoint is a historical curiosity in the mid-twentieth century. We are only too acutely aware that the natural course of development in religion and morals both for individuals and nations is as often downward as upward. No Old Testament historian of today would any longer be attracted by the old schema, since for him the history of Israel's religion follows a zigzag line, with primitive and highly developed forms of religion side by side in most periods. But it was convincing to an earlier day and contributed heavily to the triumph of historicism. Today the viewpoint of the prophets themselves is taken more seriously — that moral and spiritual progress in Israel was directly dependent upon the relation of the nation to God.

Another factor in the background that exerted strong pressure on Biblical studies was the trend away from doctrine and theology that was widely characteristic of Protestantism in the latter half of the nineteenth century. The beginnings of the trend can be seen in Schleiermacher early in the century. Reacting against the wooden doctrines of both the orthodox and the rationalist theologians, he was trying to find a way of speaking of the Christian faith in which words would correspond to realities. For him the basic reality of which he had immediate knowledge was the experience of God in the lives of Christian people. Religion was not adherence to a set of theological propositions but a life that a man lived in God. In his approach to the cultured despisers of religion, for whom all logical arguments on behalf of Christian doctrines were unconvincing, he sought to show them that already in their response to life they had bowed before realities and experienced feelings that were of the essence of religion. The inner experience was the core of the matter, and all else in Christian faith and doctrine was simply a tracing out of the implications of the inner experience.

This emphasis upon experience, combined with the contemporary enthusiasm for the methods of natural science, seemed to offer theology a new and objective basis. In religious experience it would have a body of data upon which it could go to work in a thoroughly scientific manner and thus gain for its conclusions an objective validity that no reasonable man would be able to resist, any more than he could resist the findings of other sciences. After Schleiermacher's time the scope of the investigation was progressively widened, first to take in all Christian experience through the ages, and then, as advancing knowledge of non-Christian religions exhibited striking parallels to the Christian, to include all the data of human religion. But since it proves ever more difficult to draw a line between religious experience and other experience, eventually all human experience must be comprehended by such a science. Thus arose the modern science of religion,[10] which was expected to remove mystery and confusion from the subject by defining for us with scientific accuracy the nature of religion. It is fitting to recall that at the end of the first quarter of the twentieth century, this viewpoint was so dominant that the discipline of systematic theology seemed likely to wither and vanish, to be replaced by the history and philosophy of religion. In a period so completely dominated by the idea of a science of religion based upon experience, it was not strange that Old and New Testament scholars should see their task to be the accurate description of religious phenomena in Israel, Judaism, and the New Testament church.

The broadened interest in the history of religion was in a large measure a product of the modern missionary movement. The missionary who wished to deal intelligently with the adherents of non-Christian religions had to become a careful student of those religions, and he brought home with him materials and concern that gave birth to the study of comparative religion. Also in mid-century, the opening up of various Near-Eastern cultures through archeology and the decipherment of ancient writings brought a wealth of religious parallels that were henceforward to form a background for the study of the Bible. Biblical history ceased to be the story of an isolated people and became one strand, the most significant strand,

---

[10] John Baillie's *The Interpretation of Religion* is an excellent example of this scientific approach which he was to abandon for a very different one in the course of his life as a theologian.

in the history of the Near East. These latter developments focused the attention on the problems of comparative languages, literature, and religious phenomena, and the field became so complex that it was easy for the Biblical scholar to feel that theology was a subject that he could safely leave to someone else. Perhaps the new developments also attracted to Biblical studies scholars who were more interested in the philological, literary, and historical aspects of the subject than the theological. These factors were undoubtedly accentuated by the extreme hostility that was widespread in the churches, both in Britain and America, toward all critical scholarship. It was dangerous for the scholar to meddle with theological questions. It was much safer to confine one's attention to language, literature, and history.

THE PROTEST ON BEHALF OF REVELATION

In the early nineteenth century on the Continent the major Biblical professorships were occupied by critical scholars, and orthodoxy was thrown decidedly on the defensive. But because it still had strength in the church, it was able to place its representatives in a few strategic chairs. The wholesale rejection of the developments of one hundred years in Biblical study could not be maintained by men who professed to be scholars. They too were children of their time and had to take account of the new historical approach if they expected to be heard. Their viewpoint on most questions, however, was extremely conservative, and they were prevented by their cautious conservatism from making a bold approach to most of the critical problems.

At one point they had now a real vocation: speaking out on behalf of the revelational character of Scripture. They might confuse the issue by identifying the text of Scripture directly and without qualification with the revelation of God, but at least they led men to expect in Scripture something more than the story of a succession of ancient religions. Rudolf Kittel tells of the profound religious impression J. T. Beck (1804–1878) made upon him, even though he found himself forced to follow a course in Biblical research that Beck could not approve,[11] and it was undoubtedly this influence

[11] E. Stange, ed., *Die Religionswissenschaft der Gegenwart in Selbstdarstellungen.* Vol. 1 (1925), p. 114.

combined with that of his evangelical home that made him dissatisfied with a Biblical science that no longer considered itself a ministry of the church. Beck elaborated a hermeneutic in which Scripture was described as having body, soul, and spirit. The body was the historical-grammatical text; the soul, the psychological content; and the spirit, the divine meaning. The inspiration of Scripture was primarily the inspiration of the holy men from whom it came. Spiritual exegesis had to penetrate to the divine meaning, which, when grasped, was found to comprehend also the psychological and the historical-grammatical. The succession of inspired persons constituted a sacred history in the midst of the world. This was far removed from the static orthodoxy of a century earlier.

J. C. K. von Hofmann (1810–1877) is usually remembered as the elaborator of the conception of sacred history. Like Beck, he broke away from the old orthodox identification of revelation with revealed doctrines and recognized that, in Scripture, God is portrayed as revealing himself in history. The heavenly order presses in upon the earthly ever more and more until Christ comes. The revelation does not merely occur in history but rather weaves itself into history until it forms an objective, visible, linear course of development. The goal of the sacred history is Jesus Christ, and the record of it is Scripture. To understand this history, however, one has to stand within it by faith and be enlightened by the Holy Spirit, so that interpretation combines spiritual and historical understanding, with the former being primary. The revelation in sacred history was the revelation of the meaning of all history, so that Scripture contained within it the explication of all events that would ever happen in the life of the world. This seemed to make room both for the recognition of God's self-revealing activity and for the historical investigation of Scripture. But it created an insoluble problem in identifying revelation with a specific strand of human history within the history of Israel and the church. It assumed that when the Spirit-enlightened historian examined the history of Israel, he would be able to lay bare in an objective way this strand of revelation. The question had still to be faced whether the revelation of God in any form could be grasped and represented by historical means. Most certainly the revelation-event, whether it is Isaiah's vision of God or Peter's understanding of the secret of Jesus' being, is an event in history and can be reported by the human witness, but the historian is not bound to give the events the same interpretation that they received from Isaiah and Peter. It has still to be decided whether the sacred history is really sacred or is the product of an agelong delusion.

A pupil of von Hofmann's, Aug. Köhler, saw the problem and redefined the sacred history as the history of the revelations of God reflected in the consciousness of Israel as the church of the Old Testament.[12] It was clear to him that its interpretation was a theological rather than a historical task. Ernst Sellin, a pupil of Köhler's, thought him the apostle of a new time because he preserved the scientific character of Old Testament studies and at the same time their theological and churchly character. Sellin in his own work tried to combine the historical and the theological. For J. Köberle, however, the revelation was not in a sacred strand of history but in the profane history of the nation, recognizable at three points: in the unique historical experiences of the nation, in the unique prophetic interpretation of these experiences, preceding and accompanying them, and in the appropriation of this interpretation by an ever-greater section of the nation. The sacred history was thus hidden in the entire history of Israel, so that no simple line could be drawn between the sacred and the secular. Here one sees the origin in conservative scholarship of those conceptions of sacred history which hold a prominent place in present-day theological discussions.

Martin Kähler [13] in 1896 made a significant contribution to the understanding of the relation between revelation and history in the New Testament. After twenty years of investigating the origins of the New Testament writings, he came to the conclusion that, important as such research was, no assured results could ever be reached by a purely historical method. It was only too clear that the conclusions of liberal and conservative scholars alike were what they were because of the assumptions with which they approached the sources. It was intolerable that Christians should be dependent for their knowledge of Jesus Christ upon a historical scholarship that could reach no certain conclusions, at least in common or for any

Kähler

important
as point
of reference

p. 304

[12] Franz Hesse, "Die Erforschung der Geschichte Israels als theologische Aufgabe, *Kerygma und Dogma*, Vol. 4 (1958).

[13] Martin Kähler, *Der sogenannte historische Jesus und der geschichtliche biblische Christus.*

length of time. Equally intolerable was it that conservative scholars should make salvation contingent upon an infallibility of doctrine received directly from Jesus through apostolic eyewitnesses, since one's eternal welfare would then depend upon a proof of authorship.

Kähler therefore took a new starting point. The Biblical writings, he observed, were not written as historical documents but as witness to God. It was this witness which founded the church, and throughout history it has proved its power to bring renewal in the church. The writings are perfectly adapted to this purpose, even though to science they may seem to be defective historical documents. Their intention was not scientific biography but the awakening of faith in Jesus as Savior through the proclamation of his saving activity. The revelation in them is beyond the reach of historical research, and so also is the action of God by which he brought the Gospels into being. Therefore, we must not attempt to go behind the kerygma of the early church that we have in the New Testament, for the revelation is embodied for us in the kerygma, and when we try to re-create a Jesus of history other than the Biblical Christ who is proclaimed in the kerygma we only bring ourselves into confusion. "The historical Jesus of the modern author conceals from us the living Christ." "The real Christ is the Christ who is preached." He is known only to faith, but no man need seek him in the Scriptures in vain. What Kähler is saying is that if we would know Jesus Christ, we must receive the apostolic witness so that we know him in the fellowship of his apostles, seeing him through their eyes, the eyes of faith, and not merely seeing some kind of reconstructed figure of Jesus of Nazareth, shaped as much by the modern scholar's assumptions as by the New Testament material. Kähler, like others we have considered, represents a revolt against the general trend of scholarship and had to wait a quarter century for his work to bear fruit.

Mention should be made of one conservative scholar in Britain who might be classed to some degree with Beck and von Hofmann, James Orr of Glasgow. His *Revelation and Inspiration,* published in 1910, admits the necessity of critical scholarship but puts the emphasis upon revelation. "The one thing criticism can never expunge from this book, the Bible, is what we speak of as the gospel — its continuous, coherent, self-attesting discovery to man of the mind of God regarding man himself, his sin, the guilt and ruin into which his sin has plunged him, and over against that the method of a divine salvation, the outcome of a purpose of eternal love, wrought out in ages of progressive revelation, and culminating in the mission, life, death, atoning work, and resurrection of his Son Jesus Christ, and in the gift of his Spirit to the church and believers." It is the hearing of this gospel that is the only proof men can have that the Bible is God's Word. God's revelation of himself was in divine acts, saving acts, that formed the basis of the prophet's knowledge of God and confidence in him. Revelation was not inconsistent with a progress in understanding and doctrine in Israel, at each stage those elements which were accidental and temporary falling into the background and all that was vital and permanent in the preceding stages being carried forward. Thus far Orr's development of the subject is promising, but when the revelation is identified by him as being " practically synonymous and coextensive " with Scripture, it becomes necessary for him at all costs to defend the veracity of the Biblical narrative in every detail. Historical investigation begins then to lose the freedom to do its work, and the discussion of Scripture becomes an interminable apologetic for everything that stands written that might be offensive to the mind of modern man.

ON THE BORDER BETWEEN THEOLOGY AND HISTORY

Conservative scholars failed in their protest on behalf of revelation because they were unwilling to grant history its full rights. The demand for an honest historical approach to Scripture was too strong to be resisted, and there could be no limits placed upon it, no line drawn beyond which it dared not go. It had to learn for itself the inherent limitations of its method. But as the nineteenth century drew to its close there appeared two works that had a strong appeal in many quarters because they were both historical and theological. They sought to give full scope to the claims of history and yet to maintain a theological interpretation of the Old Testament. We need to ask why with them the theological interest died.

The first is a two-volume work by Hermann Schultz [14] in which he defined Old Testament theology as " That branch of theological science which gives a historical presentation of revealed religion during the period of its growth. . . . The task of Biblical theology

---

[14] H. Schultz, *Old Testament Theology*, pp. 2, 10.

is thus purely historical." " We must determine by purely historical tests what were the moral and religious principles which at each separate period of Israel's history were either expressly asserted or else implied in its forms and ceremonies." The two key words, " revelation " and " religion," are combined into one entity, and the revelation in religion clearly consists of moral and religious principles. Revelation has been denatured and no longer has its specific Biblical meaning. Schultz was aware that the standpoint of any historian must influence his conclusions. " No spiritual movement can or will reveal itself in all its truth except to one who, having come under its charm, keenly appreciates its real meaning and takes an interest in all its peculiar characteristics." But to be charmed and interested was something less than participation with one's existence through faith. It meant only a sympathetic attempt to understand the religion from within. Schultz also saw the need to establish a clear distinction between Biblical and systematic theology. " It is one of the most important and difficult tasks of modern theology to put an end to this vague confusion between Biblical theology and systematized evangelical doctrine." " The subject matter of the Bible cannot be the immediate foundation of Christian belief. . . . Scientific theology has become conscious that the old evangelical presupposition that the doctrine of the Bible and the Christianity of the church are in perfect harmony, is no longer tenable. . . . Systematic theology has to present in one harmonious whole the moral and religious consciousness of an evangelical Christian of the present day. . . . Biblical theology has to show, from a purely historical standpoint, what were the doctrinal views and moral ideas which animated the leading spirits of our religion during the Biblical period of its growth."

Much of this is quite valid, but Schultz went on to describe the Biblical period as " not merely the beginning but also the classical standard of all Christian literature and Biblical theology (as) the description of that perfect typical development by which all later ecclesiastical work must be measured." He wanted to free the church from the old slavish subservience to whatever " doctrinal views and moral ideas " might be proved to be present in the Scriptures and yet to retain something in Scripture as the criterion and authority over the church's life. But where in Scripture could he find that " perfect typical development "? What he was looking for in Scripture was a form of religion, in the midst of the varied religious phenomena, that could be accepted as the true and genuine religion by comparison with which the truth and genuineness of religion through the ages might be measured. But the forms of religion in each age in Scripture have characteristics that belong to that age alone. The religion of Jesus and of Paul is, in some respects at least, the religion of devout Jews of the first century. The error of Judaistic Christianity was in making the religious practices of Jesus authoritative for all time. Approached merely as the record of religion or religions in Biblical times, the Bible thus confronts us with so many and varied forms of religion that it becomes very difficult to discern what is authoritative.

The weakness of this work is that in attempting to preserve in some measure the nomenclature of revelation and theology while writing a history of Israelite religion, it succeeded only in confusing the two. The " religion of revelation " cannot be identified directly with the religion of Israel or with selected " doctrinal views and moral ideas "; rather, it was the religion of only a segment of the nation and existed always in tension with prevalent beliefs and practices. The term itself is highly questionable. It makes revelation merely one of the significant characteristics of a religion, while in Scripture revelation always cuts across and sets in question the existing religion. Revelation is God in action, a God who refuses to become even the most significant element in man's religion. Schultz has essentially lost the basis for a Biblical theology.

The second borderline work was A. B. Davidson's *Theology of the Old Testament.*[15] He too found himself torn between the two tasks, the theological and the historical, but, unlike Schultz, he did more justice to the former than to the latter. It is difficult to know the final issue of his thinking from a book that was put together after his death from notes left by him. In the earlier pages (which may not be earlier in time), he uses the characteristic phrase of the historical school: " We do not find a *theology* in the Old Testament; we find a religion. . . . Hence our subject really is the history of the religion of Israel as represented in the Old Testament." But two pages later he makes a directly contrary judgment: " The Old Testament contains almost exclusively a *theology,* or doctrine, of

[15] A. B. Davidson, *The Theology of the Old Testament.*

Jehovah the God of Israel." It is this second standpoint which is supported by the body of material in the book, and it is in no sense a history of the religion of Israel. But an Old Testament theology that was no surer of its validity than this could be no match for a "religion of Israel" that proceeded with confidence and scientific definiteness. Because the relation of a Biblical theology to the descriptive history of religious phenomena in the Bible remained undefined, the theological interest slowly but surely sank out of sight as the nineteenth century ended and the twentieth century began. The historical approach had gained a complete victory.

[IX]

THE DEATH AND REBIRTH
OF BIBLICAL THEOLOGY — II

WE HAVE SEEN how a variety of forces conspired to bring about the death of theological concern in Biblical studies. The development had in it a certain inevitability. The weakness of the earlier varieties of theological approach and the necessity that the historical method, once established, should not have its conclusions dictated to it in any degree, determined the course that was followed. The more devoted a Biblical scholar was to his science, the more he found himself impelled to lay aside his theological interest and become purely a historian. We now turn to the developments of the past fifty years, which may seem to be history in reverse, as scholars are pushed beyond a purely historical approach to a theological one. It might appear at first sight to be a reactionary movement that is attempting to revive an old approach that has already been weighed in the balances and found wanting. Frightened by the radical consequences of a completely honest historical science, are scholars compromising themselves as historians in order to be able to assert dogmatically the absolute truth of certain Biblical doctrines without which the Christian faith as we have known it would be unlikely to survive? Have the systematic theologians, backed by a church that has become slightly hysterical about its doctrinal confusion in the face of aggressive non-Christian faiths and philosophies, pressured the Biblical scholars into a theological groove that really diverts Biblical studies from their own proper and most fruitful task?

The only way to answer these questions is to show what happened to the interpretation of the Bible when a pure historicism had its full freedom, unchallenged. We shall see that, just as tensions produced by an inadequate method in the theological period made the experiment of pure historicism necessary, so the tensions produced by the inadequacies of historicism have made it necessary to reconsider the nature of a Biblical science that, like any good science, should let its method be determined by the character of the object that it is to investigate. If the Bible is only a complex of human events, ideas, and experiences, then a purely historical science is called for. But if it is witness to the words and acts of God in relation to man, it has to be both historical and theological in order to fulfill its appointed task of Biblical interpretation.

It is significant that whereas the all-conquering " history of Biblical religion " denied to Biblical theology the right to live, and still today in a few rare instances feels its existence threatened by the contemporary rebirth, the revived Biblical theology usually affirms the necessity for the continuation of the most thorough historical studies. There may in some quarters be the delusion that Biblical theology validates a direct, uncritical, unhistorical approach to Scripture, enabling the student to get at the real content of Scripture without the labor of working his way through the literary and historical problems. But no scholar of any rank in the field of theology proposes any such approach, and those who have worked most fruitfully at the tasks of Biblical theology show on every page of their work that they are willing to face the literary and historical problems with as open a mind as any who have preceded them. They are fully aware that to let dogma dictate the answers to historical questions leads back into a hopeless wilderness and not forward into the freedom of the truth. Biblical theology in its rebirth has been not a reactionary movement but rather the next step forward that had to be taken by a responsible Biblical science.

A Historical Account of Israel's Religion

Oesterly and Robinson's *Hebrew Religion* (1930) offers an excellent example of what competent historians were able to make of the religion of Israel when they attempted a purely descriptive and untheological account. At the very outset they state that the study of Semitic comparative religion " abundantly proves " Hebrew religion to have been " made up of elements common to the religion of all early Semites " (p. xvii). This conception dominates the book, the attempt being made constantly to demonstrate that all but the very highest aspects of Hebrew religion may be explained as quite natural developments from general Semitic religion.

The earliest period, the pre-Mosaic religion of the Hebrews, is admittedly difficult to reconstruct. Since the traditions regarding the patriarchs gained their present form in a later age, it is hard to discern what pertains to the earlier and what to the later time. But these historians, dismissing in its entirety the tradition of a faith existing in the earlier day that, whatever it was, was something much more than superstition, insist upon reconstructing the period wholly from the relics of superstition that persisted into later times and have parallels in primitive Semitic religion. Animatism, animism, polytheism, totemism, taboo, and ancestor worship are taken to have constituted the faith of Moses' ancestors. That these may have been factors in the religion of partriarchal times is not to be doubted. But there is no evidence upon which to base the assertion that the religion of the patriarchs had in it no other elements than these.

The second period, beginning with Moses, is explained as owing its degree of progress to the taking-over by Moses of the nomadic religion of the Kenite tribe of the Midianites, with the deliverance from Egypt serving to set a divine imprimatur upon Moses' work in the eyes of his people and so to consolidate his achievement. Thus, the general nature of the religion of this period is assumed to have been about the same as that of any nomad people. "We may be fairly sure that Israelite theology in Moses' day did not differ materially from that of other peoples at the same stage of development." (P. 136.) Therefore, the Mosaic religion is reconstructed from what is known to have been the general nature of nomadic religion, and again the Hebrew tradition of a greater and purer faith is ignored, being regarded as entirely a reading back of later developments into the time of Moses. If this is valid, one may well ask whether there has ever been a nation so mistaken in its memory of its own beginnings. The God of Moses is described as "a mountain 'El," and a "mountain 'El" is elsewhere defined as one stage lower than a Baal! He is a "combination of mountain spirit, storm and volcanic deity, and wilderness guide." The terms of the Mosaic covenant that survive the ruthless trimming of the tradition are the demand that Israel should worship only this mountain 'El, that no other divine name should be used in taking an oath, and perhaps also an insistence upon some kind of observance of the Passover and the Sabbath. The ethical advance of this period, which caused the prophets of later times to look back upon it as approaching the ideal, was due to the adoption of the " fairly high moral standards " of the desert nomad! These nomad standards are, indeed, rendered high honor! Not only are they held responsible for the Mosaic reforms, but, we are told, they broke through in Elijah and Amos and " in the end proved to be the decisive factor in making Israelite religion unique in the ancient world " (p. 151). What the prophets attribute to a personal revelation of God is here plainly regarded as a natural product of nomadic religion.

The third period begins with the settlement in Palestine. We are asked to accept as a fact of history that Israel now took over in its entirety the culture and religion of the Canaanites. " It seems, in fact, that they simply adopted the culture of Palestine en bloc." (P. 169.) The analogy is used of the Teutonic invaders of Rome in the fourth century after Christ, who adopted both the culture and the religion that they found in the invaded land. " While, then, the name used in worship was that of Yahweh, the details of the cultus were, we may believe, very much what they had been in Palestine from time immemorial." (P. 176.) " From being an 'El, Yahweh had now become a Baal." (P. 177.) Since a civil code and a form of ecstatic prophecy are found in Palestinian life before the Hebrew conquest, the conclusion is drawn that " Israel inherited both the Law and the Prophets from her predecessors in Palestine " (p. 178). A third time the Hebrew tradition is assumed to be wholly wrong, and the details of Israel's religion are inferred from an alien source. How a nation that apparently had nothing unique of its own and that in its first three stages of development merely swung, leaders and people alike, from one form of paganism to another afterward pro-duced a faith that was unique not only in the ancient but in the modern world as well, is not easy to understand. Moreover, this theory is at direct variance with the sustained consciousness in Israel of a peculiar calling and destiny that can be traced far back in the records of the nation's life.

At last the period is reached when the Yahwist revival took place, carrying Israelite religion to its highest achievements and accounting for some of its most impressive records. But even this is attributed to the working of merely natural forces. It is explained as the result of two factors: the fact that the southern and eastern tribes, having remained in a pastoral nomadic state, had resisted Canaanite demoralization and the fact that " the national spirit was aroused when Jezebel sought to give her own Baal supremacy over Yahweh, the Baal of Israel " (p. 184). Nomadic standards of ethics plus Hebrew nationalism equals the great prophets of Israel. We have a right to rebel against a fantastic historical arithmetic of this kind. " The supreme place which must be ascribed to the Israelite prophets is due to the fact that they dared to identify God with the good, and asserted that his character was at least as high as that of man. It was here that the ancient tradition of nomadic Israel had its effect." (P. 194.) One fears that no place of supremacy would ever have been ascribed to the prophets had they done no more than make their God as good as a nomadic man. It is also significant of the general tenor of the book that 32 pages suffice to describe the importance of the prophets for the whole religion of Israel, while 192 pages are required for the exposition of pagan elements.

The term " revelation " occurs at several points, perhaps in deference to those who still feel that a history of Israelite religion should have something to say about revelation. But the use of the term is curious. After denying any great spiritual experience to Moses and explaining his achievements as due merely to what he learned from Jethro about a nomadic God and nomadic morals, the writer proceeds to describe this latter as a " very real " revelation of God. " The revelation of Yahweh to Moses was very real, but it was accorded by means of the instrument which he chose," i.e., Jethro. (P. 114.) Such a use of the word " revelation " seems unlikely to produce anything but confusion. Again, it is said in regard to Second Isaiah: " The natural evolution of ideas does much to deepen and enlarge men's thought of God; but there come moments when to such development there is needed the self-revelation of God himself (we may not know how or by what means) " (p. 260). " Here was one of the men to whom God vouchsafed to reveal himself in a very special way, and there are not many to whom such revelation has been accorded, but when there is response, as in the case of Deutero-Isaiah, they become landmarks in the history of religion."

(P. 261.) Where the line between the natural evolution of ideas and the personal revelation of God is to be drawn is not at any point expressly stated. One may surmise that the attempt to draw such a line and yet leave the two in direct continuity might be fraught with difficulty. It looks very much as though in this case the category "revelation" had been drawn in as a last resort to explain what even those most devoted to naturalistic theory would hesitate to call a merely natural development of primitive Semitic religion.[1]

One rises from the reading of the book with the idea that, if no more than this can be said, then, as far as Christians of today are concerned, the Old Testament may safely be ignored. Perhaps that impression is not wholly just, but it is impossible to deny that such a presentation of Israelite religion is well calculated to produce it. The religion described appears to be only of antiquarian interest. Persons whose experience of the Old Testament is intimate though unscientific are likely to object rather strenuously that this is not the religion of the Old Testament as they know it and to think that there is something curiously wrong with an investigation of the Old Testament that arrives at such conclusions. Either these scholars have gone wrong somewhere in their method of investigation or the church through the centuries has been wrong in maintaining the Old Testament alongside the New as a book of revelation.

Objection might also be raised against the arid intellectualism of the method. T. K. Cheyne once said of Heinrich Ewald: "Our critic never treats the Old Testament as if he were a medical student dissecting the dead." That could not be said of the presentation we have been considering. Religion is treated as a dry composite of ideas, customs, and institutions, never as a faith by which men once lived. It seems to be forgotten that even the most primitive religions have this dignity, that by them men were attempting to deal with the deeper realities of life and to come to terms with their destiny.

The use of this book as an illustration of the inability of a purely historical approach to get even near the content of the Old Testament may be contested on the score that other historians have more recently drawn a very different picture in which, for instance, a much

---

[1] G. E. Wright's *The Old Testament Against Its Environment* contains a strong and thorough protest against the validity of this interpretation of the religion of Israel.

more significant place is given to Moses and the exodus. It cannot be denied, however, that the Oesterly-Robinson history is representative of its period, that the inability of the authors to take account of the reality of a revelation of God was a universal dilemma of historians, and that as a consequence the content of the Old Testament was presented not as a witness to God's revelation of himself in Israel but rather as the unfolding of a complex mass of diverse religious phenomena in which the higher forms developed naturally out of the lower. Certainly the historian can come to a quite different conclusion concerning Israel's religious development when he approaches it with different presuppositions, that is, with a different theology.

One has only to examine the evaluation by A. C. Welch [2] of religious developments in Israel in the centuries before Amos to realize that Canaanization is not the whole story. Also, most Old Testament scholars today would agree with H. H. Rowley [3] that the history of Israel is inexplicable apart from a prophetic achievement of Moses and a national experience of deliverance in the Mosaic era. But these revised evaluations belong not to the period of pure historicism but to the period of reaction, which owes its impulse to new theological insights. To the untheological historian the conviction of Israel that it stood in a unique relation with Yahweh as his chosen people was interpreted against the background of Near Eastern religious ideas; parallels to it were found in other Palestinian and Mesopotamian cults, and it was considered to be a religious expression of national egotism. But when the call of Israel was understood in the light of the call of individual prophets and the connection was seen between the Israel of the Old Testament and the church as the New Israel of God in the New Testament, the conception of Israel's chosenness took on a totally new significance. It could no longer be dismissed as a primitive religious phenomenon that has no significance for the Christian of today. In short, the interpretation of the historical facts depends to a large extent upon the context in which they are seen, and the ultimate context is determined by the historian's conviction concerning the significance of Scripture as a whole.

[2] A. C. Welch, *Prophet and Priest in Old Israel.*
[3] H. H. Rowley, *The Biblical Doctrine of Election.*

A Historical Account of New Testament Religion

A parallel but less radical illustration from the area of New Testament studies would be Maurice Goguel's two volumes: *The Life of Jesus* and *The Birth of Christianity* (cited as L.J. and B.C.).[4] His concern at every point is to be the objective historian. " The business of the historian is only to establish the facts and set them out in order by their mutual connection. It is not his job to evaluate them and to disengage their deep significance and their spiritual meaning or even to discover if they correspond to a transcendent reality." (B.C., p. 11.) He recognizes, however, that more than facts are required to form a history. The history of Jesus is the history of his thought, so that one has to penetrate behind the words to the thought by psychology and intuition. " In order to understand Islam we must look through the eyes of a Muslim, and in order to understand the thought of Jesus we must have or we must acquire the spirit of a Christian." (L.J., p. 215.) Also, the events of the life of Jesus must be seen in the larger context formed by the consequences in later history. Goguel stops short of saying that the meaning of the events is comprehensible only to one who stands within the Christian faith. He assumes, rather, that the historian can imaginatively place himself in that situation, an assumption that is open to challenge. It is at least evident that he is conscious of some difficulty in the posture of complete objectivity. He would not trust the complete objectivity of a historian who had no sympathy with " the spirit of a Christian."

Goguel's approach to the New Testament accounts of the resurrection of Jesus brings out several facets of his dilemma. As a historian he declares that it is impossible to make sense of the earliest stage of Christianity apart from the honest conviction of the disciples that their Master had risen from the dead. " The creative source of Christianity was the faith in the risen and glorified Jesus." (B.C., p. 29.) " No fact was more important for the primitive faith than the resurrection of Jesus; yet on no fact is the tradition so diverse and incapable of being reduced to a unity." (B.C., p. 58.) The multiplicity of stories of the resurrection Goguel explains as the product of

[4] Maurice Goguel, *The Life of Jesus* (Eng. tr., 1933); *The Birth of Christianity* (Eng. tr., 1953).

a multiplicity of visions. An actual appearance of Jesus to the disciples seems to be automatically excluded from consideration by him. He therefore interprets the resurrection visions as psychological experiences of the disciples that were the consequence and expression of the revival of their faith in Jesus, a faith that had been crushed by his death. There was a resurrection not of Jesus but of the disciples' faith in him. He does not appear to be conscious that in this judgment he has made an evaluation of the facts that carries him far beyond the function of a historian and that the judgment is determined by the theological assumptions with which he approaches the documents.

The problem of objectivity appears sharply also in Goguel's portrayal of the relation between Jesus and John the Baptist. The known fact of Jesus' baptism at the hands of John must, according to Goguel, have been a source of great embarrassment to Christians. Therefore, they would be likely to conceal any indication of a dependence of Jesus on John and would emphasize Jesus' superiority to John from the very beginning. On this basis he develops a theory that preceding Jesus' ministry there was an extended period in which Jesus worked in close association with John. " Jesus appears in the light of history for the first time as a member of the circle that surrounded John the Baptist, and . . . it was from him that he received his first impulse to action." (L.J., p. 264.) Thus " Jesus began by preaching and baptizing in the same way and in the same spirit as John; . . . he then severed his connection with John because he had changed his views on the question of purification; that is to say, about the efficacy of baptism. . . . After Jesus had left him John only saw in him an unfaithful disciple and almost a renegade " (L.J., pp. 275, 279). Needless to say, it requires a radical readjustment of the texts concerning Jesus and John to produce these conclusions. One rather suspects that the whole reconstruction results from the frustration of the historian at being unable to find evidence of growth and development in the Jesus of the New Testament records. History should mean movement and change. Therefore, the historicity of the figure of Jesus extracted from the New Testament remains suspect unless some development in his attitudes and thought can be demonstrated. But fatal to Goguel's theory are the facts that the Christian church (and not Judaism) remembered John the Baptist with gratitude, and that each of the four Gospels gives him a place of prominence at the very beginning of the Gospel story, Matthew and Luke indicating his great independent stature as a prophet. It is not unreasonable to suppose that a prophet of such insight as John might have discerned in some degree how far beyond him Jesus was. The judgment of the Gospels concerning the relation of Jesus to John seems to have been based on that of Jesus himself as expressed in Matt. 11:7-19, a passage that bears upon it the marks of belonging to the earliest tradition, combining, as it does, the affirmation both of the greatness of John as a prophet of God and of the measure in which the Kingdom transcends John's movement.

The purpose of this critique is not to disparage the value of such historical work as that of Goguel but merely to indicate its limitations. Every student of the New Testament is grateful to him and recognizes the usefulness of such historical labors. We cannot be satisfied to receive the testimony of the New Testament authors in its finished canonical form and to make no attempt to unravel as best we can the threads of history that are as often concealed as revealed in the documents. Whether it is in relation to the story of the early church or in relation to the life of Jesus, the attitude that we should leave off any attempt to get at the historical facts and be content with the message of the canonical documents is not likely to be acceptable to Christians for long. Usually such an attitude assumes, perhaps unconsciously, and most likely uncritically, certain answers to historical questions. The task of the historian is to investigate with every means available the human story of the Scriptures, but he will perform his task most objectively when he is most conscious that within the human story of the Scriptures, as its central core, is the story of God's word and action, the living God dealing with his people in the midst of history, a story that cannot be reduced to a succession of human ideas and experiences without perverting its reality. Goguel's presentation is not radical in its results when compared with some other works (such as those of Wilhelm Bousset) in which the origin of the Christian Church is portrayed as the end product of the interaction of various religious ideas and forces in the first century A.D., and the figure of Jesus in its various permutations is " explained " in much the same way as the prophets were " explained " by Oesterly-Robinson, as a natural development in the evolution of religion. It could only be a matter of time until such an incredible explanation would create a reaction in the opposite direction.

Since our concern is with the death of the theological interest in Biblical studies and the disclosure of the forces that brought it alive again, we are justified perhaps in passing over the whole complex development in the later *religiongeschichtliche* school represented by Bousset. Historical judgments so extreme that they were highly embarrassing to Christianity were combined with a mysticism that professed to make Christianity independent of history but that actually provided an excuse to substitute Goethe and German idealism for Jesus Christ and the Trinity. The continuity of Christianity with its origins was decisively threatened. But we must not underestimate the importance of this school in its influence upon the more recent situation and in the shaping of the minds of eminent interpreters. Both Rudolf Bultmann and Martin Dibelius were moving in a direction marked out by it when in their form-criticism they tended toward a radical separation between the Jesus of history and the Christ of faith. Bultmann's determination to find a basis for the Christian faith that will make it independent of any one historical expression of it has here its roots. Erik Esking has recently traced some of these lines of development as background for his study of the work of Ernst Lohmeyer in theological exegesis.[5]

DISSATISFACTION AND REVOLT

The exclusion of theological interest and the transformation of the Biblical disciplines into strictly historical sciences had serious consequences in many different directions. Before all else it involved the scholar himself in a form of schizophrenia. In most instances he had been led to the study of Scripture not by the fascination of literary and historical problems but by a conviction concerning the importance of the Bible as a revelation of God to mankind. But now, in the interests of objective historical scholarship, he felt compelled to put all his Christian interests and convictions in a separate compartment of his mind and life where they would have no influence upon his investigation of Scripture.

[5] Erik Esking, "Glaube und Geschichte in der theologische Exegese Ernst Lohmeyers."

Needless to say, many scholars found this impossible. But where they were successful in suppressing the conscious theological concern, there arose in many minds a confusion about the relation of these Biblical sciences to other departments of theology. They seemed more in place in the context of sciences for the investigation of ancient cultures than in the church. Also, commentaries on Scripture from a purely historical viewpoint were singularly dry and academic in the eyes of the Christian preacher and teacher who wanted help in making the message of the Bible relevant to the life of ordinary human beings. A Biblical science that cut itself loose from the concerns of the church soon began to lament the unconcern of the church about the Bible and the disregard of seminary graduates for Biblical problems. In short, a Biblical science that refused to be theological threatened, in spite of the earnestness and devotion of countless scholars, to dissolve the relation between the church and the Bible and to leave itself no future except as one department of research in Near Eastern culture. It is not surprising that, wherever scholars retained their conviction that the Bible is before all else the source of the church's knowledge of God, there was dissatisfaction with such an order. But so firm was the grip of historicism on men's minds that it took years, and many severe shocks, for this dissatisfaction to bear fruit. One of the first to see the inner logic of the historical method and to recognize the drastic consequences of a pure historicism for the Christian faith was Ernst Troeltsch. His writings were important in preparing the way for a new development.

Rudolf Kittel, who had experience in a parish for some years before he established himself as an Old Testament scholar and who felt himself under suspicion as a scholar for that reason,[6] was one of the first to speak out. In an address at Leipzig in 1921,[7] he laid emphasis upon the inadequacy of merely literary and historical investigation and called for the " elucidation of the specifically religious values " in the Old Testament as that which alone can give Old Testament science a relationship of theology. Of the history of religion he said: " We came near apologizing for the very existence

---

[6] R. Kittel, in *Die Religionswissenschaft der Gegenwart in Selbstdarstellungen.* Vol. I.

[7] R. Kittel, " The Future of Old Testament Science," ZAW, XXXIX (1921), p. 84.

of our Old Testament people and its religion. . . . Thus it was no wonder that an outsider such as Harnack misunderstood us." There must, therefore, be an undertaking of the wider task of a systematic presentation of the essence of Old Testament religion and a delving into the secret of divine power in which it has its ground.

In 1923, Eduard König, whose investigations had consistently been of a conservative character, produced a volume on Old Testament theology [8] in which he took issue with the practice of making the common religion of the people the starting point in dealing with the religion of Israel. The true starting point, he asserted, is "the legitimate religion of Israel." This rested upon the valid insight that the religious phenomena in the life of Israel cannot be treated as a unit, since they include the most radically contradictory elements, and that our attention should be concentrated upon a particular religious tradition in Israel which alone has abiding significance. But at once the objection was made, and made rightly, that there are a number of legitimate religions of Israel. As Eissfeldt phrased it, "Legitimate religion stands at odds with legitimate religion." History may expose these varied religions to our view, but it requires something other than historical science to deal with the question of legitimacy.

In 1925 an essay by Carl Steuernägel, in the memorial volume in honor of Karl Marti, drew attention to the need that Old Testament theology should be set free from the chains of a history of religion in which it was threatening to pass away completely. Steuernägel did not deny that the history of religion has its proper place, but he insisted that justice cannot be done to the contents of the Old Testament unless alongside the history there is an Old Testament theology. "The other theological disciplines have a right to demand that we present to them the Old Testament materials which they require in such a form as is necessary for their purposes, and we Old Testament scholars have no right to refuse this demand as long as we make the claim to be theologians." The systematic theologian has no right to dictate in what scheme the materials are to be treated, but he has the right to ask of the Old Testament scholar what the Old Testament says concerning God, man, salvation. A satisfactory answer to these questions requires something more than a history

[8] E. König, *Theologie des Alten Testaments* (Stuttgart, 1923).

of religion, and an Old Testament science that refuses to take these questions seriously has gone a long distance toward dissolving its connection not only with theology but with the life of the church.

In 1926 appeared Johannes Hempel's *Gott und Mensch im Alten Testament,* in which the author, recognizing the inadequacy of the preceding historical presentations, attempted to get beneath the surface of Israel's religion by the use of a psychological method. It is still a history that he writes, but a history of the spiritual experience of the Israelites rather than of their religious forms, ideas, and institutions. What Hempel tries to do is to extend the net of the historical method by this addition of a psychological approach in order that it may be adequate to take in those deeper elements in Israel's religion "which come from God and lead to God, and which also lead us to God." But the same objections may be raised against a purely descriptive psychological method as are raised against a purely descriptive historical method. It cannot divorce itself from judgments of value or from pronouncements that are theological in their nature. Nor can any purely descriptive method, historical or psychological, do justice to the theological content of the Old Testament. Hempel's work, however, illustrates the growing consciousness that the current histories of Israel's religion had been failing, for some reason, to take account of a very essential part of the religious phenomena.

Also in 1926 appeared an article by Otto Eissfeldt, "History of Israelite-Jewish Religion and Old Testament Theology," [9] which recognized that this particular problem was but an aspect of the general problem of theology. "The tension between the Absolute and the Relative, between Transcendence and Immanence, is at present *the* problem of theology, and for Biblical science this general problem narrows down to the particular one: History and Revelation." Two principles of interpretation have long stood over against each other, the historical demanding that the religion of Israel be investigated by the same historical methods that have validated themselves in other spheres, and the theological insisting that the real essence of the religion of the Old Testament cannot be known except through faith — "faith" meaning something far more than mere sympathetic penetration. The justification of the historical is

[9] ZAW, XLIV (1926), 1 ff.

that through it alone can dependable knowledge be gained of the varied phenomena that constitute the religion of Israel. The justification of the theological is that the Old Testament bears witness to an absolute and transcendent reality that eludes historical science and makes itself known only to faith. " The historical and the theological approaches belong on two different planes. They correspond to two different functions of our spirit, knowing and believing. . . . The knowing mind is conscious that in spite of all its efforts it cannot reach out beyond the limited world of space and time; faith knows itself laid hold upon by an eternal reality. . . . Thus the necessity of both methods of approach is rooted in our spiritual nature and we have only the choice either to make a compromise between the two or to recognize and prosecute each of them in its own place and in its own way."

Eissfeldt is emphatic in his protest against the former of these alternatives, believing that it can result only in confusion. Both Schultz and Procksch serve for him as examples of such confusion. " The more thoroughly the two methods of approach are kept separate from each other, the more fruitful will be their influence upon each other." But both must be kept alive. The error of orthodoxy was that it let history disappear in the revelation, while the error of the historical method in the nineteenth century was that it threatened to let the revelation disappear in the history. Thus, there must be two sciences: the one presenting the phenomena of Israel's religion in a completely objective fashion and withholding all judgments concerning truth and value, so that men of various confessions and even non-Christians may work together at this task; the other, thoroughly scientific but presenting what the Old Testament revelation means to the religious community of which the scholar is a member and having the character of a witness the validity of which is limited to the circle of those whose piety is the same or similar to that of the author. At this latter task members of different religious communities cannot work together, but one community can only overcome the other through mightier demonstration " of the Spirit and the Power."

Hans Windisch develops a similar point of view for the New Testament in *Der Sinn der Bergpredigt* (1929). Historical exegesis, he says, " has to do with the document, theological exegesis with the object " with which the document deals, which is God. Since the object is known only through the document, the two are in a very close relation to each other, but they must be kept strictly separate. What must be avoided at all costs is a theological exegesis that will make the ideas of the text serve the ends of a particular theology that lies beyond the text, subordinating the text thus to a special, confessional, philosophical, and personally determined point of view. Historical exegesis is a science that may be practiced by non-Christians as long as their methodology is valid. But, for the understanding of the deepest concerns of the New Testament authors, a theological exegesis is necessary that will take all texts as witness of the church and seek God's authoritative Word in them for us; it attempts to liberate the meaning from its antique form and to make it comprehensible to the God-seeking man of the present. Windisch agrees with Eissfeldt that " each form of theological exegesis can have validity only for a certain circle of persons," so that various forms may have equal validity and each should recognize the legitimacy of the other. Also, Lutheran theological exegetes should direct their attention to texts congenial to them and leave alone those which are Jewish or Catholic in content, not attempting to extract a Lutheran theology from them. The assumption of Windisch is that it is only the theologian who is unable to get free from dogmatic presuppositions.

Eissfeldt and Windisch both fail to recognize that neither the historian nor the theologian is able to approach the records of Israel's religion wholly uninfluenced by his particular theological prepossessions; nor do they seem to see the peril of an Old Testament or New Testament theology that seeks merely to embody in systematic form what the religious community of the scholar makes of the revelation of Scripture. That can too easily become a matter of each religious community merely finding in Scripture a basis for its own particular viewpoint. History and theology are too closely intermingled in the same text to be made the subject matter of two separate disciplines.

In 1929 there appeared an article by Walther Eichrodt in the *Zeitschrift für die Alttestamentliche Wissenschaft,* entitled "Has Old Testament Theology Still Independent Significance Within Old Testament Science? " Taking account of the revived interest in an

Old Testament theology, Eichrodt explained it as due to the growing conviction that "by historical means it is impossible for us to penetrate to the essence of Old Testament religion." Judgments of truth and value belong not in a historical science but in philosophy and dogmatics. This limitation, however, he says, has never been properly recognized in the Old Testament field. Its recognition leads to the combining of a systematic method with the historical one in order to gain a critical apparatus adequate to interpret the very essence of Old Testament religion. Eichrodt also pointed out the impossibility of complete objectivity in handling such a subject and suggested that the scholar, instead of priding himself upon his objectivity, should rather make full allowance for the conceptions that are already present in his own mind and are likely to influence the direction of his thought and interpretation.

After 1930 there was a perfect flood of literature upon the subject. In 1933, Ernest Sellin, in the preface to his *History of Israelite and Jewish Religion,* showed his sympathy with the movement toward theology: " It seems to me high time for Old Testament science to remember that it is not merely a historical discipline but also a discipline in Christian theology." Immediately he gave substance to this conviction by publishing his volume on Old Testament theology. Also in 1933, Eichrodt completed the first of his three volumes on Old Testament theology. Then in 1935 came Wilhelm Vischer's *The Witness of the Old Testament to Christ* and in 1936 Ludwig Köhler's *Theologie des Alten Testaments.*

In the area of New Testament studies the situation, at least on the Continent, was more dramatic. Historicism still held its position essentially unshaken by such conservatives as Adolph Schlatter when Barth's *Romans,* with its brazenly theological exposition, was flung into the arena in 1919. It was like the explosion of a bomb, or better, like the introduction of a chemical substance that had the effect of separating the divergent elements that had been mingled together in New Testament scholarship. The origin of *Romans* was in the frustration of two Swiss pastors, Karl Barth and Eduard Thurneysen, as they tried to fulfill their ordination vows to be ministers of the word of God to their people. Both had been thoroughly trained in historical criticism and had no sympathy with the conservative repudiation of it. But none of the modern commentaries seemed to them to take them far enough into the Scriptures. They dealt only with the linguistic, literary, and historical questions and stopped short of the point where Scripture asks to be taken seriously as an absolutely unique revelation of God to man. Yet this was the very point at which they, as ministers of God, had to have something to say. Therefore, they began, in close association with each other and comparing notes as they made their way, to explore this farther journey into Scripture.[10] And the Bible opened to them as though it were a book they had never seen before.

All kinds of influences were mingled together in enabling them to break through the established patterns of their world and to look at Scripture with fresh eyes. Hermann Kutter and the Christian Socialist Movement had encouraged a sensitiveness to social issues and an impatience with the corrupt and complacent middle-class individualism of the church. Dostoevsky had shaken them loose from any tendency to identify Western civilization with Christianity.[11] The war of 1914–1918 had shown them how easily a cultural Protestantism could become a nationalistic Protestantism. Christoph Blumhardt of Bad Boll, with his understanding of the power of the living Spirit of God and his freedom from any elements of pietism, reinterpreted to them what it meant in the early Christian community to be born of the Spirit and to live in the power of the Spirit.[12] Luther and Calvin helped them to see what could happen in the life of a church when the word of God that is to be heard nowhere except in Scripture recovers its true authority and when there is a ministry that has the courage to speak a word today in which Jesus Christ together with his prophets and apostles will be speaking afresh. Kierkegaard made his contribution by cutting through the immanentalism and intellectualism of modern theology and by underlining the central Biblical truth that God is God and man is man. These and yet others were heard alongside the Scriptures, but the decisive factor was that the Scriptures themselves were heard and preached, and these two men became more and more convinced that what they were hearing would have to be heard much more widely

[10] Letters between Barth and Thurneysen in *Antwort* (1956), and *Gottesdienst-Menschendienst* (1958).

[11] Eduard Thurneysen, *Dostoiewski* (1930).

[12] E. Thurneysen, *Christoph Blumhardt* (1926).

in the church. They were aware that what they were preaching was not much understood elsewhere, and that involved in it was an approach to Christian theology that was radically different from all approaches with which they were familiar. In 1915 they knew already that a theological battle lay before them, and they hoped to have ten years to prepare themselves for it. The publication of Barth's *Romans* precipitated the battle. Some of the offense that it gave to scholars was that a village preacher, of no standing in the world of New Testament studies, should challenge the validity of a tradition of interpretation that was the laborious creation of a century of scholarship. All manner of flaws were found in the volume itself, and it was pronounced on every hand to be a monstrous piece of eisegesis. But somehow it refused to be brushed aside. It raised questions that a self-respecting New Testament discipline could not refuse to consider. And, in the answering of them, many who repudiated Barth's *Romans* found themselves forced to recognize the legitimacy of the theological concern.

The pressure upon New Testament studies exercised by Barth's *Romans* has given rise to the impression that the theological concern was injected into or forced upon New Testament scholars by a systematic theologian. On the contrary, it was a preacher-theologian who as yet had no knowledge that he was to teach systematic theology and who was merely trying to find the meaning of the Bible for modern life. His commentary was the roughhewn product of his own wrestling with Scripture, so roughhewn that he began to rewrite it completely almost as soon as it was published. Its power lay not in the perfection of its exegesis but in its assertion in positive fashion that a whole new approach to Scripture had to be devised if the words were to have today the same kind of power as witness to God that they had when they were first written. But, had there been no Karl Barth, the transition from a purely historical scholarship to one that has room for both historical and theological concern would eventually have taken place, most likely at a much slower pace. That is evident in the manner in which scholars who stand at the opposite pole from Barth theologically have nevertheless made the transition from pure historicism to a recognition of their theological responsibility. It is evident also in the fact that a New Testament scholar such as Rudolf Bultmann, who represented the most thorough and radical application of the principles of historical and critical research, recognized the necessity of a theological as well as a historical approach if exegesis was to penetrate beyond the surface of the Biblical text.

Barth and Bultmann followed widely different courses. While Barth was jubilantly rediscovering the strange new world within the Bible as he faced the dilemmas of a pastor, Bultmann was working on the frontiers of New Testament scholarship. The tradition into which he was drawn was the radical one of Reimarus, Strauss, Johannes Weiss, Bousset, and Wrede. With Strauss and Kähler he relinquished all hope of recovering from the New Testament documents a historical figure of Jesus. With Weiss and Albert Schweitzer he accepted the thesis that Jesus' ministry was focused upon a future coming of the Messiah and that he made no claim to be more than a Jewish teacher and prophet. With Wrede he agreed that Mark's story of a gradual revealing of a Messianic secret of Jesus was a post-resurrection invention. And with Bousset he drew a sharp line between a Palestinian Christianity which remembered Jesus as a rabbi and prophet but awaited his coming as the Messiah and a Hellenistic Christianity in which, under gnostic influence, Jesus was worshiped as a heavenly being, the Lord who came from heaven into the world of men to redeem them, and, having completed his task, returned again to heaven. Bultmann's own project of form criticism, at which Martin Dibelius and Karl Ludwig Schmidt were working also, each in his own way, had even more radical consequences for his assessment of the New Testament. The criteria that he developed to distinguish between the various strata in the New Testament tradition were highly subjective and tended to furnish him with evidence to support his picture of the early stages of Christianity. Beginning in a very simple way as the consequence of the impact of the life and death of a Jewish teacher upon his Jewish followers, an impact that for some strange reason opened a new life to them and began a new era in the life of man, the new faith expressed itself first in the eschatological language of the Jewish world, but, when it broke into the Hellenistic world, adopted the more highly mythological language of that world. For Bultmann it was axiomatic that neither the Jewish modes of expression nor the Hellenistic could be adequate for the modern man. The mythological world of the ancients is gone, never to return. Therefore as early as 1921 he saw the task confronting the Christian theologian of translating the gospel out of its ancient formulations that are a needless hindrance for the man of today into terms that are meaningful in the world we know. Liberalism had tried to liberate Christianity from its mythological framework but had failed to see the reality that was expressed in the mythology, and so had lost the gospel itself from sight. What was needed was not to eliminate the mythology but to translate its meaning into our own language. The project of demythologizing the gospel which Bultmann proposed in 1941 in his famous essay on "The New Testament and Mythology" was therefore a direct and natural outcome of the earliest developments in his scholarly interests.

This was, however, only one aspect of the early Bultmann. There was another aspect that brought him for a brief time into close association with Barth. Like Barth he found himself in strong reaction against the dominant theology of the early twentieth century. He saw the emptiness of a historical method that could get at only the outside of historical events, and followed Dilthey in his proposal of a new approach to history by which the inner reality of men's lives where history is made would be disclosed. He repudiated the immanentalism which found God somewhere in man and identified religion with culture, and, with Kierkegaard's infinite qualitative difference between God and man as the motto of his theology, longed for the liberation of religion from being harnessed to the various individual and social purposes or programs of man. The essence of religion for him was the fulfillment of man's life in God. The predicament of man was his engrossment in a world apart from God, his life empty even in the midst of his cultural riches. The glory of the gospel was that in it God came to man in his Word to reveal to him his emptiness, to free him from his dead past, and to open to him as a sheer gift of grace his own true future. The cross was the symbol of this coming of God to man, for, with the revelation of the emptiness of his life in the world without God, man had to die, but in his death to the world he came alive in a new life with God. We can understand why Bultmann welcomed Barth's *Romans*. It was a blast against an arid type of historical exegesis and had in it a recognition of the interpreter's theological involvement with his text. It spoke without embarrassment of a word from God in which God judged and redeemed humanity. It freed religion from all forms of legalism and moralism and set it to its own true task of reconciling man with God and with himself. But Barth was to Bultmann only one element in the dawning of a new day, and he had serious reservations concerning Barth's approach to Scripture. Where Bultmann saw in much of Paul's expression of the gospel a Hellenistic gnosticism from which the true kerygma had to be disentangled, Barth saw only indispensable elements of the revelation of God in Jesus Christ. For Bultmann, Jesus could not be more than the *bearer* of the divine Word to man, the incarnation being a mythological expression of that truth; while for Barth, Jesus in his human person was actually the incarnation of God, and all that we know of God as Christians is revealed to us in the years of his earthly life. Bultmann, in his review of Barth's *Romans,* confessed himself at a loss to understand how an inbreaking of God into history in the life of a first-century Jew could be conceived. To him this was simply a fragment of an ancient gnostic mythology.

Bultmann has thus both a positive and a negative significance in the rebirth of Biblical theology. He saw more clearly and earlier than any other New Testament scholar that the purely historical school was incapable of reaching the ultimate content of Scripture as a revelation of God to man and that a theological content demanded a theological interpretation. But so absolutely did he draw the line between God and man, between the Beyond and this world, that he had to deny the possibility that God could become man in Jesus Christ or that the Holy Spirit could dwell in man as in a temple. Not only this, but he had to deny that man could at any time speak truth concerning *God.* God, even in his coming to man in his word, remains the Unknown, so that all human statements have to be understood as statements about what has happened to man's self-understanding as a consequence of the revelation. We can speak only of the *effect* of the revelation, not of the God who reveals, only of our own death and resurrection in confrontation with the cross, not of God's redemptive action in the Christ of the cross, only of the benefits of Christ in us, not of the nature of Christ. Theology thus becomes anthropology and Christology becomes soteriology, so that Bultmann by this development closes the door upon the possibility of a Biblical theology.

DEVELOPMENTS IN GREAT BRITAIN AND AMERICA

The long, slow, steady process of action and reaction in European scholarship was not reproduced in Great Britain and America for a number of reasons. Because the establishment of a critical approach in theological seminaries and in the church was a century later than on the Continent, there was a necessary telescoping of developments and a total absence of some important factors. In America at the close of the nineteenth century the transition was made in many instances directly from an uncritical orthodoxy to a pure historicism such as characterized German scholarship at that time,[13] the result being a radical antithesis between uncritical evangelicals and critical liberals. In Great Britain this antithesis was considerably softened and the acceptance of a critical approach in the church was facilitated by the fact that many who devoted themselves to critical studies were strongly evangelical and resisted the extreme historicism that had become dominant in Germany. Between 1890 and 1920 a long succession of books appeared in Great Britain by scholars such as G. A. Smith, J. E. McFadyen, W. Sanday, Bishop Gore, C. F. Burney, etc., which had as their purpose the demonstration that the higher criticism did not need to have a destructive effect upon the preaching of the Old Testament in the church. The term " revelation " was not abandoned. Burney called his book *The Gospel in the Old Testament* and asserted that " the Old Testament still points forward to Christ, who draws together in his single person its different spiritual ideals and fulfills beyond all human expectation their highest possibilities." [14] It is surprising that neither in Great Britain nor in America do conservatives such as Beck, von Hofmann, and Kähler seem to have exerted any influence at this time. In America they would have broken the paralyzing false antithesis that prevailed by demonstrating the possibility of a conservative

[13] See B. W. Bacon, in V. Ferm, *Contemporary American Theology* (1932) for a description of the sudden transition in Yale Seminary that took place in the last decade of the nineteenth century.

[14] C. F. Burney, *The Gospel in the Old Testament* (1921).

evangelicalism that did not close its eyes to the historical problems. The British brand of critical evangelicalism that had its representatives also in America was too liberal in its theological premises to bridge the gap.

More recently this British avoidance of the extreme developments that were characteristic of German Biblical scholarship has made many British scholars unsympathetic to the theological reaction against historicism, inclining them to see in it merely another " extreme " development. The rather dangerous impression has grown in some circles of British and American Biblical scholarship that whereas the Europeans have always fluctuated wildly between extremes in an unbalanced fashion, " we " have ever followed a more balanced, sane, middle-way tradition. Our history does not support such pretentions. Our middle way has only too often been an eclecticism in which we have tried to have the best out of contradictory theologies without ever facing clear-sightedly the issues that divide them. Also, the assumption that the truth is always to be found " somewhere in between " and never at the extremes has not been singularly productive in our theological dialogue; our movements tend only too often to be slight shifts to the right or left of center in order to take account of the " emphases " of " extreme " theologies.

We must also be honest in acknowledging that theological and critical developments in Great Britain and America have followed in general the patterns established on the Continent, with variations, and usually with a delay of twenty years or more. Except in Biblical archeology, contributions by British and American scholars have rarely established new trends, although at many points they have pursued an independent course within the established pattern. Thus, at the very time that historicism began to be challenged by Biblical theology on the Continent, works began to appear in Great Britain that were in line with the most extreme products of the " history of religion " school.[15] This would suggest that, with the passage of time, what once appeared objectionable as an extreme position becomes familiar, then attractive, then reasonable. It is not surprising, then, that in the 1920's and 1930's the new development of a theo-

---

[15] Oesterly-Robinson, *op. cit.;* S. H. Hooke, ed., *Myth and Ritual* (1933); *The Labyrinth* (1935); *Myth, Ritual, and Kingship* (1958).

logically oriented Biblical scholarship on the Continent was regarded in Great Britain with disgust and dismay as a wild and erratic extremist movement in which no really well-balanced scholar could be interested. As late as 1950, C. H. Dodd could dismiss the whole thing as " flourishes against historismus," and could find no work of a similiar trend in Great Britain between 1919 and 1949 that he thought worth mentioning.

Yet Dodd himself has never been content to be a historian and nothing more. He has busied himself consistently with theological questions that are intermingled inextricably with the historical. For all his concern with historical and critical questions, his primary interest has been the interpretation of the gospel. In his inaugural lecture at Cambridge in 1936 [16] he pointed out that the tendency of the " history of religion " school to dissolve the uniqueness of the New Testament phenomena constituted " a direct challenge to the student of the New Testament to conceive the Canon as the expression of a distinctive movement of life and thought," that is, to take the canon of Scripture seriously, and he saw the field of scholarship degenerating into sterility unless it got on with the task of interpretation. The period of analysis that left the New Testament in fragments should be succeeded by a period of interpretation. " Our task is . . . to grasp the whole first-century gospel in its temporary, historical, and therefore actual, reality, and then to make the bold and even perilous attempt to translate the whole into contemporary terms." He seems never to have realized that this was the very task at which those scholars were already hard at work whose concern was theological exegesis and Biblical theology. In his *Authority of the Bible* (1928), which we have already examined (Chapter VII), he showed his concern that the Bible should recover its place of influence in Protestantism, but he could not get beyond historical and psychological categories in interpreting the prophets and apostles and introduced revelation only to do justice to the uniqueness of Jesus, an indication that he was not sufficiently aware of the confusion in his own theological approach. The same con-

---

[16] C. H. Dodd, *Thirty Years of New Testament Study,* Morse Lecture. *The Present Task in New Testament Studies.* In *The Bible Today* (1946), Dodd shows a profound theological change in his approach to the Bible, asserting strongly the uniqueness of the Biblical revelation, the unity of the Testaments, and the necessity of a Christological interpretation of the Old Testament.

fusion appears in his *Apostolic Preaching,* in which the " facts " and " historical events " of the kerygma turn out to be not the kind of events that are accessible to the historian but divine events in the midst of history, such as the resurrection, that are known only to faith. In his overeagerness to establish the historicity of the gospel and its origin in the real life of a real person who really lived on earth among men, he is led into speaking as though the revelation of God in Jesus would have its original power for us if only the historian would do his work adequately and set the Jesus of history before our eyes. He seems never to have taken seriously Kähler's argument that, since our salvation depends upon our relation to Jesus Christ, our knowledge of him cannot be contingent upon the fluctuations of historical scholarship; he must be available more directly through the witness of the Scriptures themselves.

It was not until the 1930's that the first signs of theological concern showed themselves in British Old Testament scholarship. Two books by W. J. Phythian-Adams [17] probed into questions of theology. First, however, he attempted, by a new analysis of the early traditions of Israel, to establish the presence in them of a larger body of valid historical material than had long been credited. Unfortunately, he based his argument in part upon an ingenious theory of volcanic disturbances that would account for the miraculous accompaniments of Israel's deliverance from Egypt, and thereby drew attention away from what he had to say concerning the historicity of the exodus and the antiquity in Israel of the consciousness of a destiny as the peculiar people of God. He pointed out the importance, in understanding the election of Israel, of seeing it in the light of the election of the New Israel in the church, and vindicated the compatibility of a belief in God as the God of all men with a belief in God's choice of a particular people through which he might accomplish his purposes on behalf of all men. Phythian-Adams drew attention to the increasing neglect of the Old Testament: " The entire volume . . . has now been virtually abandoned, as if the revelation which it contains were too imperfect to be spiritually profitable to Christians." " For the world which has rejected this revelation of sacred history, all human history must remain devoid of significance." God has revealed himself in word and act in Israel that

[17] W. J. Phythian-Adams, *The Call of Israel; The Fullness of Israel.*

through Israel he may be known to all men. Jesus Christ is the climactic moment of the revelation: " He is in himself the anointed Israel of God." But cut apart from the Old Testament, he ceases to be understood.

A. G. Hebert [18] in 1941 spoke out against what he called the new Marcionism of a critical approach to the Bible that either expurgated the Old Testament or reduced it to a level that was sub-Christian. He recognized the " deep theological difference between this new apologetic and the faith of the Bible itself, which it seeks to interpret," and the inevitable confusion that must follow if the Bible is interpreted on the basis of theological assumptions that are alien to it. A spectator scholarship whose underlying assumptions are those of humanistic science is inadequate. The scholar must interpret the world of Biblical thought and life from within, from the standpoint of a faith that " believes passionately in the mighty acts of God in delivering Israel out of Egypt and choosing Israel to be his people." The text cannot be understood until its claim is taken seriously that it is witness to a redemptive action of God that is incomplete in the Old Testament and comes to its completion in Jesus Christ in the New. He proceeds, therefore, with a study of the Messianic hope as the central theme of the Bible that gives to the two Testaments their unity. In this and in later writings Hebert lets his concern for the unity of the Testaments lead him into typological and allegorical interpretations (cf. Ch. IV, above), but this should not be allowed to conceal his pioneer achievement in Great Britain in demanding attention for the basic theological problems in Biblical research.

The posthumous publication of Hoskyns' work on the Fourth Gospel [19] by F. N. Davey in 1940 laid before the English-speaking world a concrete example of theological exposition in which the problems of historical scholarship were by no means neglected. The commentary, in spite of the great unevenness of its quality that resulted from its being put together from fragments, pointed the way beyond philological, literary, and historical notes to the elucidation of the faith that comes to expression in the text. It was a demonstration that Scripture is of a character that it discloses its meaning only

[18] A. G. Hebert, *The Throne of David: A Study of the Fulfillment of the Old Testament in Jesus Christ and His Church.*
[19] E. C. Hoskyns, *The Fourth Gospel.*

to a scholarship that recognizes both the human and the divine in its content and is prepared to deal with both historical and theological realities. Hoskyns was deeply influenced in his approach by his translation of Barth's *Romans* in 1933.

In the 1940's it became evident that an increasing number of Biblical scholars in Great Britain and America were finding the theological questions inescapable. Alan Richardson's *Preface to Bible Study,* in 1943, though small in size, was the most balanced and thorough treatment of the relation between the historical and the theological in Scripture that had as yet appeared in English. Then in 1944, G. Ernest Wright published *The Challenge of Israel's Faith,* in which he pressed beyond any mere study of the history of the evolution of Israelite ideas to the question of the permanent significance of Israel's faith. Paul Minear's *Eyes of Faith* in 1946 was a penetrating study of the unique " angle of vision," or way of seeing things that is characteristic of the Biblical writings. The Biblical author, because he writes not as an impartial individual observer of the spectacle of life and religion but as a man who is bound to-gether with God and with his fellow man, sees everything differently from the modern man, or scholar, who has been taught by a long tradition to abstract himself from his world and his fellows and, above all, from God. What Minear does, then, is to take us through the words into the inside of the Biblical faith that we may under-stand it from within, making plain to us, however, the risks and decisions we must encounter on that journey.

An equally provocative contribution to hermeneutics was made by Minear in 1954 in his chapter on " Christian Eschatology and His-torical Methodology " in *Neutestamentliche Studien für Rudolf Bultmann*. Here he is concerned to show that the content of Scripture demands of the historian a methodology different from that with which he is accustomed to operate. The historian's usual method forces him to exclude from consideration essential elements in the Biblical witness. He assumes, for instance, a conception of time in which there is no room for the Biblical understanding of time. The fact that Minear draws the illustration of his argument from eschatology makes the presentation doubly complex. The problem reflected in the contrasting conceptions of time has its center in the contrast between the Biblical understanding of history as an unceasing dialogue between God and man and the modern conception of history in which there is room only for man.

Also in 1944 appeared Millar Burrows' *An Outline of Biblical Theology,* which undertook to present in orderly form what the Bible has to say concerning revelation, God, Christ, the universe, man, the people of God, sin, salvation, priesthood, etc. But Burrows proceeds with his task with unbroken confidence in the competence of historical investigation to lay open the theological content of the Bible. At no point does he even discuss the historian's problem that is posed by the interference of his own theological assumptions in his understanding of the theology of the Biblical authors. As a consequence, his categories of interpretation remain largely those of the historical school. He repudiates the tendency of some scholars " to define revelation in terms of something other than the communication of definite ideas." Therefore, revelation, as encounter with a personal God as it is in the prophets, or as the coming of God himself to man to take possession of his life as it is in the New Testament, remains outside the scope of his definition. The ultimate criterion for him of what is divine revelation in Scripture is " the test of experience," a judgment of truth and value on our part that we recognize as " a witness of God's spirit in our hearts." " What is ultimately authoritative for us is that which commands the assent of our own best judgment." The revelations of the Bible are " the highest ideals and most profound truths given to man." Thus, although this book has the form of a Biblical theology, it belongs on the whole to the earlier period of scholarship and represents largely a reorganization of what formerly appeared as a history of Biblical ideas.

Otto Baab,[20] like Burrows, has unbroken confidence in the ability of historical science to describe the theological ideas of the Bible with complete objectivity. Anyone, whether Protestant, Roman Catholic, or Jew, should be able to produce the same results in a historical theology of the Old Testament. The hope of such a theology, therefore, is that it should unify all scholars, providing

---

[20] Otto Baab, " Old Testament Theology, Its Possibility and Methodology," in H. R. Willoughby, ed., *The Study of the Bible Today and Tomorrow;* Otto Baab, *Theology of the Old Testament;* quotations are from the chapter in *The Study of the Bible Today and Tomorrow.*

them with " ' grass-roots ' theology, capable of empirical confirmation and social application." " Theology, when written descriptively and with scientific objectivity, becomes communicable to representatives of all faiths and cultures, provided that the principle of objectivity in the study of religion is recognized. . . . This opens the way to a general knowledge and possible acceptance of the truths contained in the Old Testament." " Knowledge of the nature of the God of Israel " is scientifically available to all men. The absurdity of this position is fully exposed when it is stated in New Testament terms: the nature of the God revealed in Jesus Christ can be known by any man who is willing to investigate the New Testament with a scientific historical method. Faith is unnecessary to a knowledge of God! On this basis not only a Jewish or Buddhist scholar but even an atheist scholar who is objective in his approach should be able to write a satisfactory Biblical theology for use in the Christian church!

Two Significant American Developments

A significant contribution to the discussion of the problem of interpretation has been made in the writings of John Knox.[21] He is conscious, as neither Burrows nor Baab is, that Christian faith cannot be made to depend upon the fluctuating researches of historical scholars. The church cannot wait in suspense for the solution of critical questions before it affirms its faith in the God whom it knows in Jesus Christ. It cannot live in fear that some new development or discovery will rob it of the object of its faith. Neither can it identify the revelation of God with any pattern of religious or theological ideas that it may extract from Scripture. Revelation is an event in which God comes to man for his salvation. The event comprehends the life, death, and resurrection of Jesus, but it does not end there but rather comes to its culmination in the church. In its essence the event is the coming of the Spirit, that is, the coming of God to man, in Jesus and his church. The gospel is the proclamation of his coming. There is, then, a double witness to the divine event, the New Testament Scriptures and the church in which, in so far as God's Spirit dwells in it, the event remains a present reality. We know of the event never solely through the Scriptures but because we participate in the life of the community that had its origin and

[21] Particularly in *Criticism and Faith*.

has its existence in and through the event. And it is this present immediate knowledge of God in the church through the indwelling Spirit which enables the church to interpret the New Testament and to discern in its documents the true nature of the event in which it had its origin. In traditional terms this means that the God who reveals himself in the Scriptures can be known only when in the power of his Spirit he actually comes to man now through the community of faith. Without an interpreting church the Scriptures remain dumb. Yet, the Scriptures in which the earliest church set down its memory and interpretation of the saving action of God in Jesus retain their primacy in the church as the means through which the reality and meaning of the event remain alive and powerful and authoritative in the church. The fact that the church belongs to the very essence of the event itself through the Spirit that possesses it does not endow it with the right to set its own continuing traditions and judgments on a par with the New Testament.

This is perhaps the most important contribution to the problem of interpretation alongside that of Paul Minear which has been made by any American Biblical scholar. Difficulties arise, however, at several points. The event of revelation is validly distinguished from the New Testament documents, which preserve the memory of it and by means of which it is reconstructed by the church, but these documents seem then to have served their purpose, so that an authority of the event itself can be asserted quite apart from any authority of Scripture. " It is not what was written that has authority, but what happened. The Bible has value only because it brings us a firsthand account of that happening. The event is the important thing, not the account, and we must interpret the account to recover the event." [22] Why are the authority and importance of the Scriptural account deprecated, if not denied, and a purely instrumental function assigned it, particularly when it is being emphasized that the church belongs to the essence of the event itself, so that it must through the ages participate in its importance and authority? Does not this subordinate Scripture to the church in a decisive fashion? But we must ask, How long does the church continue to belong to the essence of the event when once its ears become closed to the message of Scripture? Also, it may be asked whether the term " re-

[22] J. Knox, *op. cit.*, p. 80.

construct " can be used in relation to an event that is at once human and divine. Is it through a reconstruction of the life of Jesus and of the history of the early church that God reveals himself or through the Biblical witness to God's action in that series of happenings? Is it through a reconstruction of the history of Israel that God is revealed or through the Old Testament witness to God's dealings with Israel, even though the historical picture may not be accurate in every detail? It is true that the Biblical witness to the event must never be confused with the event of revelation itself. The Scriptures are witness to the Word and not the Word itself. (John 1:6; 5:39.) But equally it must be asserted that without continual openness to the witness of Scripture the church swiftly loses its genuine memory of the event and ceases to mediate any true knowledge of it. Both Paul and the author of John's Gospel had good reason to emphasize the inseparableness of the Word and the Spirit, the Word being unrecognized without the Spirit and the Spirit ever coming to man through the Word.

Again, there is some vagueness about what is meant by the " recovering of the event " which is the task of the historian. The mystery of the divine action in the event is emphasized; so also is the succession of happenings in the human scene in which the action of God occurs. The historian by his research sets the New Testament documents in their proper order and reconstructs the human happenings. This is necessary if the event is to appear in its full dimensions. This rather suggests that the event in its *full* dimensions is accessible to historical investigation and description. But if the central reality of the event is the coming of God to man, statements concerning it will be both historical and theological, and theological judgments should not be presented as though they were historical evaluations.

It is also notable that in the description of the revelation-event no reference is ever made to the Old Testament. The event is the coming of the Spirit in Jesus and his church. What, then, is the relation of the Word and Spirit that possessed the prophets to the Word and Spirit that were known in Jesus and his church? The New Testament claims that there is continuity here in spite of all discontinuity (Matt. 5:17; John 1:6-14; Heb. 1:1). The event that extends forward into the church also extends backward into the Old Testament and gives unity not only to the diverse writings of the New Testament but also to the much more radically diverse writings of the Old Testament.

The second contribution, by a systematic theologian, is an acute analysis of the relation of history and theology in the interpretation of the Christian tradition. Richard R. Niebuhr [23] brings the problem to a focus by considering what historians and theologians have been able to make of the resurrection of Jesus. Historical criticism in the nineteenth and early twentieth centuries found itself confronted with an insoluble problem in the New Testament stories of the resurrection. Because such a resurrection seemed to be an event of a character that historians did not find present elsewhere in human history except as myths or legends, they felt compelled to deny that Jesus actually rose from the dead. But in doing this they removed the actuality of the one event that was central for the New Testament authors and was the clue to the meaning of all other events that had to do with Jesus. A principle of explanation had then to be found quite different from that which was inherent in the documents. What no one asked, however, was whether or not the presuppositions of the historians and theologians were adequate to the task of interpretation to which they had set themselves. But now Niebuhr asks this question and submits the concepts of history and nature that have been dominant among theologians and exegetes to a searching scrutiny. He finds that, for more than a century, scholars of widely varying standpoints have taken over from natural science, and from a historical method based on the methods of natural science, assumptions concerning history and nature in which by their very definition there could be no room for a resurrection of the dead — and, he might well have added, no room for a living God who speaks and acts in history. He calls, therefore, for a redefinition of nature, history, and historical reason that will take as its starting point a world and a history in which the resurrection of Jesus Christ is recognized, together with the crucifixion, as the event in the midst of time that is of crucial significance for the interpretation of all other events in time.

Niebuhr's insistence is that the resurrection is an event in history and that it could have had no significance for human beings had it not been in the context of history. The whole " sacred history " tra-

---

[23] Richard R. Niebuhr, *Resurrection and Historical Reason.*

dition he deplores as a removal of the events of revelation to a special realm beyond ordinary history in order to protect their unique character, but actually because of a failure to understand history itself as the realm in which God's encounter with man must take place if it is to occur at all. Barth's placing of the resurrection of Jesus in a special " time " of its own he classifies as one form of this error, but he does not take account of Barth's insistence that revelational events are events in history even though they may be such as to elude the historian. Bultmann's dilemma concerning the resurrection, from which he seeks to escape by eliding it with the crucifixion, Niebuhr traces to Bultmann's uncritical adoption of a conception of nature as " a self-contained nexus of mechanical law " and a conception of history as by definition a realm of purely human occurrences that stand all of them under the sign of death. Niebuhr's bold claim is that the Christian theologian must draw his understanding of history and of nature from within that which he knows as a Christian standing in the full stream of the Christian tradition. What he says of the resurrection could be expanded to apply to the revelation of God in every part of Scripture. The witness of the people of God from earliest Old Testament times is to a history in which God has dealt with them in judgment and mercy. History is for them a story in which both God and man are active and no event can be rightly understood except within the context of this dialogue between God and man. Therefore, a historical method that would interpret the significance of that story for our own time must be of a character that can take full account of both the human and the divine factors in the story without reducing them to flat abstractions as complexes of merely human ideas. Such a method must be both rigorously historical and rigorously theological.

THE MODERN FLOOD OF OLD AND NEW TESTAMENT THEOLOGIES [24]

During the past twenty-five years, the rebirth of Biblical theology has been celebrated by the publication of three theologies of the New Testament, plus one work on Christology that may be classed with

[24] E. Sellin, *Alttestamentliche Theologie;* W. Eichrodt, *Theologie des Alten Testaments;* L. Köhler, *Theologie des Alten Testaments;* W. Vischer, *The Witness of the Old Testament to Christ;* O. Procksch, *Theologie des Alten Testaments;* E. Jacob, *The Theology of the Old Testament;* T. C. Vriezen, *An Outline of Old*

them, and not less than nine theologies of the Old Testament, more if one includes the works of Burrows and Baab. Then there have been the massive theological dictionary of the New Testament edited by Kittel, and the equally massive Dogmatik of Barth, which must be recognized as making major contributions to the problems of Biblical theology. Beyond this are numerous books and articles that deal with special aspects of the subject.

The fact that no Biblical theology basing itself on the whole of Scripture has appeared (except the outline by Burrows), but only Old or New Testament theologies, suggests that the unity of the Biblical revelation is still far from adequate recognition. Eichrodt, Jacob, Vriezen, *et al.* may assert in principle that the Old Testament finds its completion in Jesus Christ, and Richardson may consider the Old Testament the primary context of the New, but all of them alike conform to the now traditional separation of the two, and nowhere has sufficient attention been drawn to the fact that the problems of the one are in essence the problems of the other. The doctrine of God's creation of the world and man cannot be cut apart from the doctrine of God's creation of a new world and a new man in Jesus Christ without concealing something of the meaning of both. The election of Israel and the election of a new Israel in Jesus Christ belong together as two segments of a single story in which each segment illumines the other. The process of criticism and reinterpretation of Israel's understanding of God's purpose with it in the Old Testament comes to its climax in the decisive reinterpretation in the gospel of all that has gone before. Neither Testament can be seen in its full context except in a Biblical theology.

There has also been a tendency, which we have already observed in Burrows and Baab, to carry over the mentality and assumptions of the nineteenth-century historical approach into the theological, as though the theological task were merely one of description, setting the Biblical phenomena in order not so much in their historical sequences as under the traditional theological themes. What is

---

Testament Theology; G. von Rad, *Theologie des Alten Testaments;* G. A. F. Knight, *A Christian Theology of the Old Testament;* R. Bultmann, *Theology of the New Testament;* E. Stauffer, *New Testament Theology;* A. Richardson, *An Introduction to the Theology of the New Testament;* O. Cullmann, *The Christology of the New Testament.*

achieved, then, is little more than a rearrangement of the material to make it more readily accessible in an era when interest is keen in systematic theology. Even as history such an approach is deficient, since it abstracts the ideas from the living relationship between God and definite human persons in which they were expressions of the realities of life itself and presents them as dead relics of a distant past. A theology of the Old Testament fails if it is merely a museum of Old Testament thought and does not re-establish the living participation of the Old Testament authors in the theological dialogue that is essential to the life of the Christian fellowship.

Even a superficial examination of the recent Old and New Testament theologies reveals how mistaken it is for anyone to think that they represent a theological movement of a unified character.[25] Bultmann and Richardson stand at opposite poles on most questions, and Stauffer represents a conservative position in which none of the others would find themselves at home. Von Rad and Eichrodt approach their subject very differently. Martin Buber from Judaism contributes to the discussion while coming to very different conclusions from the Christian theologians and yet commands a hearing from them. Hebert stands in an Anglo-Catholic tradition in theology, and the marks of it are plainly evident in his Old Testament interpretations. Far from there being any deadly uniformity in the ranks of Biblical theologians, the diversity of their theologies constitutes one of the major problems of the present and future.

We have seen earlier how, in the first stage of critical Biblical scholarship, the theological interest was discredited by the manner in which each theologian discovered his own theology in the Scriptures. Historicism was an attempt to escape from that perversion and attain a more objective picture of Biblical developments. But historicism in turn produced evidence of the involvement of the scholar's subjective convictions in his representation of Biblical material. Barth and Bultmann, as we have seen, wrestle with this problem, recognizing the inevitability of the scholar's subjective involvement and trying to show how it can be kept from resulting in largely subjective judgments. But there is a danger that the inevita-

---

[25] J. R. Branton, "Our Present Situation in Biblical Theology," *Religion in Life* (Winter, 1956, 1957), p. 5, speaks of "the Biblical theologians" without any indication of the variety.

*The recovery of the unity of the Church must accompany and result
from the emergence of a central consensus on the message of
the Bible — The two are inseparable.*

bility may be taken as a permission and validation of a subjective approach in which the conclusions are dictated not so much by the
content of the Scriptures as by the theological position of the scholar.
Down this road lies the certainty of a renewed discredit for Biblical
theology.

An examination of the various theologies of the Old and New
Testaments does not lie within the scope of this study. Our concern
has been limited to the problems that underlie the existence of a
Biblical theology, and in particular it has been focused upon the
relation of history and theology in the investigation of Scripture.
The task of a scholarship that hopes to penetrate the surface of the
Biblical text and to lay open its ultimate content to the contemporary
world is to bring history and theology into a unity that will correspond in some measure to the unity of the human and divine elements in the Scriptures themselves. The story of the death and rebirth
of Biblical theology has been largely an account of tensions and
conflict between the historical and theological interests. If the future
is to hold better things in store for us, we need not only to take warning from the experiences of the past but also to look sharply at some
of the trends that are developing under our very eyes.

Present Tendencies to Reversion

Having sketched the course of Biblical interpretation across two
centuries, we are naturally concerned to know in what direction it
seems to be going at present. Some might be inclined to conclude
from the substantial body of literature that now exists that a new
historical-theological approach is firmly established and that we
have reached a new plateau in scholarship on which we shall soon
be able to speak again of " assured results." Perhaps the abundance
of theological summaries is an evidence that the new time of assurance has already arrived.[26] It may be salutary, therefore, to indicate
certain signs that seem to point backward rather than forward,
developments that claim to be new but that are possible only when

[26] Raymond Abba, *The Nature and Authority of the Bible,* seems at first to
grasp the dimensions of the problem but fails then to explore them with any decisiveness and becomes content with summarizing the results of recent scholarship
in the English-speaking world. He assumes too quickly that the newly exposed
problem is solved.

scholars ignore what is plainly written in the church's experience with the Bible in the past.

Allegory and typology have received thorough consideration in Chapter IV. In the second century A.D. they saved the Old Testament for the church, but the church was to pay dearly for it as through the succeeding centuries the text of Scripture was buried so deep beneath the mass of allegorical and typological interpretations that it was no longer able to speak with disturbing clarity into the life of the Christian community. The Reformers restored to Scripture its freedom to speak, with revolutionary consequences for the church; but with the return of a free use of allegory and typology, Scripture was once more subordinated to the doctrinal tradition of the church. Yet, as we have seen, these methods of interpretation are being encouraged today in many quarters. Men who have been pioneers in cutting through the existing traditions of scholarship to make possible a new and more profound theological interpretation seize upon these ancient and outworn devices in their zeal for a Christological interpretation of the Old Testament. In short, they overreach themselves in their emphasis upon a valid truth and at this point lead the way backward into one of the blind alleys of interpretation that the church explored quite sufficiently and thoroughly in the past.

From Germany come reports of an even more serious form of reversion. Gerhard Ebeling [27] describes how the reaction against liberal Protestantism that has dominated German theology since 1920 has in some influential quarters become a repudiation of historical-critical scholarship. According to Erwin Reisner,[28] historical science, which has made itself judge over all things and even over the truth of God, belongs to a sinful world that one who responds unconditionally to God's revelation must renounce. Helmut Echternach [29] has proclaimed the infallibility of the text of Luther's translation of the Bible and demanded that any exegesis that fails to agree with the Lutheran confessional statements should be branded

[27] G. Ebeling, "Die Bedeutung der historisch-kritischen Methode für die protestantische Theologie und die Kirche," ZTK (1950), p. 1.

[28] E. Reisner, "Revelation-Faith and Historical Science," *Der Anfang,* Heft 3 (1947).

[29] H. Echternach, *Es steht geschrieben.*

as false. Attempts of scholars to get at the original meaning of passages he declares to be futile; all one can do is to discern their present meaning for us. Hans Asmussen,[30] a prominent churchman and theologian, in a study preparatory to the Amsterdam conference of the World Council of Churches, adopted an interpretation of Isa., chs. 40 to 66, that assumed it to be written a century and a half before the events reported in the text. These three writings are known to the author only through the above essay of G. Ebeling. Ebeling suggests that many sections of the German church are susceptible to these tendencies because of a craving for security and a desire to escape from problems, motives that are strong today as a consequence of the distressing years that lie directly in the past. Similar tendencies, however, seem to be encouraged in some parts of the English-speaking world by an uncritical enthusiasm for Luther and Calvin that proceeds as though their theological ideas and Biblical interpretations could be transported unchanged into the present scene.

Perhaps the same influences account for the curious conservatism of E. Stauffer's *New Testament Theology*.[31] It has many characteristics that would appeal to literal-minded Christians. The Johannine literature is all assumed to have been written by the apostle John. Gen., chs. 1 to 3, is quoted as though it were a narrative of historical events. The doings of Satan are described with the same factuality as the doings of any other Biblical characters. Since both John's Gospel and the Apocalypse are assumed to be by an apostle, their theological content is taken to be an expression of Jesus' own mind. The focus of the book is on what is called a " Christocentric theology of history." The author extracts from Scripture a plan of history from the Creation to the parousia that unfolds on two levels, the cosmic and the earthly. Events on both levels were determined by God before the beginning. God appointed Satan on the cosmic level to an office in the divine ordering of the world and in the predestined plan for history. The world's tragic involvement in sin and destruction is due as much to Satan's fall from heaven as to Adam's fall on earth. Luke 4:5 is interpreted as showing that God " has, as a temporary measure, handed over political power to Satan since the Fall;

[30] H. Asmussen, *Law and Gospel.*
[31] E. Stauffer, *New Testament Theology.*

and Satan gives it to whom he will." Our redemption thus had to take place on two levels, through the eternal Christ on the cosmic level, and through the incarnate Christ on the earthly level. Most striking is the relative unimportance of the figure of Jesus in the whole scheme except as the divine validator of this " theology of history." Revelation seems to be nothing more or less than this " Biblical plan," so that there is no room for any thorough consideration of the event of revelation in Jesus Christ, which alone created and sustains a Christian church.

THE QUEST FOR THE JESUS OF HISTORY

Another form of reversion stands at the opposite pole from the examples we have been considering, the project of a number of scholars who have been close to Bultmann to take up afresh the quest for the Jesus of history. They have reacted against Bultmann's dictum that " we can know almost nothing concerning the life and personality of Jesus, since the early Christian sources show no interest in either." [32] Bultmann stood in line with Strauss and Kähler in affirming that the New Testament documents are not of a character to provide us with materials for a biography of Jesus. His work in form criticism, which created great uncertainty about which elements in the Gospels are to be attributed to Jesus and which to the early church, added to his restraint. He asserted that we possess only the preaching of the early church and have knowledge of Jesus Christ only through it, so that we cannot go behind its mingling of faith and history to reconstruct a purely historical figure. In this he had and has the enthusiastic support of Barth. But there has always been a strong dissent at this point, particularly in Great Britain and America, where one may therefore expect strong interest in the new quest. The piety of the past century has been deeply attached to the figure of the Jesus of history, even though the content of the figure has been so variously conceived, perhaps for the very reason that each person has been able to make him the incarnation of his human ideal. The most marked reversion is evident in a study of the new quest written by an American scholar who has been strongly influenced by the German school.[33]

---

[32] R. Bultmann, *Jesus and the Word.*
[33] J. M. Robinson, *A New Quest of the Historical Jesus.*

Käsemann

Ernst Käsemann's judicious probing of the question in 1954[34] was such as to command wide assent. He expressed the conviction that when form criticism has done its work, there remains a larger body of authentic historical material concerning Jesus than has been recognized, as, for instance, in the solid core of tradition concerning the Passion story. But the tradition has a complex and not a simple direct form because of the unique way in which a living church remembered and proclaimed its gospel that was centered in Jesus. It had no interest in any mere repetition of facts concerning Jesus because for it he was the Christ, the Lord, the Son of God, the Savior of all mankind, and its memory of him as a human person was from the beginning penetrated and intermingled with its knowledge of him as the risen Lord of the church. Not only in John's Gospel, where it appears most clearly, but also in Mark's, the events of Jesus' life are narrated and at the same time interpreted in the light of the faith engendered in the church by the resurrection and under the guidance of the Holy Spirit. This eliding of historical memory and theological interpretation gives to the Gospels their seemingly mythical character. A historical Jesus apart from the risen Lord would have been an abstraction for the early church, but equally would the risen Lord have been an abstraction apart from Jesus of Nazareth, and the whole New Testament insists upon the importance of the earthly life of Jesus, a life in history.

With great restraint, therefore, Käsemann undertakes to establish criteria by which to distinguish the historical figure of Jesus in the midst of the interpretations in which it is embedded. His method is to eliminate whatever elements in the tradition can be explained as originating either in Judaism or in any part of the early church. He finds samples of authentic tradition in the antitheses of Matt., ch. 5, where Jesus speaks with an authority that transcends the authority of the Scriptures, in the claim of Jesus in Matt. 12:28 to expel demons by the power of the Spirit, and in the evident consciousness of Jesus in Matt. 11:12 ff. that with his mission the Last Days are breaking in. These passages, coupled with the evidence that Jesus saw his Kingdom coming to his hearers in his very words, convince Käsemann that Jesus set not his person but his mission at the center of his preaching, and that the church was merely drawing out the full

[34] E. Käsemann, "Das Problem des Historischen Jesus." ZTK (1954), p. 125.

implications of this when it proclaimed him Messiah and Son of God. There is no encouragement here to the writing of a life of Jesus [35] but only a recognition that it is possible to discern an actual historical mission and a unique person and gospel in the midst of the church's reinterpretations. The purpose is not to find a Jesus of history on whom faith can focus in such a way that the risen Lord becomes irrelevant but rather to preserve the unity between the person whom men knew as Jesus of Nazareth and the person whom they acknowledged as Lord of the church. No valid criticism can be made of these findings.

Ernst Fuchs [36] approaches the problem differently but in part with much the same result. He begins with the Pauline faith in Jesus as Lord that, together with Paul's apostleship, depends wholly upon his vision of the risen Christ. This faith brought Paul a totally new understanding of himself and of all things and the joy of salvation from judgment, death, and anxiety. Fuchs then analyses passages in the Gospels in which Jesus dares to set himself in God's place, as in his forgiving of men's sins and in his demanding of them a decision in relation to himself and his gospel that is nothing less than a decision for or against God. In the parable of the prodigal he sees Jesus defending his own conduct by portraying God as showing the same attitude to sinners as his own. It was the monstrous claim inherent in this that infuriated the religious authorities and brought about Jesus' death. But, for those who responded to Jesus' absolute claim upon their loyalty, he was already the Lord in reality though not in name.

Fuchs, however, does not stop here. He seems concerned to explain this recognition of Jesus' Lordship as a human process. It was because Jesus, reflecting on the meaning of John the Baptist's death for himself, made an absolute decision for God, that his words and his death had power to call men to decision in such a radical fashion. To believe in Jesus was to repeat his decision and so to enter with him upon a new relation with God that would create tension with the existing community and exact a cost in suffering. This new life was life in the eschatological community, resurrection life, so that only

---

[35] Günther Bornkamm's *Jesus von Nazareth,* which is another expression of the new quest, is not in any sense of the word a " life " of Jesus.

[36] E. Fuchs, " Die Frage nach dem historischen Jesus," ZTK (1956), p. 210.

within it had Jesus' resurrection any meaning. The resurrection brought to expression the triumphant character of that life. Also, it is significant that Paul's missionary purpose is said to be " that his hearers should participate in the same self-understanding that was disclosed to him in the name of the Lord Jesus." There is at least a suggestion here that what is presented as the revelation of God in the New Testament is actually a communication by Jesus to his apostles, and then by them to others, of a self-understanding, a relation with God, an eschatological existence, an ultimate decision in the face of death, which is a human phenomenon and as such available to historical description.

J. M. Robinson [37] is much less restrained than Käsemann or Fuchs in his confidence concerning historical method. What was wrong with the old quest for the historical Jesus, he says, was not that the realities of Jesus' life were of a nature that they were beyond the grasp of the historian but only that the historical method was too superficial. With its empiricism it could get at only the outside of history and not its interior psychological reality, which is the womb in which events are created. It was this deficiency in method which made the earlier New Testament historians unable to reach solid and dependable conclusions concerning the historical life of Jesus. But now, thanks to Wilhelm Dilthey in the nineteenth century and R. G. Collingwood in the twentieth, we have a new approach to history. Because we participate in the same stream of history of which the men and events of the past were a part, they are alive in us and we can relive their experiences, thereby discovering the meaning of the events for them. The meaning of Jesus was transmitted across the centuries in the church's kerygma, and the church until now has had no other way of knowing Jesus than by responding to the kerygma in faith. But in the kerygma it has always been impossible to separate the original image of Jesus from the church's interpretations of him. The attempt of C. H. Dodd to do this, to distill a residuum of historical facts out of the kerygma, failed because it did not take sufficient account of the interpretative character of the kerygma itself. The church, through the years, has had to endure the embarrassment of being unable to speak with certainty about the historical life of Jesus. The knowledge it had through the kerygma was

[37] J. M. Robinson, *op. cit.*

sufficient for its needs, yet the historical question remained a thorn in the church's side.

Now, however, the new historical method has made possible a decisive answer to this question. Scholars have an instrument whereby they can penetrate the inmost secret of Jesus' being. "Jesus' understanding of his existence, his selfhood, and thus in the higher sense his life, is a possible subject of historical research." [38] The old quest failed because " it was an attempt to avoid the risk of faith by supplying objectively verified proof for its ' faith.' " [39] The new historical method declares that real historical understanding of the inner meaning of events is impossible unless there is a dialogue between the historian and the past in which the historian's existence is laid unconditionally open to the reality of the past. This openness is actually another name for faith.

What we seem to have offered us, then, is a double route to the meaning of Jesus, the kerygmatic and the historical. Jesus is "a historical person to whom we have a second avenue of access provided by the rise of scientific historiography." [40] Neither is a substitute for the other. Both should be kept in operation — although it is not too clear why the kerygmatic needs to be continued once the historical route is established, particularly since the latter is likely to have a much stronger modern appeal in an age that is impatient with revelation and confident in reason. The recent exclusive preference for the kerygmatic route has threatened us with docetism, he says, from which we can be protected only by a new emphasis upon the historical. But there seems to be nothing in the kerygmatic knowledge that is not present in much plainer unmythical and untheological terms in the historical knowledge. In fact, the kerygma, when its mythological expression is decoded, proves to be " decidedly an evaluation of the historical person." [41] In spite of all disclaimers, this seems to be either of two things: a reduction of the kerygma by demythologizing so that the action of God in Jesus Christ, which it proclaims, is simply another name for what happens when the " transcendent self " of Jesus impinged upon other human

[38] J. M. Robinson, *op. cit.,* p. 72.
[39] J. M. Robinson, *op. cit.,* p. 44.
[40] J. M. Robinson, *op. cit.,* p. 85.
[41] J. M. Robinson, *op. cit.,* p. 90.

selves, or the provision of a rational knowledge of Jesus by historical method through which the church will be able to prove to itself
and others the validity of the content of the kerygma. The former is
the dissolution of theology into anthropology; the latter is a modern
version of the old structure of rational orthodoxy in which the revelation of God in the Gospel was bolstered from without by what the un-
aided human reason was able to say about God.

The warnings of Reimarus and Strauss seem to have been forgotten. The wisdom of Kähler is turned to folly. The historical
method of Dilthey and Collingwood is invested uncritically with
the dignity of a new and superior channel of revelation. But, above
all, confidence is restored in the capacity of the historian to tell us
the ultimate truth concerning Jesus Christ, at least in so far as he
is willing to be an existentialist historian. In spite of the novel elements in this project, it is surely not unfair to evaluate it as a form of
reversion.

These illustrations are sufficient to show the problematic character
of some of the present developments in Biblical theology. There are
no assured results, and there is no clear indication of the road that
should be taken. It is this confused situation which makes one impatient with theologies of Old or New Testament that proceed as
though there were no serious preliminary problems that demand
attention. We have entered upon a new theological era in Biblical
scholarship, but, unless the basic theological questions receive more
responsible and more thoroughly critical consideration, it can become an era of hopeless confusion and wasteful reaction. We do not
emerge into a paradise of easy solutions in Biblical interpretation
when we acknowledge that scholarship must be competently theological as well as competently historical. Rather, the task is made
more complex and the danger of misinterpretation greater than ever
before.

Biblical Theology must take theology seriously.

CONCLUSION

IT MAY SEEM unduly pessimistic to conclude this study of interpretation on a critical note and with the suggestion of a clouded and uncertain outlook toward the future. But earlier the conviction has been emphatically expressed, and evidence offered to support it, that we have for some years now been moving into one of those periods in the history of the church and of mankind when doors of understanding come open and the Bible speaks with new clarity and power. That this is happening is not the result of our cleverness or an indication that at last we have found the key to the Scriptures. It is simply God's mercy to us in our time of need. Perhaps more than anything else it indicates that in the dilemmas of our time we have lost confidence in our own devices and have become willing to hear what God has to say to us through the Scriptures as a totally new word to our generation, not a supplement to what we already knew, but instead a word that cuts directly across all that we thought we knew. It makes both an end of us and of all our works and at the same time a new beginning. But if there is one thing that we have learned from the history of interpretation, it is that great new insights can be very quickly lost and that a most promising beginning can be deflected into a blind road. Very often what looks like a period of consolidation is actually a period of confusion and compromise in which the road forward that was opening is no longer seen. We need to remember also that unconsciously even Luther and Calvin helped prepare the way for the confusion and compromise that succeeded the era of the Reformation.

The purpose of this book is, on the one hand, to mark out more clearly the road on which we are traveling, that, seeing whence we

gospel

have come, we may at least avoid some of the pitfalls of the past, and, on the other hand, to lay bare the problems of interpretation that demand of us a solution before they will let us past them into the future. It is not pessimism to point out that a Biblical theology or a theological exposition that seems to have forgotten those pitfalls or to be passing lightly over those essential problems is in danger of losing its way.

His positive word –

Since so much consideration has been given to differing methods of interpretation, it should perhaps be said once more that there is no method of interpretation by which we can compel Scripture to give forth its meaning. The mystery remains of why the gospel is heard in Scripture by some men and not by others, also in some generations and not in others; and what deepens the mystery is that those who fail to hear are sometimes those who study the Scriptures most industriously. Our principles of interpretation must be determined by the nature of the text itself. Because it was written by Hebrews, we must study the forms of Hebrew thought and speech. Because it has to do with events in human history, our method must be historical. Because God is as much concerned in the events as is man, our method must be theological. And because no line can be drawn between the divine and human either in the person of Jesus Christ or in any of the events that Scripture reports, history and theology are married to each other in the text of scripture and they must remain married in our Biblical interpretation. But that the text itself should speak to us as God's word and that in this word God himself should confront us in our present existence is not in the power of any interpreter to effect. All that he does is preparatory.

The confrontation that brings understanding remains God's free act. It is his will in love to reveal himself to us and to make the light of his truth shine in our darkness. But there is a resistance to him in us that no hermeneutical method can overcome. Israel in the Old Testament failed to understand the words of the prophets not because of hermeneutical difficulties but because their hearts and minds were hardened against God; they willed not to hear what would disturb their order of life. So also in Jesus' ministry most of those who heard him speak failed to grasp what he was saying; they were not prepared for the revolution in the life of Judaism and in their personal lives that would have been the cost of really hearing him. So also today when we fail to understand Scripture, not just in the Christian congregation but also in our Christian scholarship, the difficulty may be not in our hermeneutics but in ourselves, that like our predecessors in Israel we are not unconditionally open toward a God who kills in order to make alive and who roots up what we have planted and tears down what we have built, theologically as well as practically, in order that he may clear the ground for a planting and building of his own.

BIBLIOGRAPHY

Abba, Raymond, *The Nature and Authority of the Bible*. James Clarke & Company, Ltd., 1958

Asmussen, Hans, *Law and Gospel*. 1947.

Baab, Otto, *Theology of the Old Testament*. Abingdon Press, 1949.

Baillie, John, *The Interpretation of Religion: An Introductory Study of Theological Principles*. Charles Scribner's Sons, 1928.

Barth, Karl, *The Epistle to the Romans*. Chr. Kaiser Verlag, 1922; Eng. tr., Oxford University Press, 1933.

—— *Die Kirchliche Dogmatik,* Vols. I–IV. Evangelischer Verlag, 1932–1959.

—— *David Friedrich Strauss als Theologe 1839–1939*. Evangelischer Verlag, 1948.

Baumgärtel, Friedrich, *Verheissung: Zur Frage des evangelischen Verständnisses des A. T.* Bertelsmann, 1952.

Blackman, E. C., *Biblical Interpretation*. The Westminster Press, 1957.

Bornkamm, Günther, *Jesus von Nazareth*. W. Kohlhammer, 1956.

Branscomb, B. H., *Jesus and the Law of Moses*. R. R. Smith, 1930.

Bultmann, Rudolf, *Jesus and the Word, Deutsche Bibliothek,* 1926. Eng. tr., Charles Scribner's Sons, 1934.

—— *Theology of the New Testament,* Vols. I and II. Charles Scribner's Sons, 1951–1955.

—— *Glauben und Verstehen,* Vol. I. J. C. B. Mohr, 1954.

—— *Essays Philosophical and Theological*. The Macmillan Company, 1955.

—— *Marburger Predigten*. J. C. B. Mohr, 1956.

—— *Jesus Christ and Mythology*. Charles Scribner's Sons, 1958.

Burney, C. F., *The Gospel in the Old Testament*. T. & T. Clark, 1921.

Burrows, Millar, *An Outline of Biblical Theology*. The Westminster Press, 1946.

Cairns, David, *The Image of God in Man*. Philosophical Library, Inc., 1953.

Cadbury, H. J., *The Peril of Modernizing Jesus*. The Macmillan Company, 1937.

Cheyne, T. K., *Founders of Old Testament Criticism*. Charles Scribner's Sons, 1893.

Collingwood, R. G., *An Autobiography*. Penguin Books, Inc., 1944.

—— *The Idea of History*. Oxford University Press, 1946.

Cullmann, Oscar, *The Christology of the New Testament*. J. C. B. Mohr, 1957; Eng. tr., The Westminster Press, 1959.

Davidson, A. B., *The Theology of the Old Testament*. Charles Scribner's Sons, 1904.

Davies, W. D., *Paul and Rabbinic Judaism: Some Rabbinic Elements in Pauline Theology,* S.P.C.K., 1948.

Diem, Hermann, *Grundfragen der biblischen Hermeneutik. Theologische Existenz Heute,* N. F. 24. Chr. Kaiser Verlag, 1950.

—— *Dogmatics*. Eng. tr., Oliver and Boyd, Ltd., 1959; The Westminster Press, 1960.

Dodd, C. H., *The Authority of the Bible*. James Nisbet & Co., Ltd., 1928. Reprinted 1938 and 1952.

—— *The Bible and the Greeks*. Hodder & Stoughton, Ltd., 1935.

—— *The Present Task in New Testament Studies*. Cambridge University Press, 1936.

—— *The Apostolic Preaching and Its Developments*. Hodder & Stoughton, Ltd., 1936.

—— *The Bible Today*. Cambridge University Press, 1946.

—— *Thirty Years of New Testament Study*. 1950.

—— *According to the Scriptures: The Substructure of New Testament Theology*. James Nisbet & Co., Ltd., 1952.

Driver, S. R., *The Book of Genesis*. Methuen & Co., Ltd., 1904.

Ebeling, G., *Kirchengeschichte als Geschichte der Auslegung der Heiligen Schrift,* J. C. B. Mohr, 1947.

Eichrodt, Walther, *Theologie des Alten Testaments,* Vols. I–III. J. C. Hinrichs Verlag, 1933–1939; 5th ed., Vol. I, Ehrenfried Klotz Verlag, 1957.

Echternach, H., *Es steht geschrieben*. 1937.

Eltester, W., ed., *Neutestamentliche Studien für Rudolph Bultmann zu seinem 70 Geburtstag*. Topelmann, 1954.

Esking, Erik, " Glaube und Geschichte in der theologische Exegese Ernst Lohmeyers. Zugleich ein Beitrag zur Geschichte der n.t. Interpretation." Gleerup Publishers, 1951.

Essays and Reviews. 7th ed., Longmans, Green & Co., Inc., 1861.

Ferm, Vergilius, *Contemporary American Theology. Theological Auto-*

biographies. First Series. Round Table, 1932.

Goguel, Maurice, *The Life of Jesus.* The Macmillan Company, 1933.

—— *The Birth of Christianity.* George Allen & Unwin, Ltd., 1953.

Goppelt, Leonhard, *Typos: Die typologische Deutung der Alten Testaments im Neuen.* 1939.

Grant, Robert M., *The Bible in the Church: A Short History of Interpretation.* The Macmillan Company, 1948.

—— *The Letter and the Spirit.* The Macmillan Company, 1957.

Harnack, Adolf, *Das A. T. in den paulinischen Briefen und in den paulinischen Gemeinden.* 1928.

Hebert, A. G., *The Throne of David: A Study of the Fulfillment of the Old Testament in Jesus Christ and His Church.* Morehouse-Barlow, 1941.

—— *The Authority of the Old Testament.* Faber & Faber, Ltd., 1947.

Henry, C. F. H., ed., *Revelation and the Bible.* Baker Book House, 1958.

Hempel, Johannes, *Gott und Mensch im Alten Testament.* W. Kohlhammer, 1926.

Hirsch, Emanuel, *Das A. T. und die Predigt des Evangeliums.* J. C. B. Mohr, 1936.

Hooke, S. H., ed., *Myth and Ritual.* Oxford University Press, 1933.

—— *The Labyrinth.* Oxford University Press, 1935.

—— *Myth, Ritual, and Kingship.* Oxford University Press, 1958.

Hoskyns, Sir Edwyn, *The Fourth Gospel,* Vols. I and II, ed. by F. N. Davey. Faber & Faber, Ltd., 1940.

Humbert, P., *Etudes sur le récit du paradis et de la chute dans la Genèse,* Neuchâtel, Secretariat de l'Université, 1940.

Jacob Edmond, *The Theology of the Old Testament.* Eng. tr., Harper & Brothers, 1958.

Johnson, Robert C., *Authority in Protestant Theology.* The Westminster Press, 1959.

Kähler, Martin, *Der sogenannte historische Jesus und der geschichtliche biblische Christus.* 1896. Reprinted, Chr. Kaiser Verlag, 1956.

Knight, G. A. F., *A Christian Theology of the Old Testament.* John Knox Press, 1959.

Knox, John, *Criticism and Faith.* Abingdon Press, 1952.

Köhler, Ludwig, *Theologie des Alten Testaments.* J. C. B. Mohr, 1936; Eng. tr., Lutterworth Press, 1957.

König, Eduard, *Theologie des Alten Testaments.* Chr. Belser, 1923.

Kraeling, Emil. *The Old Testament Since the Reformation.* Harper & Brothers, 1955.

Kümmel, W. G., *Promise and Fulfillment.* S.C.M. Press, Ltd., 1957.

—— *Das Neue Testament. Geschichte der Erforschung seiner Probleme.* Verlag Karl Alber, 1958.

Kraus, H. J., *Geschichte der historisch-kritischen Erforschung des Alten Testaments von der Reformation bis zur Gegenwart.* 1956.

Lampe, G. W. H., and Woollcombe, K. J., *Essays on Typology.* Alec R. Allenson, Inc., 1957.

Matthews, I. G., *The Religious Pilgrimage of Israel.* Harper & Brothers, 1947.

Minear, Paul, *Eyes of Faith.* The Westminster Press, 1946.

—— *Horizons of Christian Community.* The Bethany Press, 1959.

Mowinckel, Sigmund, *The Old Testament as Word of God,* 1938; Eng. tr., Abingdon Press, 1959.

Niebuhr, Richard R., *Resurrection and Historical Reason: A Study of Theological Method.* Charles Scribner's Sons, 1957.

Oesterly, W. O. E., and Robinson, T. H., *Hebrew Religion, Its Origin and Development.* The Macmillan Company, 1930.

Orr, James, *Revelation and Inspiration.* Charles Scribner's Sons, 1910.

Parker, T. H. L., *The Oracles of God: An Introduction to the Preaching of John Calvin.* Lutterworth Press, 1947.

Phythian-Adams, W. J., *The Call of Israel.* Oxford University Press, 1934.

—— *The Fullness of Israel.* Oxford University Press, 1938.

Procksch, Otto. *Theologie des Alten Testaments.* Bertelsmann, 1950.

Reid, J. K. S., *The Authority of Scripture: A Study of the Reformation and Post-Reformation Understanding of the Bible.* Harper & Brothers, 1957.

Richardson, Alan, *An Introduction to the Theology of the New Testament.* S.C.M. Press, Ltd., 1938.

Richardson, Alan, and Schweitzer, W., eds., *Biblical Authority for Today.* The Westminster Press, 1951.

Robinson, James M., *A New Quest of the Historical Jesus.* Alec R. Allenson, Inc., 1959.

Rowley, H. H., *The Biblical Doctrine of Election.* Lutterworth Press, 1950.

—— *The Unity of the Bible.* Carey Kingsgate Press, Ltd., 1953.

Sanday, William, *Inspiration.* Eight lectures on the early history and origin of the doctrine of Biblical inspiration. Longmans, Green & Co., Inc., 1893.

Schultz, Hermann, *Old Testament Theology,* Vols. I and II. T. & T. Clark, 1895.

Schweitzer, Albert, *The Quest of the Historical Jesus: A Critical Study of Its Progress.* J. C. B. Mohr, 1906; Eng. tr., A. & C. Black, Ltd., 1910.

Scott, E. F., *The Fourth Gospel: Its Purpose and Theology*. T. & T. Clark, 1906.

Sellin, Ernst, *Geschichte des israelitische-jüdischen Volkes*. Quelle & Meyer, 1924–1932.

—— *Alttestamentliche Theologie auf religionsgeschichtlicher Grundlage*. Quelle & Meyer, 1933.

Smart, James D., *The Rebirth of Ministry*. The Westminster Press, 1960.

Smith, Henry Preserved, *Essays in Biblical Interpretation*. Marshall Jones, 1921.

Stange, E., ed., *Die Religionswissenchaft der Gegenwart in Selbstdarstellungen*. Vol. I, Verlag von Felix Meiner, 1925.

Stauffer, E., *New Testament Theology*. Eng. tr., The Macmillan Company, 1955.

Thurneysen, Eduard, *Christoph Blumhardt*. 1926.

—— *Dostoiewski*. 1930.

—— *Festschrift. Gottesdienst-Menschendienst. Zum siebzigsten Geburtstag*. Evangelischer Verlag, 1958.

Vischer, Wilhelm, *The Witness of the Old Testament to Christ*. Evangelischer Verlag, 1935. Eng. tr., Lutterworth Press, 1949.

Von Rad, G., *Theologie des Alten Testaments,* Vol. I, Chr. Kaiser Verlag, 1957; Vol. II, 1960.

Vriezen, T. C., *An Outline of Old Testament Theology*. Eng. tr., Basil Blackwell & Mott, Ltd., 1958.

Wallace, Ronald S., *Elijah and Elisha: Expositions from the Book of Kings*. Oliver and Boyd, Ltd., 1957.

Warfield, B. B., *Revelation and Inspiration*. Oxford University Press, 1927.

Welch, A. C., *Prophet and Priest in Old Israel*. S.C.M. Press, Ltd., 1936.

Willoughby, H. R., ed., *The Study of the Bible Today and Tomorrow*. University of Chicago Press, 1947.

Windisch, Hans, *The Meaning of the Sermon on the Mount*. 1929. Eng. tr., The Westminster Press, 1951.

Wolf, E., ed., *Antwort. Karl Barth zum siebzigsten Geburtstag*. Evangelischer Verlag, 1957.

Wood, James D., *The Interpretation of the Bible: A Historical Introduction*. Gerald Duckworth and Company, Ltd., 1958.

Wright, G. Ernest, *God Who Acts: Old Testament Theology as Recital*. Henry Regnery Company, 1952.

—— *The Challenge of Israel's Faith*. University of Chicago Press, 1944.

—— *The Old Testament Against Its Environment*. Alec R. Allenson, Inc., 1950.

Zimmerli, W., *Das Alte Testament als Anrede*. Chr. Kaiser Verlag, 1956.

INDEX

313